A NEW
EURO-MEDITERRANEAN
CULTURAL IDENTITY

Editor
STEFANIA PANEBIANCO

Routledge
Taylor & Francis Group

LONDON AND NEW YORK

First published in 2003 in Great Britain by
FRANK CASS PUBLISHERS

This edition published 2012 by Routledge

Routledge
Taylor & Francis Group
711 Third Avenue
New York, NY 10017

Routledge
Taylor & Francis Group
2 Park Square, Milton Park
Abingdon, Oxon OX14 4RN

Routledge is an imprint of the Taylor & Francis Group, an informa business

British Library Cataloguing in Publication Data

A new Euro-Mediterranean cultural identity
    1. Euro-Mediterranean Partnership 2. Group identity –
Mediterranean Region 3. Multiculturalism – Mediterranean
Region 4. Mediterranean Region – Politics and government –
1945–
I. Panebianco, Stefania
320.9'1822

ISBN 0-7146-5411-6 (cloth)
ISBN 0-7146-8477-5 (paper)

Library of Congress Cataloging-in-Publication Data

A new Euro-Mediterranean cultural identity / edited by Stefania
Panebianco.
    p. cm.
Includes bibliographical references and index.
ISBN 0-7146-5411-6 (cloth)
    1. European Union countries–Relations–Mediterranean Region.
2. Mediterranean Region–Relations–European Union countries.
3. Political culture–Mediterranean Region. 4. European Union– Mediterranean
Region. 5. Democracy–Mediterranean Region.
6. European Union countries–Economic policy. 7. Human rights–
European Union countries. 8. Human rights–Mediterranean Region. I.
Panebianco, Stefania.

D1065.M43 N48 2003
303.48'2401822–dc21   2002041139

Contents

Notes on Contributors

Antonio Badini, Ambassador, is director-general for Mediterranean and Middle Eastern countries, Italian Ministry of Foreign Affairs, Rome.

Fifi Benaboud is senior adviser to the executive director of the North South Centre of the Council of Europe and coordinator of the Trans-Mediterranean Programme. She has published many articles on civil society and is a member of several networks dealing with Euro-Mediterranean relations.

Abdelwahab Biad (doctorate in law) is professor of international relations, international law and human rights at the Université de Rouen. He is a member of the research team of the Centre de Recherches et d'Études sur les Droits de l'Homme et le Droit International Humanitaire (CREDHO) and has published several articles on these issues.

Béchir Chourou (PhD in political science) teaches international relations at the University of Tunis I (Higher Institute of Languages). His research interests include Euro-Mediterranean relations, with a focus on the political and economic dimensions.

Raymond Cohen is professor of international relations and former chairman of the Department of International Relations at the Hebrew University, Jerusalem. He has published books dealing with diplomacy, conflict resolution, intercultural negotiation and the international relations of the ancient Near East.

Justin Hutchence (MA) is a lecturer in international relations in the Politics Department and in the Graduate School of European and International Studies, both at the University of Reading. He is currently finishing a PhD thesis on EU foreign policy-making with an emphasis on EU–Middle East relations.

Annette Jünemann (PhD in political science) is associate professor at the University of the German Armed Forces in Munich, Faculty of Social Sciences. Her main publications concern the Euro-Mediterranean Partnership. Her main field of interest is the EU and international relations.

Youssef Mouawad (docteur d'état en droit), lawyer and historian, is professor of business law at the Lebanese American University, Beirut. He also lectures on the 'law of war' at Nôtre Dame University, Lebanon.

Stefania Panebianco (PhD in international relations) is a political science researcher at the University of Catania. As a former holder of the Italian Chair of Mediterranean Diplomacy and Relations she lectured for two academic years at the Mediterranean Academy of Diplomatic Studies, University of Malta. She has published a monograph on lobbying at EU level and several articles on EU politics and policies.

Rodolfo Ragionieri is professor of international relations at the University of Sassan. His research interests and publications concern conflicts and security analysis in the Mediterranean and the Middle East, the theory of conflict and issues related to the relationship between abstract systems and the theory of international relations.

Mohammad El-Sayed Selim (PhD) is professor of political science at the Faculty of Economics and Political Science, Cairo University, and director of the Centre for Asian Studies at Cairo University. He has authored books and articles on international relations, foreign policy analysis and EuroMed cooperation projects.

Jamila Houfaidi Settar is professor of law and international relations and director of the Euro-Mediterranean Training and Research Unit at the Université Hassan II in Casablanca.

Stelios Stavridis (PhD in international relations) held a Jean Monnet chair in European political studies in the Politics Department of the University of Reading until December 2002. He was the director of the Centre for Euro-Mediterranean Studies, the Graduate School of European and International Studies, also at the University of Reading. He has held visiting posts at the Institut d'Études Européennes of the Université Libre de Bruxelles, the European University Institute (Florence), and the Hellenic Foundation for European and Foreign Policy (ELIAMEP) (Athens). He is now (2002–03) an Onassis Fellow at the Hellenic Centre for European Studies (EKEM) in Athens and an Honorary Fellow at the Hellenic Observatory of the LSE European Institute in London.

Foreword

I welcome this volume on the human dimension of security as I consider a better understanding of basic values as timely and relevant for advancing the Euro-Mediterranean Partnership (EMP), which was launched in Barcelona in November 1995.[1] Today the greater focus in carrying on the Barcelona Declaration has been placed on economic cooperation. But when the document was signed in the Catalan capital in November 1995, one of the main reasons for heralding it as a turning point in relations between the European Union (EU) and its Mediterranean partners was, and rightly so, its three-pronged strategy in dealing with the region's stability.

The great merit of the Barcelona Process is the global nature of its approach, which encompasses all the components – political, economic, social and cultural – for reinforcing overall stability. The widely held conviction that a greater integration among the countries of the two shores of the Mediterranean is in their best interest, and the most viable alternative to the marginalization of the region, provides fertile soil for the new model of relations to stand up to disruptive factors. We can say that despite adverse events in the area and the complexity of the challenge, the EU and its Mediterranean partners seem very firmly set to move the Process on.

I feel confident in predicting that the EMP will withstand crises and renewed tension in the region. The Barcelona Process has shown itself able to function as a 'counterweight' capable of influencing positively, although still modestly, Arab and Israeli behaviours and perceptions, thus fulfilling the task entrusted to it by the Barcelona Declaration.

However, the new framework of relations set up by the EMP will remain fragile unless it gets sufficient grass-roots support in the societies of both Mediterranean shores. Meetings mobilizing relevant organizations and scholars contribute very much to improve mutual understanding and confidence. They are useful in dispelling suspicions and counteracting misunderstandings and fears. This is instrumental to the partners' goal of pooling together resources and creating a more integrated marketplace. In the future a greater emphasis should be placed on efforts to bridge the gap between societies and make cultural diversity an enriching factor for the moral, economic and cultural growth of the region, as it has been in the past.

The search for a platform of shared values is paramount. The establishment of an area of more equal development, with all that this implies, is hardly conceivable in the absence of core values that are recognized and applied by all.

Convergence towards agreed values and rules is a compelling task to be fulfilled with resolve in parallel with progress in the other areas, especially the economic sphere.

Cultural diversity should not be seen as an obstacle to building up mutual understanding with a view to fostering common behaviours and consequently enhancing predictability, which is the main source of greater confidence. In this respect, the goal of advancing good governance provides a practical and useful opportunity to reconcile divergent views and rules stemming from the current inadequate homogeneity in the socio-political systems.

The joint commitment to take the EMP further should promote a greater interchange among the nations of the area without compromising essential standards. An intensified and upgraded dialogue such as the one that would be brought about by the Euro-Mediterranean Charter on Peace and Stability is of great value and should be urgently sought. The charter cannot rival the Barcelona Declaration, but rather must represent a functional instrument for its correct implementation and therefore would provide an appropriate institutional framework.

Italy has already suggested that the ministers of foreign affairs should play a central role by meeting in partnership councils. At the same time, MEDA funds should be used in ways that would mobilize the actors of development and civil society, who currently appear as co-opted and bridled witnesses rather than actual players. To this end EU regulations and rules of procedure should be adapted to the spirit of the partnership and the need for collective endeavours that stem from it.

Antonio Badini
Former Italian Ambassador in charge of the Barcelona Process

NOTE

1. The representatives of the EU member countries plus Algeria, Cyprus, Egypt, Israel, Jordan, Lebanon, Malta, Morocco, the Palestinian Authority, Syria and Tunisia convened in Barcelona in November 1995 adopted the Barcelona Declaration, by which the EMP was launched.

Abbreviations

ACP	Africa, the Caribbean and the Pacific
AMC	Alternative Mediterranean Conference
APEC	Asia-Pacific Economic Cooperation Conference
ASEAN	Association of South-East Asian Nations
CBMs	confidence-building measures
CEECs	Central and Eastern European countries
CFSP	Common Foreign and Security Policy
CSCE	Conference for Security and Co-operation in Europe
EC	European Community
EEB	European Environmental Bureau
EEC	European Economic Community
EIB	European Investment Bank
EMHRN	Euro-Mediterranean Human Rights Network
EMP	Euro-Mediterranean Partnership
EP	European Parliament
EPC	European Political Cooperation
EU	European Union
EuroMeSCo	Euro-Mediterranean Study Commission
FIS	Front Islamique du salut
FoE	Friends of the Earth
FYROM	Former Yuglosav Republic of Macedonia
ICJ	International Court of Justice
IMF	International Monetary Fund
MAI	Multicultural Agreement on Investment
MECUs	million ECUs
MEDA	Measures d'ajustement
MEFTA	Mediterranean free trade area
MEPP	Middle East Peace Process
MIO	Mediterranean Information Office
MNCs	Mediterranean Non-member Countries
MPCs	Mediterranean Partner Countries
NAC	North Atlantic Council
NAFTA	North Atlantic Free Trade Agreement
NATO	North Atlantic Treaty Organization
NGO	non-governmental organization
OECD	Organisation for Economic Co-operation and Development

OSCE	Organization for Security and Co-operation in Europe
PBMs	partnership-building measures
PHARE	Poland and Hungary Aid for the Reconstruction of the Economy
RAED	Arab Network for the Environment and Development
REDWG	Regional Economic Development Working Group
RMP	Renovated Mediterranean Policy
SAP	structural adjustment programmes
TRNC	Turkish Republic of Northern Cyprus
UMA	Union of the Arab Maghreb
UN	United Nations
UNESCO	United Nations Educational, Scientific and Cultural Organization
WEU	Western European Union
WTO	World Trade Organisation
WWF	World Wildlife Fund (Worldwide Fund for Nature)

Preface

For decades the Mediterranean has represented the clear-cut border of the North–South cleavage distinguishing Europe from North Africa and the Middle East, economic relations being at the forefront of their relationships. But it is nowadays widely acknowledged that the improvement of North–South relations cannot rely upon economic achievements only and that other instruments have to be adopted. Once the Mediterranean has offered a new focus of analysis, namely the Islam–West confrontation as a cultural component of the North–South economic cleavage, it is essential to foster a unified culture respectful of differences, assuming that cultural cooperation does create the basis for more stable political and economic relations.

The thread running through this volume is the question whether we are moving towards a Mediterranean cultural identity. Is there a balance between cultural globalization and localism? The Mediterranean is currently facing a dilemma. On the one hand, once we acknowledge a certain complementarity between local specificity and modernity, we might move towards a more integrated area, encouraged by political and economic incentives; on the other, by pleading for the incompatibility between the 'West' and the 'South', we might be inclined to strengthen an ideal cultural wall dividing the northern from the southern shores of the Mediterranean. The cultural dialogue, which is the essential key to the coexistence of different peoples and cultures, guides this exchange of visions of civil society, democracy and human rights and points out the necessity of overcoming the culturalist–universalist debate in the name of multiplicity and plurality.

The aim here is not to make prescriptions, nor to provide the reader with recipes for achieving stability in the Mediterranean, but rather to offer, through an interdisciplinary approach, a pluralistic vision of democracy, civil society, human rights and dialogue among civilizations, the aspects of the human dimension of security in the Mediterranean that represent the major components of the third *volet* of the Euro-Mediterranean Partnership (EMP).

These debated issues are tackled to indirectly highlight achievements or impediments to the Barcelona Process. The EMP is a long-term process aimed at realizing the ambitious goals of an area of stability and prosperity in the Mediterranean and the fostering of human and social development. But all too often misunderstandings between the partners of the EMP arise, due to different definitions of concepts and strategies, or to wrong images of each other. Despite the common heritage of the actors involved in the Barcelona Process, agreement on crucial issues, including the protection of human rights and fundamental freedoms or fostering of democracy in a coherent manner, is far from easy.

This volume does not review the content of the EMP; it focuses more upon actors and values than upon procedures and specific projects. What are the contradictions of democratization? If it is difficult to define what civil society is, how can the EMP strengthen and support civil society? Is there a unique scale of values when dealing with human rights? To what extent does a dialogue among civilizations lead to compatibility and coexistence? Some reflections are devoted to the identification of crucial issues uniting or differentiating the actors involved in and addressed by the EMP.

Aimed at offering some speculations on the actors involved in the process and by focusing upon their peculiarities and specific interests, this book contains contributions that do not necessarily adopt the same research perspective nor rely upon a unique definition. Researchers from both shores of the Mediterranean are contending, by means of theoretical tools and empirical evidence, with different concepts, which are made the object of intervention within the EMP framework. Browsing through the chapters, an ideal loop can be envisaged from the use of a common language as a means of communication to a common civilization, yet passing through the debate on 'global' values, human rights and democratic freedoms by often adopting a critical perspective towards both the EU and the Mediterranean Partner Countries (MPCs).

Most of the chapters are the result of the fruitful exchange of views that occurred at the international workshop on 'The Human Dimension of Security and the Euro-Mediterranean Partnership' funded by the Italian Chair of Mediterranean Relations and Diplomacy at the Mediterranean Academy of Diplomatic Studies at the University of Malta, which took place in Malta on 14–15 May 1999. Most of the authors took advantage of that occasion to share their ideas with colleagues from different countries. For two days various aspects of the human dimension of security in the Mediterranean area and the chapter of the Barcelona Declaration on Partnership in Social, Cultural and Human Affairs were debated in a friendly but constructive atmosphere. Those papers are now edited in this volume with the aim of making a contribution to the further development of mutual understanding in the Mediterranean and of stressing the potential for a Mediterranean cultural identity that is respectful of specific cultural trends.

As editor of this volume, I have accumulated many debts of gratitude. First of all, thanks are due to the researchers who, sharing my interest in the human dimension of security, contributed with enthusiasm to this research project and patiently waited for the publication of this book. Thanks also go to Ambassador Antonio Badini, who after having participated in the workshop, kindly agreed to write the foreword to this volume. I am grateful to Richard Gillespie, who helped in the very early stages of publication. Finally, I owe many thanks to Fulvio Attinà, whose assistance since the planning stage of this research project I found extremely useful.

Stefania Panebianco
Catania, July 2001

Introduction

The Euro-Mediterranean Partnership in Perspective: The Political and Institutional Context

STEFANIA PANEBIANCO

The Euro-Mediterranean Partnership (EMP) is a multi-dimensional initiative of North–South cooperation aimed at turning 'the Mediterranean basin into an area of dialogue, exchange and cooperation granting peace, stability and prosperity' (Barcelona Declaration, 1995). In order to provide the reader with the regional cooperation framework in which issues such as democracy, civil society, human rights and cultural dialogue in the Mediterranean are currently dealt with, this introduction will focus upon the political context in which the EMP has been launched and developed. The institutional features of the EMP will then be briefly outlined, so as to offer a framework in which to put the *tesserae* of the human dimension of Euro-Mediterranean cooperation. Finally, the three-*volet* (or chapter) structure of the EMP will be analysed in order to demonstrate that the EMP is aimed at integrating the two shores of the Mediterranean, not just at political or economic levels, but also at social and cultural levels through the Partnership in Social, Cultural and Human Affairs. This is useful to remember, as not all the authors of this volume address directly initiatives laid down in the Barcelona Declaration, but instead tackle their topics from more technical and specific points of view.

Regional Integration Patterns in the Mediterranean

To set the Barcelona Process in the international political context, it can be interpreted through the theoretical perspective of regional integration and assimilated to the regional processes that are evolving in other areas of the world as much as in the Mediterranean.

Many scholars participate in the debate as to whether a purely Mediterranean region already exists or is in the process of being created. By reviewing the main trends and approaches of regionalism with specific attention to the concept of the international region, Stephen Calleya denies that the Mediterranean can be regarded as a region, stressing that 'post-Cold War

Mediterranean realities portray a picture of fragmentation' (Calleya, 1997: 229). Conversely, Fulvio Attinà depicts the regionalization process that is taking place in the Mediterranean as a reaction to globalization and regards the Mediterranean as a 'mediterranean' region, that is a 'region[s] surrounding [a] mid-land sea[s] and including different sub-systems of states linked by their own ties, institutions and people's identities' (Attinà, 1996: 9). In fact, in the Mediterranean three sub-regional groupings linked by strong political, cultural and historical ties can be easily singled out: Europe, the Maghreb and the Levant. These sub-systems of states do not preclude the emergence of all-encompassing regional cooperation; they can be instead the founding units of the nascent Euro-Mediterranean security system.

With the collapse of the bipolar international system, regionalization has become a prominent feature of world politics. Regionalist trends have emerged not just in the three economic macro-regions (Europe, North America and the Asian Pacific), but also in other areas of the world such as Latin America and the Caribbean (Katzenstein, 1996: 125). NAFTA (North Atlantic Free Trade Agreement), ASEAN (Association of Southeast Asian Nations) and APEC (Asia-Pacific Economic Cooperation Conference), for example, are cooperative economic integration projects based upon free trade. Besides the economic factor, regionalism also involves political, social and cultural aspects.

There are, however, different patterns of institutionalized regional cooperation. There is a big difference, for example, between *de jure* regional integration that exists in Europe and *de facto* regional integration in Asia (Katzenstein, 1996: 126). In western Europe through the Organization for Security and Co-operation in Europe (OSCE) and in Asia through ASEAN, for instance, security communities are being set up based upon the creation of multilateral institutions, the adoption of rules of the game, the agreement on principles and a learning process of getting together through seminar diplomacy (see Adler, 1998 and Acharya, 1998). Multilateralism and region-building are long-term non-linear processes, involving also the Mediterranean. But the Mediterranean has not developed the conditions for a security community yet, and disappointment of the partners involved might even stop the process.

Moreover, as a reaction to globalization, localism has spread to many areas of the world in order to fight against social and cultural homogenization deriving from globalization (Rosenau, 1997: 361) and to find common solutions to the new challenges. In a post-Westphalian world where states are no longer the only actors of the international system, since both state and non-state actors are interrelated across global, regional and national levels, regional integration and globalization are two complementary processes. Analyses of the current patterns of interaction at world level stress that the emergence of a global governance is accompanied by local integration experiences, both at the economic level, to create stronger economic blocs, and also as a result of the increasing awareness of the necessity to find common solutions to new security threats (Attinà, 1996). On the one hand, the global system is faced with centrifugal forces in which, in order to compensate for the tendency to stronger international interdependency, rising regional entities and fragmentation forces react against homogenization with local policies and politics. On the other hand, due to the intensification of global interconnectedness, states' capacities of self-governance have been reduced. 'Information, pollution, migrants, arms, ideas, images, news, crime, narcotics, disease, amongst other things, readily and frequently flow across national territorial boundaries' (McGrew, 1997: 6), which have become increasingly porous.' The permeability of borders challenges the ability of states to provide for the security of their citizens (Strange, 1997: 369). Many contemporary security threats derive from the failure of states to provide minimal conditions of order within their borders (Fawcett and Hurrell, 1995: 312).

A post-modern world characterized by complexity, fragmentation and uncertainty requires common strategies. In this context, multilateral institutions are created to help states to manage common problems by providing information and reducing the costs of transactions. Through limited collective action states achieve objectives unattainable through other means (Keohane, 1993: 274). Through the creation of collective security systems based upon confidence-building measures (CBMs), states facilitate communication, information and transparency. To tackle the new sources of conflict, cooperative security seeking to prevent conflict is more suitable than deterrence or containment strategies used to prevent classic inter-state conflict (Fawcett and Hurrell, 1995: 312).

With the end of the Cold War a European approach to security based upon cooperation through transparency and information, the CSCE/OSCE multidimensional concept of security, has emerged by default as a successful model. Now that European Union (EU) and NATO (North Atlantic Treaty Organization) enlargements include the Central and Eastern European countries within the European security structure, the Mediterranean border assumes a much higher relevance in terms of European security. And security does not imply only the traditional military challenges, but also includes economic, societal and environmental threats as well.

The comprehensive concept of security is at the basis of the EMP. One of the most innovative aspects of the Barcelona Declaration concerns, indeed, the definition of security itself. The redefinition of a security streamline that emerged in the post-Cold War world, due to the rising of challenges and threats stemming not just from hard security but prominently from political and economic challenges and 'soft' security, is reflected in the EMP, where the conventional definition of security is replaced by a comprehensive concept. A broad definition of security is adopted when promoting initiatives to prevent illegal migration, terrorism, organized crime, drug trafficking, or economic and social insecurity. These 'soft' security issues are widely admitted to be trans-regional and must be tackled within a regional security regime based upon mutual cooperation.

3

Through the EMP new forms of regional institutionalized cooperation might emerge, with the ultimate goal of creating a new security community (Adler, 1997) involving both shores of the Mediterranean. The ongoing institutionalization of Euro-Mediterranean relations is providing for a wide range of levels of interaction. There are quite clear patterns of cooperation based upon, on the one hand, intergovernmental interaction and, on the other, the increasing involvement of the grass-roots level through decentralized cooperation. Alongside governments and state actors, various other actors, processes and forces form a complex web of interaction linking 27 Euro-Mediterranean partner countries.

Strong interdependence due to geographical proximity and geopolitical constraints imposes a common approach to deal with sources of instability such as racism and xenophobia, national and religious extremism, and arms and drug trafficking. The EMP has been conceived as a cooperative initiative to cope with non-military challenges such as the increasing development gap, political and societal instability. This global approach derives from the acknowledgement that threats come as much from political instability and conventional intra-state tensions as from societal instability, economic inequalities and social and political dissatisfaction (Spencer, 1998a: 136). The long-term aim of the EMP is the creation of a security regime through CBMs (Tanner, 1996) as an alternative to the traditional dilemma of security relying upon military means (Attinà, 1998).

Thus, with the EMP, common institutions are in the process of being set up to cope with the challenges produced by globalization through regional cooperation. The Barcelona Process has institutionalized a multilayered system of cooperation in the Mediterranean, but the speed of this regional process is accelerated or reduced by contingent political factors.

Exogenous and Endogenous Factors Leading to the Adoption of the Euro-Mediterranean Partnership

The EMP can be regarded as a turning point in EU Mediterranean policy as it has adopted a different strategy compared to the previous EC/EU initiatives addressing the Mediterranean countries. Long before the adoption of the EMP, the EU had established links with the Mediterranean Partner Countries (MPCs). For centuries Europe, North Africa and the Middle East have been linked by close historical ties, cultural exchange and trade, despite the dark chapter of colonization. Mainly due to French colonial ties with the Maghreb countries, the European Community (EC) established a special relationship with North Africa.[2] Since the Treaty of Rome creating the EC, cooperation instruments were to be found in commercial and association agreements, which were basically conceived to defend special economic links with the MPCs. However, these were limited in nature and in scope and were basically economic, as only a few industrial products were taken into account. In the 1960s, then, there was no specific EC Mediterranean policy. The non-European Mediterranean countries were linked to the EC with the type of instruments used in EC relations with the Third World countries (i.e. preferential commercial agreements) in order to maintain pre-existent preferential commercial regimes. The association agreements with European countries such as Greece, Turkey or Spain were different in nature, as they had full membership as the ultimate goal, excluded instead for non-European countries. A complete lack of coordination was quite evident.

To replace this piecemeal approach and provide a more coherent strategy to the several existing agreements with MPCs, the Paris Summit of 1972 adopted the Global Mediterranean Policy, which introduced technical and financial cooperation beyond economic cooperation. But this soon proved to be ineffective, first due to the critical international economic situation following the 1973 oil crisis, and second due to the post-colonial logic that formed the basis of the Mediterranean policy: the export-led principle was wrongly conceived as economic development conducive to the MPCs. In the early 1990s EU Mediterranean policy was reformed and changed into the Renovated Mediterranean Policy, which was aimed at strengthening cooperation at a horizontal level, and a new mechanism of 'decentralized cooperation' was introduced.

Several changes in the early 1990s, both internal and external to the EU, favoured the restructuring of EU Mediterranean policy and the launching of the EMP in 1995. Among the endogenous factors leading to the EMP, there is, primarily, the major role played by the reshaping of EU external policy with the adoption of the Maastricht Treaty and consequently of the Common Foreign and Security Policy (CFSP). After Maastricht the EU was looking for a more cohesive CFSP, following the indication that the Western European Union would become the military pillar of the EU. The direction was towards a more 'European' foreign policy, particularly regarding the EU periphery. Second, the EU wanted to re-equilibrate towards the Mediterranean the EU *Ostpolitik* that had followed the fall of the Berlin Wall.

However, exogenous factors were as effective as endogenous ones. First of all, economic internationalization imposing the creation of larger markets had a certain impact on Euro-Mediterranean relations by favouring the creation of a free trade area in the Mediterranean. Second, as mentioned above, the post-Cold War reorganization of the international arena in geostrategic terms allowed for the reassessment of power and a more active international role of the EU to deal directly with challenges to security in the Mediterranean. The EU's aim of having a more coherent and visible Mediterranean policy was therefore faced by new prospects of a primary role for Europe in the Mediterranean region and in the ongoing Middle East Peace Process (MEPP).[3] To some extent the adoption of the EMP can be regarded as the result of the redefinition of the role of the EU in the post-Cold War international system.

In 1995 the political conditions were favourable to a restructuring and relaunching of existing EU Mediterranean policy. During the Barcelona Conference on 27–28 November 1995, representatives of 27 countries (all 15 EU members plus Algeria, Cyprus, Egypt, Israel, Jordan, Lebanon, Malta, Morocco, the Palestinian Authority, Syria, Tunisia and Turkey)[4] adopted the Barcelona Declaration, aimed at creating a zone of peace and prosperity based upon a Mediterranean free trade area (MEFTA) by the year 2010 and the development of human resources, the promotion of understanding between cultures and exchanges between civil societies. An inclusive and global approach to tackle both 'soft' and 'hard' security concerns was then adopted. This was the launching of the EMP, or Barcelona Process, based upon, on the one hand, multilateral cooperation between the EU and MPCs and, on the other, upon bilateral cooperation with the signing of the Mediterranean association agreements between the EU and each Mediterranean partner country. South–South cooperation was strongly recommended as well.

Such an event was welcomed as a new era in Euro-Mediterranean relations. This was due, first, to the newly adopted concept of 'partnership', which in principle puts all the parties involved on the same footing,[5] second, to the increasing of EU funds devoted to the MPCs and third, to the two levels of cooperation – bilateral and multilateral – that were laid down, the latter leading eventually to a more integrated region. Nevertheless, evaluations of the results achieved since the launching of the Barcelona Process are quite controversial.

The Institutional Framework of the EMP: a Multilayered System of Regional Cooperation

With the EMP, Euro-Mediterranean cooperation has been channelled into an institutionalization process and structured through several levels of interaction. The Barcelona Process has set up political institutions aggregating individuals from 27 countries acting at both governmental and non-governmental levels. Within the general framework laid down in the Barcelona Declaration, periodical and sectoral meetings take place at different levels for advancement in each policy domain. A minimum complex of explicit rules has been agreed upon, indicating periodic meetings as the fora at which to advance on social norms and a common culture. A closer look at each interaction level proves that, despite regional political constraints and territorial disputes, the process is viable. Political leaders, senior officials, civil society representatives and experts from the 27 partner countries regularly meet within the EMP institutions, participate in the process and revitalize it. Different perspectives and points of view are compounded within common institutions aimed at facilitating cooperative behaviour. However, even though they follow a step-by-step approach, interaction is not free of contradiction, and expectations of both state and non-state actors are not always convergent. Cooperation is structured by a shared system of rules that is still in the making.

The Barcelona Process deals with three fields of action – the Political and Security Partnership, the Economic and Financial Partnership and the Partnership in Social, Cultural and Human Affairs – which are closely intertwined, according to the assumption that political stability and human development are necessary for economic investment initiatives. Following the OSCE structure, these three areas of cooperation are part of the same project, but at the same time are distinct and each one can advance regardless of the success or failure of the others. By adopting the OSCE style of three different baskets, the EMP has transposed this comprehensive approach to an area that is marked by political tensions and economic disparities but yet is rich in historical and cultural heritage.[6]

The current format of the EMP derives from the EU experience of cooperation with other regional areas and the necessity of overcoming the volatile nature of previous Euro-Mediterranean relations. In fact, the EMP is a long-term process aimed at avoiding weaknesses and deficiencies of the former EC Mediterranean policy. The Euro-Mediterranean partners have formalized stable relationships primarily to reduce uncertainty. Security needs, considered in the wide meaning adopted by the EMP, are the main impetus towards this kind of institutionalization. The engine behind the process is the mutual interest of managing resources, the necessity of facing sources of insecurity in order to create a regional security regime, the improvement of economic conditions and the fostering of better understanding among peoples. Actors are aware of the benefits of cooperation: to maximize utilities and minimize costs of cooperation. But the difficult task is to find an equilibrium between the interests of all the actors involved.

The Barcelona Declaration has indicated several policy domains, some of which have progressed towards policy formulation, while others are still at the declaratory stage. In some areas a certain agreement has been reached to formulate common policies and rules of the game have been already adopted. All in all, the structural component of institutionalization has preceded the normative and cognitive aspect of the EMP institutions. It is difficult to share models of behaviour, as the values suggested by the EU are to some extent criticized by the MPCs. However, agreement on normative values applies more easily at lower levels, within policy communities or networks of non-governmental organizations (NGOs), chambers of commerce, experts, representatives of civil society, academics, etc. With the creation of institutions and the agreement on goals, procedures and strategies the tortuous path of institution-building has started and is on its way, despite the low speed of its advancement.

To explore the conditions under which Euro-Mediterranean cooperation occurs, it is useful to identify each interaction level. The process of institutionalization is taking place at both intergovernmental and non-state actor level (see Figure 1). The leading role is played by the governmental actors, who

7

FIGURE 1: THE EMP INSTITUTIONAL FRAMEWORK

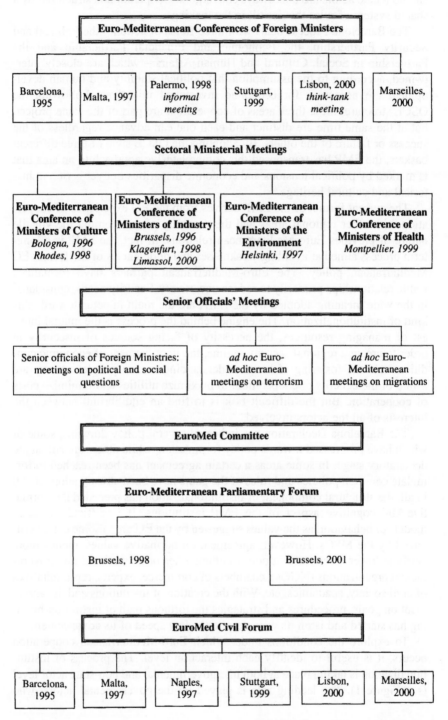

agreed to launch the process by adopting the Barcelona Declaration[7] and the Work Programme enclosed. After Barcelona in 1995, Conferences of Ministers of Foreign Affairs took place in Malta in 1997, Palermo in 1998 (although it was an informal meeting), Stuttgart in 1999 and Marseilles in November 2000. In May 2000 a think-tank meeting of Euro-Mediterranean foreign ministers also took place in Lisbon to prepare for the Marseilles conference. Foreign ministers' meetings take place to review the implementation of the EMP and revive the process itself.

Inter-state relations and political or territorial disputes can influence the pace of advancement of regional cooperation. While the Malta meeting was a hostage of the stalemate of the MEPP,[8] the *ad hoc* informal Palermo meeting was quite successful in revitalizing the Partnership after a couple of years of *relantissement* due to the breakdown of the Arab–Israeli peace process. The Stuttgart meeting made substantial political statements to advance the Barcelona Process, both with specific EMP projects and the MEPP. The Marseilles interministerial conference was again frozen by the second *intifada*, which started at the end of September 2000.[9] However, the Barcelona Process remains in place as a multilateral regional forum.

Along the guidelines agreed upon at interministerial meetings, sectoral meetings at governmental expert level are held in each cooperation field. As a matter of fact, the formulation of single policies relies upon sectoral meetings at ministerial level and *ad hoc* conferences or workshops. For instance, projects in cultural fields are fostered during the Euro-Mediterranean Conferences of Ministers of Culture. The first conference took place in Bologna in 1996 and the second one in Rhodes in 1998. In most cases ministerial sectoral conferences have lead to the establishment of permanent dialogue structures and trans-national networks of private operators, as was the case for the regional programme 'EuroMed Heritage', which was launched during the Bologna conference.

Senior officials' meetings are an important platform for reconciling differences and agreeing upon a common project. Among their tasks is the drafting of the Charter for Peace and Stability in the Mediterranean, a political statement that has to be adopted at ministerial level by all partners, which eventually will have the same value as the Barcelona Declaration. In Stuttgart in 1999 the ministers of foreign affairs adopted the guidelines for elaborating a Euro-Mediterranean Charter as set up by senior officials. The French EU presidency was in charge of organizing the fourth Euro-Mediterranean Conference and worked hard to have the final draft of the charter adopted in Marseilles in 2000. Due to the ongoing conflict in the Middle East, the Syrian and Lebanese foreign ministers were absent to protest and the required consensus of the 27 partners was missed. However, senior officials have recently focused upon other fields of cooperation, namely terrorism, migration and human exchanges.

The institutional innovation of the EMP created a EuroMed Committee for the Barcelona Process, consisting of a high-ranking representative from each of the 27 Euro-Mediterranean partners and chaired by the EU presidency. This committee holds periodic meetings to examine activities related to the EMP and to review the progress towards the implementation of Euro-Mediterranean cooperative strategies and actions to be adopted within the framework of the EMP. Its main task, then, is to implement and monitor the follow-up meetings and work on each *volet* at ministerial and official levels. It also stimulates and approves activities to be carried out under the EMP framework.

The European Commission is in charge of the organizational function and acts as the secretariat of the EMP. It is in charge of the preparation and follow-up work for the meetings. The Commission plays the role of 'institutional entrepreneur', stimulating the creation of rules, norms, routines and suggesting behavioural models. Regarding financing decisions, the commission is assis-ted by a 'Med Committee' composed of representatives of the member states and a representative from the European Investment Bank.

Within the EMP framework parliamentary diplomacy is conceived as another fruitful instrument for creating confidence among the partners. In order to promote institutional contacts, the Work Programme annexed to the Barcelona Declaration had invited the European Parliament (EP) to take the initiative with the national parliaments of the Euro-Mediterranean partners. In October 1998 the first Euro-Mediterranean Parliamentary Forum took place, bringing together representatives from the EP and members of parliaments of the MPCs. The forum adopted a final declaration aimed at sanctioning the parliamentary dimension of the EMP. In March 1999 a Conference of Presidents of Euro-Mediterranean Parliaments took place to contribute to the Euro-Mediterranean parliamentary dialogue; the Second Euro-Mediterranean Conference of Presidents of Parliaments took place in Alexandria in May 2000. The Second Euro-Mediterranean Parliamentary Forum took place in Brussels in February 2001. The EP fully supports EU initiatives concerning the Mediterranean; in order to stress the salience of the non-governmental level of Mediterranean cooperation, in March 2000 the EP issued a Resolution on Mediterranean Policy inviting the Council and the EC to relaunch the EMP, in which decentralized cooperation and social development were regarded as key elements of the Partnership. A constraint on parliamentary cooperation, though, derives from the different representative systems and parliamentary mandates.

If incidental factors such as political constraints greatly influence the results of the institutions' activities, networking capability is much higher at non-state levels. In order to encourage the involvement of a wide circle of actors outside central governments, since the beginning of the Barcelona Process meetings of associations, NGOs' representatives and civil society accompany the interministerial meetings. In 1995 non-governmental actors took the initiative to organize and institutionalize a level of interaction parallel to the interministerial level. Representatives of civil society, mainly acting in the fields of human rights, environment, industry, business and trade unions took action and organized the EuroMed Civil Forum as an alternative to the ministerial meeting, to provide state actors with inputs from the bottom. After Barcelona, the Conferences of Ministers of Foreign Affairs held in Malta, Stuttgart and Marseilles were accompanied by EuroMed civil fora as well. Another civil forum was held in Naples in December 1997 to stimulate the process after the Malta Conference and a Trans-Mediterranean Civil Society Summit took place in Lisbon in May 2000 in parallel with the think-tank meeting of Euro-Mediterranean ministers of foreign affairs. As a result of this non-governmental interaction networks of a wide typology of social actors dealing with issues dealt with by the EMP have been set up.

The EuroMed Civil Fora have widely contributed to the spread of the concept of multiculturality and the importance of civil society. On these occasions civil society representatives adopt recommendations, official documents or final reports on issues ranging from human rights to environmental issues, from industrial relations to trade unions, from economic affairs to cultural dialogue. The Marseilles EuroMed Civil Forum produced a common declaration and individual statements from the three colleges (the NGOs' Civil Forum, the Trade Union Forum, and the Local Communities and Authorities Forum). Through participation in the civil fora, civil society representatives have become actors of the political process, drawing ministers' attention to a wide range of issues such as human rights, youth, environment and culture. If the meetings of ministers of foreign affairs are generally conceived to review the functioning of the EMP and reinvigorate the process with new ideas and cooperative programmes, through the parallel civil fora the intergovernmental level is provided with a new impetus from the grass-roots level. Non-governmental bodies have then become official actors in the partnership.

The pivotal role of civil society organizations in the creation of CBMs, or more precisely partnership-building measures (PBMs), is also enacted through the decentralized cooperation that forms the basis of several Euro-Mediterranean programmes. Following the path marked out by the Renovated Mediterranean Policy, decentralized cooperation is one of the founding mechanisms of EMP cooperation that does not see states as the only actors but, on the contrary, recognizes civil society as an important actor of cooperation. The bottom-up approach is a recurrent principle in the Barcelona Declaration, where a rough list of non-state actors to be involved in the process is provided. Cooperation programmes involving practitioners and members of civil society can be long-lasting and more effective than a top-down process, as they imply direct cultural exchanges.

The Commission itself supports the creation of Euro-Mediterranean networks to exchange experiences and know-how and to contribute to the reinforcement of the EMP through active cooperation between organizations with similar functions acting in EMP partner countries. Among these stable networks are: EuroMeSCo, a non-governmental network of foreign policy institutes; Femise, a network of economic institutes; Jemstone, a network of journalists in the EuroMed region; Remfoc, a Euro-Maghreb network for training

11

in the field of communication; Europartenariat, a forum of small and medium enterprises; ArchiMedes, a network of chambers of commerce not exclusively from Euro-Mediterranean countries; MEDAPME, a network of small and medium enterprises. Most of these networks are funded by the MEDA pro-gramme and their level of institutionalization varies according to the field of action.

Within the EMP institutional framework a variety of actors are involved in cooperation at governmental, administrative, parliamentary and civil society levels. All in all, the establishment of the institutional project has been relatively easy. But the institution-building process, which aims at reducing uncertainty, can be easily hijacked by contingent political factors and different perceptions of rules and strategies. Moreover, the scarcity of resources still represents an important constraint.

From what has been sketched out above, beyond the potential of the Barcelona Process as a regional cooperation forum, the weakness of a Euro-Mediterranean institutional process that is strongly utility-oriented emerges. Institutionalization among countries with different economic development is usually rather problematic, but not necessarily impossible. Despite different political strategies and cognitive models, the perception that a common problem-solving process had to be initiated led to the launching of the Barcelona process. Common structures have been created in order to debate and negotiate to adopt common rules and develop pluralist cognitive models. For an enduring institutional process, common norms and values are required. The development of interaction and dialogue within the third *volet* of the EMP in order to help the creation of a pluralist identity of shared values is, then, of primary importance.

Political and Security Cooperation in the Mediterranean

Political and security cooperation within the framework of the EMP is based upon a variegated typology of initiatives ranging from meetings at ministerial, junior diplomat or senior official levels, to networks of practitioners or researchers. The overall project emphasizes the creation of PBMs that are based on political and diplomatic processes instead of directly addressing the resolution of existing conflicts. The most innovative aspect of the Euro-Mediterranean relations introduced by the EMP is the multilateral cooperation that takes place via OSCE *seminar diplomacy*, i.e. meetings of diplomats, prac-titioners, civil servants and experts 'aimed at promoting political dialogue and international co-operation ... and preventing or managing conflict by means of consensual technical or normative knowledge' (Adler, 1998: 138). In Barcelona the partners agreed to improve mutual trust and understanding through PBMs in order to build an environment that is conducive, in the long term, to a regional system of cooperative security.

This translates into non-conventional initiatives such as EU-sponsored seminars for junior diplomats from all the 27 partners, or into the creation of EuroMeSCo or Strademed to regularly bring together security experts to promote transparency in security perceptions. The creation of EuroMeSCo (Euro-Mediterranean Study Commission), for instance, was expressly mentioned in the Barcelona Work Programme as a PBM under the Barcelona Process; so in 1996 a non-governmental network of foreign policy institutes in the EuroMed region was set up. Within expert networks agreement on normative values applies more easily. The emphasis, then, is on cooperation and exchange of information taking place in informal settings to foster mutual confidence and understanding, and on bringing countries with different strategic cultures a bit closer.

The Final Conclusions of the Presidency of the Marseilles Ministerial Conference reaffirmed 'the need ... to enhance the political dialogue at their level too, to contribute to clearing up misunderstandings, foster the approximation of analyses and perceptions and make it possible subsequently to agree on measures to strengthen confidence and transparency'. The key elements of PBMs are precisely the exchange of information and transparency. PBMs provide for regular consultation and exchanges of information between partners. Those agreed so far are:

- training and information seminars for diplomats;
- networks of foreign policy institutes (EuroMeSCo and Strademed);
- cooperation among civil protection services during natural and man-made disasters;
- a register of bilateral agreements; and
- an exchange of information on international conventions on human rights, disarmament and humanitarian rights.

The political and security partnership also embraces a wide range of actions dealing with 'hot' issues such as terrorism, and as a result some problems among the partner countries can arise even at the very beginning of cooperation, when specific actions are planned. So, for instance, a clear-cut definition of terrorism is usually avoided. In order to avoid complete stalemate, a pragmatic approach has been adopted and actions are taken on a step-by-step basis whenever there is a common perception of a specific threat. The difficulties and lengthiness encountered by the partners in adopting the Charter for Peace and Stability in the Mediterranean, which would provide an institutional mechanism for dialogue and crisis prevention, prove that, in this case, a 'lowest common denominator' approach is *de facto* adopted.[10] Issues are tackled only if and when there is a common will and agreement to cooperate, that is to say, there are no major unilateral vetoes. Otherwise, a project is frozen until the propitious conditions for its adoption arise.

Moreover, when dealing with human rights a 'minimal consensus' rule is often followed. It is evident that the EMP brings together 27 partners who not only have different levels of socio-economic development but also different socio-political systems that are differently ranged in the democratic development scale. In the Barcelona Declaration the commitment towards the democratization process is clearly and repeatedly stated, but democracy is a critical issue. At EU level, also, coherence is often lacking towards aggression to democratic values and processes in the partner countries, or whether democratic freedoms are to be granted without limits or controls (e.g. freedoms of expression, of association, of thought and of conscience). Critics of EU democratic policy point out that beyond the declaratory content of official documents, in practice the EU allows legitimate counterparts not necessarily to respect democratic standards.[11] A certain declaratory reference to principles such as fostering democracy and human rights has not been accompanied by a 'hard hand' of EU countries and political pragmatism has prevailed in events such as the Algerian crisis.[12] For most partners the conventional defence of borders is still an important factor and economic factors often prevail over internal crises.

Despite these contradictions, a positive result of the piecemeal approach that is at the basis of the EMP is that a *relantissement* in one field does not block the others. There are few doubts that the results achieved so far by the EMP are very poor compared to the ambitious goals indicated in the Barcelona Declaration. But the process is still in place, while other initiatives, such as the Middle East and North Africa (MENA) Process led by Washington to bring together industrialists and small and medium enterprises, have been interrupted due to political tensions in the region. Realistically, one of the main achievements of the Barcelona Process is its very existence and the fact that despite the existing political tensions among the partners, it has remained the last multilateral regional forum.

Challenges to the Economic and Financial Partnership: Some Critical Evaluations

The spread of neo-liberal economic development theories in the 1990s, leading to the state withdrawal from the economy through privatization of state assets and the rule of the free market, was the inspiring force of the EMP in economic and financial affairs. The EU has adopted the rule 'liberalization vs. protectionism' even in its external relations with MPCs. As a result, the framework of the Euro-Mediterranean Partnership on economic and financial affairs is widely based upon neo-liberal assumptions.

In the second chapter of the Barcelona Declaration emphasis is placed upon sustainable and balanced economic and social development to create an area of shared prosperity through sustainable socio-economic development, improvement of living conditions of the population and the encouragement of regional cooperation and integration. One of the main aims of the EMP is to complete by 2010 a MEFTA in industrial goods and services within the 27 partners. This is an ambitious goal, which clearly stems from the dynamics typical of the 1990s of creating large trans-national trading and investment blocs such as NAFTA, Mercosur and APEC. After EU enlargement, this achievement would open up a large market of 600 to 800 million people and about 40 countries, with all the economic opportunities this would allow.

But this framework is often subject to strong criticism. A view shared by scholars who are not necessarily from the southern Mediterranean flank stresses that a too rapid introduction of free competition rules might be detrimental to local companies, which are often inefficient small- and medium-sized enterprises. Moreover, in the short run Mediterranean countries may suffer a substantial loss, as they will lose the tariff revenue collected on imports of EU origin that account for half of imports into Mediterranean countries and governments would have to find other forms of revenue. In the immediate term this would imply major fiscal costs (Marks, 1999: 54).

Critics of the assumption that economic development will almost automatically follow liberalization stress that if, in the long run, there are the economic opportunities offered by larger markets in the global economy, in the short run there are risks stemming from the restructuring of underdeveloped economic systems often protected by tariff barriers or state subventions. Although the liberalization of trade should induce firms to improve their efficiency, weak economies relying upon state subventions and protection might reduce rather than increase their competitiveness, and liberalization then has to be accom-panied by complementary actions to improve the functioning of the economy. The EMP is likely to be beneficial to the Mediterranean countries in the long run, while in the short to middle run it is likely to be economically welfare-reducing. The *mise à nouveau* phase, the transition and modernization process to raise local standards to European levels, is therefore extremely delicate, and the operational level of local companies must be raised through infrastructure improvements, technology transfer and training.

According to some critical visions of the implementation of EMP economic prescriptions, reduced tariffs on manufactured goods will mean that those who would initially benefit the most are the European exporters, while 'the main costs are likely to be borne by southern Mediterranean economies' (Marks, 1999: 57). The Partnership will increase EU exports to MPCs while decreasing imports away from them (Tovias, 1999: 82). Without reviewing the principles upon which the EMP is based, the implementation of the EMP economic framework might create a 'leopard-spot economy' in North Africa, with North African countries even more becoming satellites of European economies (Joffé, 1999: 259). Expectations at both political and public opi-nion levels are so high that negative results from a poor or wrong implementation of the EMP might be counterproductive and even deepen the North–South divide.

For the period 1995–99 the EU allocated €4,658 billion and the European Investment Bank (EIB) granted €3,996 billion loans. For the period 2000–06 an increase has been decided, passing to an EU allocation of €5,350 billion and

€6,4 billion EIB loans. Nevertheless, the MPCs strongly criticize the EU for preferring Eastern Europe to the Mediterranean partners in terms of investments and allocated funds.

The Human Dimension of the EMP: the Partnership in Social, Cultural and Human Affairs

The institutionalization process encounters difficulties not just due to political reasons or economic disparities marking the North–South divide, but also because of a different cultural approach that does not always allow for an immediate agreement on concepts and strategies. It is exactly the third *volet* of the Barcelona Declaration, the Partnership in Social, Cultural and Human Affairs, that offers an intriguing area of investigation, with its clearly stated aim of 'developing human resources, promoting understanding between cultures and exchanges between civil societies' (Barcelona Declaration, 1995). Here, critical goals are set such as dialogue between religions, a more active role of civil society, the strengthening of democratic institutions and the rule of law. Despite the continuously recalled principle of preservation of cultural specificity, the declaratory emphasis must come to terms with reality, with the distrust of the MPCs towards 'western' values and any form of economic and cultural 'neo-colonialism', and with the price of public opinion often scarcely interested in long-term projects, but much more sensitive to everyday problems.

The scope of the EMP is much broader than previous EC/EU Mediterranean policies, which were basically economic, or other existing initiatives dealing strictly with security (e.g. the NATO Mediterranean Dialogue). The comprehensive approach of the EMP puts political, economic and human affairs on the same level as major components of the same process. The EMP is not a strategic collective security alliance, but a pervasive project dealing directly with various sectors of society. The third *volet* of the Barcelona Declaration represents the most innovative aspect of the EMP, namely the development of human resources as one of the key components of regional cooperation.

The official aim of the third chapter of the Barcelona Declaration is to promote closer relations and better understanding between their peoples and improve mutual perceptions. The basic assumption of the EMP is the existence and recognition of different civilizations and cultural traditions. This implies dialogue and mutual respect between Mediterranean cultures and civilizations. With the EMP, for the first time culture has been included in the field of cooperation between the EU and MPCs. The traditions of culture and civilization throughout the Mediterranean are an important factor in bringing people closer, promoting mutual understanding and improving the perception of the other. The development of human resources and civil society, support for democratic institutions and exchanges between societies are fundamental goals of the EMP.

Following the path marked by the Renovated Mediterranean Policy, decentralized cooperation is one of the founding mechanisms of EMP cooperation that does not see states as the only actors but, on the contrary, recognizes civil society as the major actor of cooperation. This bottom-up approach is a recurrent principle in the Barcelona Declaration, where a rough list of non-state actors to be involved in the process is provided. Through decentralized cooperation programmes, cooperation between civil societies acting in specific sectors takes place, developing pluralist cognitive models. As a matter of fact, agreement on normative values takes place more easily at lower levels, within networks of NGOs, chambers of commerce, experts and academics. Trans-Mediterranean networks are created to develop relations among public and private social actors from the 27 partners. In brief, representatives of civil society broadly conceived act as socialization actors.

Aimed at involving a wide circle of actors outside central governments, since the beginning of the Barcelona Process meetings of associations, NGOs' representatives and civil society have accompanied the ministerial meetings to provide state actors with input from trade unions, chambers of commerce, industrialists, human rights, environmental and cultural associations. The EuroMed Civil Fora have widely contributed to the spread of the concept of multiculturality and the importance of civil society.[13]

Within the third *volet* of the EMP several initiatives have been adopted to stimulate integration at grass-roots level through various methods of cultural diffusion such as theatre, cinema, media, education, arts, music, etc. Several cultural events have been conceived to enhance harmony and mutual respect among peoples. Within the cultural cooperation framework several programmes based upon decentralized cooperation have been adopted to create trans-Mediterranean networks in order to develop relations among public and private social actors from the 27 partners. At the Bologna Meeting of Ministers of Culture in April 1996 cultural heritage had been identified as a priority area of cooperation. The preservation of an intellectual heritage through the EuroMed Heritage Programme has been the most successful subject of cooperation in this *volet*.

Stressing the common cultural heritage does not imply losing specificities, but pleads instead for mutual respect and coexistence, as 'dialogue and respect between cultures and religions is a necessary condition for the reconciliation of peoples' (Barcelona Declaration, 1995). Inter-religious dialogue represents, then, another important component of the third chapter of the Barcelona Declaration. The overall aim at the basis of the EMP is the 'pursuit of a pluri-cultural consensus which strengthens the notion of human rights and reinforces the universality of human rights taking socio-cultural, linguistic and religious diversities of the Mediterranean into account' (ibid.). The EMP rests upon a constructivist approach aimed not only at promoting tolerance, but at spreading positive perception of cultural differences as well.

Conclusions: Speculations about the Future

Cooperation in the Mediterranean has become imperative for several reasons. First, due to geopolitical reasons common strategies are necessary to avoid conflicts and create an area of peaceful coexistence. Second, environmental aspects such as the ecological challenges the Mediterranean is facing (e.g. desertification, pollution, uncontrolled urbanization) require common North and South strategies. Third, economic considerations are important. Demographic increases within the MPCs are not accompanied by economic development, and so rising unemployment has an increasing influence. Finally, social and cultural solutions are required to avoid any 'clash of civilizations' (Huntington, 1998) due to misperceptions and mistrust. These are the basic assumptions that led in 1995 to the launching of the EMP to create a framework of regional cooperation.

The EMP has the potential to strengthen political, economic and cultural ties across the Mediterranean area. But so far concrete results of the Partnership have been limited when compared to the aims listed in the Barcelona Declaration. A certain rhetoric should be replaced by more effective actions. The comprehensive approach adopted in Barcelona is based upon the assumption that political stability and economic prosperity are interdependent and require social and cultural development according to a mutually reinforcing logic. Due to the *relantissement* in achieving political stability in the area and to the delay of economic development taking off, a restructuring of the Barcelona Process is now required, focusing particularly upon the initiatives aimed at dispelling any degeneration of interrelations leading to xenophobia, racism, increasing intolerance and so forth. To raise the visibility of the Process, new initiatives are essential to deal not only with the élites, but with a broader public as well.

NOTES

1. According to McGrew, in a globalized world 'governments no longer control what transpires within their own national boundaries' (McGrew, 1997: 10).
2. Among EU member countries, Mediterranean countries are traditionally linked to southern Mediterranean countries and are prone to cooperation initiatives much more than northern countries. Historically, France has played the leading role of dominant power in the region. In more recent times the Spanish government has also pushed for closer EU–Mediterranean relations through a campaign ending up with the Barcelona Conference of November 1995. The Italian government has been active in this direction as well; in 1990 Italy together with Spain

launched the proposal for a conference on security and cooperation in the Mediterranean along the lines of the Conference on Security and Cooperation in Europe (Bin, 1997). See Willa (1999: 9 ff) for a comparison of attitudes of EU Mediterranean countries towards the Mediterranean area.

3. The adoption of the EMP in 1995 was to a large extent influenced by the optimism generated by the MEPP which had started with the Madrid Summit in 1991. The EU role within the MEPP multilateral track soon revealed itself to be more prominent in the economic sphere than in the political one. The US then reaffirmed its key role in the region with attempts to revitalize the MEPP, which had been frozen by the second *intifada* of September 2000.

4. Libya remained outside the Barcelona Conference due to the Lockerbie affair. The release of the Libyan suspects and the removal of international sanctions was followed by an invitation to Libyan representatives to participate in the 1999 Stuttgart Inter-Ministerial Conference with an observer status. Some European countries, and Italy is among the promoters, are acting to have Libya in the Barcelona Process as soon as international conditions allow it, on condition that Libya accepts the *acquis* of the Barcelona Process *in toto*.

5. However, a political constraint on the concept of partnership stems from the Arab–Israeli conflict, in particular the Arab veto on holding meetings at the highest level in a 'non-neutral' country. This is one of the reasons why all conferences of foreign ministers have been held so far in EU (namely Spain, Italy, Germany, France) or neutral countries (Malta). As long as the MPCs do not host a meeting of foreign ministers, the EMP will not be a real 'partnership'.

6. The main differences between the two processes are evident: while the OSCE (at that time still the CSCE) was born in the East–West context, the EMP is embedded in the North–South context; the EMP is a purely European initiative, the USA and Russia being non-actors in this project; the European partners were culturally much more homogeneous compared to the Mediterranean partners (for a detailed comparison between the EMP and the OSCE, see Xenakis, 1998).

7. The Barcelona Declaration is not a constitution, but rather a politically binding declaration.

8. For more details on the Malta Conference and the effects produced by the critical political situation in the Middle East over the Barcelona Process, see Edwards and Philippart (1997).

9. The relationship between the EMP and the MEPP is very special. The MEPP is formally separated but *de facto* complementary to the Barcelona Process. The Europeans have repeatedly stated that these are two distinct processes. The EMP should not be hijacked by the stalemate of the MEPP, because the main security concerns of the EMP partners, namely the MEPP, are not directly addressed by the Barcelona Process. However, clear reference is made in the Barcelona Declaration to the 'land for peace' principle; the Stuttgart chairman's conclusions referred to Israel's responsibility in the stalemate of the process; and in the EU Common Strategy for the Mediterranean the MEPP is addressed as a 'prerequisite for peace and stability in the Mediterranean'. Undeniably, the political conditions of the early 1990s (the Madrid Peace Conference and the Oslo agreements) led the way to the Barcelona Conference and created the favourable conditions to commit the EU, Magreb, Mashrak and insular Mediterranean countries plus Turkey in a joint project. Following this, the Malta interministerial meeting of April 1997 proved that the Barcelona Process was seriously affected by the critical political situation. When the MEPP was at a stalemate during the Netanyahu administration, the EMP process was not completely paralysed, as interministerial meetings took place and political involvement was reaffirmed by all partners. The Marseilles interministerial meeting was again a hostage of the renewal of violence in the Middle East, with the most evident effect that the adoption of the Peace and Stability Charter was impossible. However, the very subtle distinction between the two processes allowed partners such as Syria to be involved in MEDA projects mainly pertaining to the third chapter and upon condition that Israel is not a partner in the same project. The multiple areas of cooperation listed in the Barcelona Declaration allow for a different involvement of each partner in the EMP projects according to its interest.

10. At the Stuttgart Ministerial Meeting in April 1999 the guidelines for elaborating the Charter for Peace and Stability submitted by senior officials were welcomed by ministers as a functional instrument for the implementation of the principles of the Barcelona Declaration. Nevertheless, concrete progress towards the formal approval of the charter was not made, as the ministers of foreign affairs set the vague deadline 'as soon as political circumstances allow'. In Marseilles

the ministers agreed to defer the adoption of the charter, owing to the political context *as soon as the situation permits.*

11. For a critical view on democracy in the EU see Chapters 1 and 3 in this volume.

12. A case in point is that despite the Algerian crisis, European investments in new oil, gas and pipeline activities went on regularly.

13. See Chapter 5 for a detailed analysis of the EuroMed Civil Fora.

Part I:

DEMOCRATIZATION IN THE MEDITERRANEAN COUNTRIES

1

A Challenge for EU Mediterranean Policy: Upgrading Democracy from Threat to Risk

BÉCHIR CHOUROU

The Mediterranean in EU Foreign Policy

It has become commonplace to open any discussion on the Mediterranean with statements to the effect that the Mediterranean is the cradle of civilization, the birthplace of the three main revealed religions (Christianity, Islam and Judaism), the area where several cultures interact and so on.

Without denying the relevance of such considerations, there are other – perhaps more critical – ones that ought to be kept in mind when discussing the Mediterranean. In particular, what is meant by the term 'Mediterranean', and is it an appropriate unit of analysis? The same question applies equally well to the term 'Europe'.

The Units of Analysis

Before one can proceed with any analysis, one ought to be clear about the delimitation or definition of the units to be analysed. In this particular case, the term 'Euro-Mediterranean' is clearly to be understood as a political construct that does not necessarily reflect geographical or other even less concrete features or characteristics. Thus, the word 'Europe' is used to refer to the European Union (EU), however its membership happens to be constituted. The word 'Mediterranean', on the other hand, lumps together a group of countries chosen on the basis of criteria sufficiently diverse and incoherent to be qualified as political. Thus, this group includes Jordan, which has no Mediterranean shore, but excludes Libya (which, for the time being, is considered as a non-entity) despite the fact that it is the country with the longest Mediterranean shore, just as it excludes ex-Yugoslavia and Albania, which are deemed to belong more properly to the group of Central and Eastern European countries (CEECs), since their failure to meet any of the above criteria disqualifies them from being included in the group 'Europe' or the group 'Mediterranean'.

The second point that should be made at the outset is that, however each group may be made up, neither of them is as cohesive or homogeneous as it might appear at first glance. If we start with the Mediterranean group, it includes the non-European countries that extend from Morocco to Syria. These countries constitute about half of the membership of the League of Arab States, and are part of what is collectively referred to in common language as the 'Arab world'. But despite the fact that it has a common language (at least in written form), a common religion (at least in terms of basic precepts), and a common heritage (depending on how the term is defined), the Arab world has rarely – if ever – constituted a homogeneous entity.

From the point of view of academics, diplomats and politicians, there is a distinction to be made within the Arab world between the Maghreb and the Mashrek or between North Africa and the Middle East. The former is constituted of the five countries that are members of the Union of the Arab Maghreb (Union du Maghreb Arabe or UMA), namely, Algeria, Libya, Mauritania, Morocco and Tunisia, whereas the latter (the Mashrek) includes Egypt and all the countries located to its east.

Although these two regions have some similarities and affinities, their differences are deemed sufficiently great to justify their being considered as separate entities. These differences relate to such factors as history, political orientations, alliance systems, cultural influence and economic status, among other things.

Furthermore, differences are also to be found even among members of a given group. In the case of the Maghreb, one can use numerous indicators to identify major contrasts between the countries of the region. In addition, bilateral relations are characterized by perennial open or latent conflicts, which account for the region's chronic tensions and the UMA's patent failure to make any headway.

Similarly, there are long-standing conflicts between Mashrek countries, whether over borders, the peace process or migration. Such conflicts may be temporarily set aside when circumstances so require – as was the case during the 1991 Gulf War – but invariably the region reverts back to what seems to be its natural state of division. A recent illustration of this phenomenon can be found in the failure of the erstwhile Gulf coalition to agree on a common stance when renewed tension between the USA and Iraq in September 1995 brought the area to the brink of a new war.

Consequently, expressions such as the 'Arab world' or the 'Mediterranean region' are more useful as intellectual abstracts or convenient shorthand for a certain area of the globe than as a reference to a target for foreign policy decisions.

Turning now to the term 'Europe', it is used to refer to the EU and its member states whose number currently stands at 15. In terms of orientation towards the Mediterranean, the EU members may be classified as follows.

- The majority (eight members) are neither Mediterranean nor do they have direct interests in, or active contacts with, the Mediterranean.

24

- One member (Germany), although non-Mediterranean, does take sporadically an interest in developments in the Middle East and the Muslim world on account of the large Turkish community that lives there and of the country's special ties with Israel. But it would be difficult to assert that it has an identifiable and long-standing policy towards the Mediterranean.
- One member (the United Kingdom) is not Mediterranean and its current interest in the area is minimal, despite the fact that it was at some point fairly active in the Mashrek.
- Another member (Portugal) is not Mediterranean but is showing a growing interest and involvement in Mediterranean affairs, probably because of its Iberian position.
- Yet another member (Greece) is Mediterranean but maintains little contact with its southern neighbours.
- Two members (Italy and Spain) maintained or continue to maintain a colonial presence in North Africa, which explains their continued interest in the western basin of the Mediterranean.
- The last member – France – may, for all practical purposes, be considered as the only EU member to have had a continuous presence and interest in the non-European part of the Mediterranean. Without even going back to the Napoleonic era, that presence can be traced to at least 1830, when France occupied Algiers and then proceeded to colonize the rest of Algeria and all of North Africa. In the Mashrek, French involvement was limited to the inter-war period, when France was granted a mandate over Lebanon and Syria. That mandate came to an end just after the Second World War, and by 1962 all the North African colonies had become independent. As a result of that experience close political, economic and social links were established between France and the Maghreb (and to a lesser extent with the Mashrek) and have been maintained and, in some cases, strengthened until the present day.

On matters relating to the Mediterranean, each of the members finds itself on either side of a so-called North–South divide. The main actors of the 'southern' block are France (which is often at the forefront, especially on issues relating to the Maghreb), Italy and Spain, while Greece becomes active mostly when issues relating to Cyprus and Turkey are under discussion and Portugal is seeking greater involvement in this group. The remaining EU members have tended to defer to this group on a variety of Mediterranean questions, although this attitude has been slowly changing as demands on Europe grow faster than the resources required to meet them, as members who hitherto stayed on the sidelines take an active interest in the eastern Mediterranean, and as members who are interested in Central and Eastern Europe try to keep attention from focusing too much on the Mediterranean.

Under these conditions, the Mediterranean moves to centre stage only when questions become or are made into 'major issues' (e.g. immigration, fundamentalism, terrorism), or when the EU has to make a decision on a question that particularly affects one or some of its members (such as granting import quotas to third countries, or when a member of the 'southern bloc' presides over the Union and succeeds in carrying along the rest of the members on a Mediterranean (side-)track.

However, it should be recognized that even though decisions adopted by the EU towards the Mediterranean may have been inspired or even imposed by one member or a small number of members, they are upheld and implemented by the entire membership, a fact that seems obvious but that needs to be recalled because of its impact on power relations between the EU and the Mediterranean Partner Countries (MPCs). In this respect, it is further important to recall that decisions are more and more made in Brussels rather than in national capitals.

The Mediterranean countries, by contrast, have neither the institutional means nor even the desire to formulate common stands towards Europe. Thus, none of the MPCs that have signed or are discussing association agreements with the EU ever negotiated as a group, nor did they even seek to coordinate their positions. In fact, during hearings conducted by the House of Lords in 1994 on relations between the EU and the Maghreb countries, the ambassadors of Algeria and Tunisia in London were specifically asked whether they wanted or would have preferred to have negotiations carried out within the framework of the UMA, and they both answered no.[1]

As a result, each MPC had to lobby individual EU 'patrons' to seek their support for its interests. But whatever the degree of success this approach may have had in the past, it is not likely to be very useful in the future. As EU membership expands, it becomes more and more difficult for an MPC to form coalitions in its favour or to defeat a concerted opposition to its causes. A case in point is that when a member of the House of Lords recently asked what justifications can be presented to taxpayers for the UK's 16 per cent contribution to the Community spending in the Maghreb countries, the implication was that if such justifications cannot be given, then spending should not be approved.

Such questions will very likely become more frequent in the future and as a result, members that may still want to further the interests of non-members can expect to run into more-or-less stiff opposition. Two recent examples may be used to illustrate this trend. When the Commission began discussions on the financial package for the Mediterranean, it proposed an initial figure of €6.3 billion for the period 1995–99. The ensuing debate showed that commissioners from the 'southern bloc' wanted a higher figure whereas others wanted a lower one. In the end the latter won and a figure of €5.5 billion was agreed upon, only to be brought down even further by the Cannes Summit (June 1995) to €4,685 million.

The second example relates to EU financial help to the countries of Africa, the Caribbean and the Pacific (ACP). Ever since the first Lomé Convention was signed in 1975, aid to ACP countries increased in real terms every time the convention was renewed; this was true for Lomé IV, which was signed in 1990. However, when a mid-term revision of Lomé IV was undertaken in 1995 the EU failed to grant a new increase. In fact France had difficulties convincing its partners to accept a sufficient increase to cover inflation.

In summary, it may have been possible at one time to argue that measures adopted by the northern Mediterranean towards the southern Mediterranean reflected the views of one or a few members, but from the 1980s onwards it became more and more difficult to uphold such an argument, and such measures can presently be considered as broadly European. On the other hand, it would be erroneous to consider them as measures towards the Mediterranean as a region, because they are in effect *European* measures adopted towards *individual Mediterranean countries*.

This is not to say that Europe approves of, or is responsible for, this situation; it can even be pointed out that it has called for regional and sub-regional integration among MPCs, and that it has set aside for the period 1992/96 the sum of €2,030 million (230 million in grants and 1,800 million in EIB loans) for horizontal cooperation. The fact remains, however, that relations between Europe and the Mediterranean are extremely unbalanced and this has important implications for the future evolution of those relations.

Before looking at events that led to the partnership initiative, it may be useful to examine the motives that lay behind Europe's actions in the Mediterranean and the place that the Mediterranean occupies in EU priorities.

The Mediterranean in Europe's Foreign Policy

'The southern and eastern shores of the Mediterranean, as well as the Middle East, are geographical areas in relation to which the Union has strong interests in terms of security and social stability' (Lisbon European Council, June 1992). 'The Mediterranean constitutes a priority area of strategic importance for the European Union' (Essen European Council, December 1994). It is in such terms that Europe describes its stand towards the Mediterranean. From various documents and declarations it is possible to identify more concretely the main objectives that the EU seeks to achieve:

- immigration: to stop the flow of immigrants from the south and, by the same token, check the drug traffic (although it is not clear what the linkage is between immigrants and drug traffickers);
- fundamentalism: to prevent Muslim fundamentalists from gaining power in a Mediterranean country and setting up regimes that would be hostile to Western interests;
- trade: to secure oil and gas supplies on which Europe is dependent;
- prosperity: to improve standards of living in Mediterranean countries so as to ensure social and political stability; and
- peace: to prevent internal and interregional conflicts that may make European intervention necessary or inevitable.

All of these objectives are interrelated and each one may have one or several subsidiary goals attached to it. Thus prosperity would contribute to the reduction of immigration pressures and prevent the rise of fundamentalist regimes. Similarly, internal and regional stability requires not only prosperity but also education, training, pluralism and the respect of human rights.

There is at least one additional objective that is sometimes cited as important for Europe, namely, military security. However, the possibility that one or several MPCs would consider mounting a military attack against Europe is quite remote. On the other hand, terrorist attacks are possible and have indeed taken place, but they cannot be dealt with through classical military means.[2]

In order to achieve these objectives, the EU has adopted a strategy it calls 'partnership' with the MPCs. According to its promoters, this approach seeks to put an end to a situation where the South was mostly a passive and subservient recipient of handouts, and to replace it by another situation where the MPCs and the EU would work as full and equal partners towards achieving mutually beneficial goals. This partnership has been defined and adopted by the Euro-Mediterranean Conference held in Barcelona in November 1995.

I shall now examine the historical process that led to that conference; then I will examine the first concrete agreement achieved within the framework of the Euro-Mediterranean Partnership (EMP), and in light of that I shall lastly evaluate the Barcelona Process and its impact on the Mediterranean region.

Evolution of Euro-Mediterranean Relations

From its very beginning the European integration process included the Mediterranean element within its framework. On the one hand, the Treaty of Rome that instituted the European Economic Community (EEC) left the door open to other European countries to become members (Art. 237); Greece and Spain did so, and Malta and Cyprus will follow in the near future. On the other hand, the treaty contained a section (Arts 131–6) pertaining to the association of non-European countries and territories that have special relations with the founding members (although the above-mentioned Art. 237 leaves no possibility for these or any other countries from the Maghreb or the Mashrek to become full members, as Morocco found out).

Throughout the 1960s trade agreements were signed with various Mediterranean countries granting their manufactured products free or preferential access to the EEC, and a limited access for some of their specific agricultural products. In the mid-1970s Europe adopted what it called a Global Mediterranean Policy and proceeded to sign cooperation and association agreements with various MPCs: Algeria, Morocco and Tunisia in 1976; Egypt, Jordan, Lebanon and Syria in 1977 (a free trade agreement had already been signed with Israel in 1975). In addition to traditional trade provisions, the new agreements included a financial component in the form of five-year protocols designed to support the process of economic development in the recipient countries.

From the mid-1980s onwards, several important events began to unfold and had a direct or indirect bearing on Euro-Mediterranean relations; the accession of Spain and Portugal to the European Community; the fall of the Berlin Wall and the disintegration of the communist bloc; the rise of social, political and economic crises in several countries of the southern Mediterranean; increased activism on the part of fundamentalist movements, which in the case of Algeria led to the cancellation of elections in December 1991 and the outbreak of civil war there; increased terrorist attacks inside and outside Europe against European and western interests and citizens; the Gulf War; and the launching of the Middle East Peace Process (MEPP).

As some of these events were taking place, Europe felt the need to review its policy towards the Mediterranean and eventually adopted what it called the Renovated Mediterranean Policy (RMP). As the Commission put it:

> The Mediterranean policy adopted by the Council in December 1990 reinforced existing efforts and introduced new features to make rélations with the MNCs more dynamic, backing the Community's actions chiefly by using assistance with economic reforms to encourage the process of opening up to the outside and structural reform which was under way in some of the MNCs.[3]

In addition to the traditional financial protocols that fund projects carried out in individual beneficiary countries, a new facility was – as mentioned earlier – introduced to promote regional and decentralized cooperation through projects that interest two or several MPCs; several programmes were set up to that effect, such as Med-Invest, Med-Campus, Med-Urbs, etc., and have since been replaced by the MEDA programmes.

In two separate documents relating to EU policy towards the Maghreb[4] and the Mashrek[5] issued respectively in 1992 and 1993 the Commission proposed that future relations with MPCs go beyond the financial sector to include a political dialogue between the parties, the creation of a Euro-Mediterranean free trade area, as well as social, economic and cultural cooperation. These suggestions were approved at the Lisbon Summit (June 1992) and confirmed at the Corfu Summit (June 1994).

In the meantime, negotiations with Tunisia, Morocco and Israel got under way on the basis of mandates specifying those four basic elements. Furthermore, the Essen Summit (December 1994) declared its support for Spain's intention to convene in the second half of 1995 a Euro-Mediterranean conference to carry out an in-depth examination of all major political, economic, social and cultural issues of mutual interest, and to define a general framework for a permanent and regular dialogue in these areas.

At the Cannes Summit (June 1995) the Council adopted a document defining the position that the EU would present in Barcelona. It is interesting to note that the spirit, the structure, and even the wording (with some minor modifications) of the Cannes document were faithfully reproduced in the Barcelona Declaration (cf. Presidency Conclusions, Cannes, 26–27 June 1995). It is further interesting to note that the other party to the dialogue, the Mediterranean countries, did not submit for public consideration a document of their own defining their position on what was to be discussed.

To get back to the Cannes document, it specifies in its general introduction that the multilateral approach that will serve as a framework for the EMP will complement, and *not replace*, existing or forthcoming bilateral agreements linking the EU to individual MPCs, and that such bilateral agreements will serve as 'one of the main instruments for the implementation of the measures contained in the present [Cannes] document'.

As for the Barcelona Declaration itself, it is presented in detail in the introductory chapter of the present volume. However, there is one topic of particular interest that will be underlined here, namely, democracy. In this regard, the preamble of the Declaration states that 'the general objective of turning the Mediterranean basin into an area of dialogue, exchange and co-operation guaranteeing peace, stability and prosperity requires a strengthening of democracy and respect of human rights'. The document further states in the chapter dealing with political and security partnership that the signatories are to 'develop the rule of law and democracy in their political systems'. These statements on democracy call for two remarks. First, although they appear to be straightforward, their meaning becomes uncertain when the context in which they are enunciated is taken into consideration. Thus, while the signatories promise to institute democratic political systems, the Declaration recognizes 'the right of each of them to choose and freely develop its own political, socio-cultural, economic and judicial system'. The Declaration further calls on all states to 'refrain, in accordance with the rules of international law, from any direct or indirect intervention in the internal affairs of another partner'. The inevitable implication is that a state may simply declare that its political system is democratic according to its freely chosen criteria (and in the absence of other commonly agreed ones), and that any attempt to impose a different yardstick may be considered as an undue intervention in a state's internal affairs. This issue will be discussed more fully below.

The second remark concerning democracy is that its mention in the Barcelona Declaration constitutes something of a novelty. Throughout the Cold War period, European and other western states never considered the presence or absence of democracy as a relevant criterion for the determination of their policies towards Third World countries. When did democracy become an element in EU foreign policy? What factors could explain this shift? How does the EU define democracy, and how does it determine its presence or absence? It is to these questions that I shall now turn.

Democracy in EU Foreign Policy: the Rhetoric

From the late 1980s onwards most aid donors, whether states or international organizations, began using the principle of conditionality in their aid policy, whereby recipient states were expected to meet certain criteria as a condition for obtaining various forms of assistance or for participating in cooperation programmes. Thus, the World Bank and its associated institutions, as well as the members of the Organisation for Economic Co-operation and Development (OECD), which supply the bulk of official development assistance, began linking aid to 'democratization'. Although a precise definition of this term is difficult to pinpoint, and even though there is a tendency to replace the term by the equally ill-defined concept of 'good governance' and to use both in conjunction with and/or instead of 'respect of human rights', it may surmised that donors expect recipient countries to have non-authoritarian or non-dicta-torial forms of political systems. When and why did Europe adopt the principle of conditionality, and how does it define democracy?

Democracy as an Element of EU Foreign Policy

When communist regimes in the ex-Soviet Union and in Eastern Europe started falling one after the other, many in the West proclaimed that this vindicated their long-held view that authoritarian rule and economic *dirigisme* were inferior to democracy and market economy. Soon western countries moved from merely calling for the adoption of liberal principles and practices to making that adoption a prerequisite for obtaining financial assistance. Thus, the International Monetary Fund (IMF) made various liberal practices (privatization, elimination of public subsidies and of state controls on economic activities, etc.) a cornerstone of the structural adjustment programmes (SAPs) that it 'proposed' to Third World countries in need of help for dealing with the economic crisis that hit them in the mid-1980s. The United States, for its part, has called for a 'crusade for democracy'. As for the EU, various documents issued from 1991 onwards proclaim, in the words of the Maastricht Treaty, that 'the development and consolidation of democracy and the rule of law and adherence to human rights and fundamental freedoms' are principles that the Union must respect internally as well as apply to its relations with non-members. However, this policy suffers from a number of problems, three of which appear as particularly serious: a shifting or insufficient operational definition of democracy; undue emphasis on economic liberalism at the expense of political democracy; and inconsistent implemen-tation of the policy.

Operational Definitions of EU Mediterranean Policy Objectives

Although the objectives of the EU policy towards non-members in general, and towards Mediterranean countries in particular, are clearly stated in various documents such as Council resolutions, the Barcelona Declaration, or the partnership agreements signed with Mediterranean countries, there is little effort to give specific measures that would serve for the implementation of those objectives, or for determining the extent to which such objectives have in fact been achieved. This is particularly the case for political and security objectives, and, to a lesser extent, for objectives in social, cultural and human affairs, whereas in the economic and financial areas fairly concrete measures are enunciated for achieving the stated objectives.

Thus the objective of creating an area of shared prosperity is to be sought through the creation of a free trade area by the year 2010, encouraging investments, promoting women's participation in economic and social life, etc. In fact, the Work Programme annexed to the Barcelona Declaration lists 13 areas of cooperation, each containing a number of specific actions to be undertaken towards building a zone of shared prosperity.

Similarly, the Declaration identifies eleven areas – ranging from health and migration to terrorism and drug trafficking – in which actions are to be undertaken with the aim of promoting understanding between Mediterranean cultures and societies.

However, when it comes to the establishment of an area of peace and stability, the Declaration does list a number of principles to be respected by the signatories, but the Work Programme does not go beyond calling on states to 'conduct a political dialogue to examine the most appropriate means and methods of implementing the principles adopted by the Barcelona Declaration'. Thus, it is not clear what is meant by 'develop[ing] the rule of law and democracy', or how parties go about determining whether or not there is an 'effective legitimate exercise' of human rights and fundamental freedoms.

Furthermore, it appears that there is a tendency to put greater emphasis on respect for human rights than on adopting democratic rule, even though the term 'democracy' continues to be prominent in official pronouncements. This is not to deny that respect for human rights is an important objective, or that it is an essential element of democracy, but the shift may be a convenient way of avoiding or evading the issue of defining democracy. Since hardly anyone would openly oppose democracy (or peace, brotherhood or freedom), there is much to gain, and little to lose, in using the term. However, to give a specific definition to this term may lead to major difficulties, not least of which the conflict that would inevitably arise between competing definitions, and the more than likely accusation of 'cultural imperialism' that would be levelled at anyone proposing or imposing a particular definition.

On the other hand, human rights have the advantage of being well defined, since one can simply refer to any of the many international instruments that list those rights, and that most states have ratified or at least signed. Furthermore, there are numerous supra-national – and therefore impartial – as well as national organizations that have the responsibility of verifying the respect of rights, and of denouncing any observed or suspected abuses. Finally, some acts (such as genocide or ethnic cleansing) are so widely rejected and so difficult to hide that no state can realistically hope to commit them without being discovered and denounced. As for other forms of human rights abuses, the burden of proving them would be left to those who claim their existence. In sum, unless a state is observed killing its citizens in large numbers (say beyond 100,000 or perhaps a million), or selling them off as slaves, or voluntarily starving them, or committing similarly 'gross' or 'serious' abuses, it would be considered as (adequately) respectful of human rights.

Thanks to this strategy the EU can continue to advocate democracy without having to force its members to agree on a common standard by which to evaluate its existence, and to call for respect of human rights without taking any major risks. This, however, does not adequately deal either with the problem of disrespect for other fundamental freedoms that the EU claims to consider as important, such as freedom of expression and of association, or with the view that such a disrespect is inconsistent with democracy – however it is defined. In an effort to resolve this dilemma the EU, perhaps finding inspiration in US policy, falls back on one or more of the following arguments. First, it claims that Third World countries cannot institute democratic regimes overnight, and they should therefore be given some time to make the transition towards democracy. During this period of 'democratization' countries would be expected to adopt various measures commonly associated with the democratic process, such as elections, pluralism and the emergence of civil society. Second, given the difficulty of the task, countries should neither be rushed nor judged too harshly if progress appears to be slow; one has to be patient as long as a regime appears to become less authoritarian. Finally, one has to keep in mind that countries have to proceed with economic liberalization and adopt a market economy, and they should therefore not be distracted from this task by other considerations, especially if one keeps in mind that liberalism will sooner or later facilitate the transition to democracy.

The validity of some of these claims will be discussed below. Suffice it to say at this stage that it is not clear – to this writer, at any rate – whether the EU considers democracy, human rights and economic liberalism as synonymous, or whether, if that were not the case, it has ranked them in any particular order, or whether, and this is the most likely alternative, the whole issue of democracy is totally irrelevant as far as EU policy towards the Mediterranean is concerned. This last view is justified not only because the EU has failed to go beyond mere declarations to take any concrete actions favouring the emergence of democratic regimes in the Mediterranean, whereas such actions *have been taken* in Eastern Europe, but also because, as it will be argued below, the EU took and continues to take actions whose effect can only be the effective blocking of any move towards democracy in the Mediterranean.

Inconsistent Implementation: The Mediterranean versus Eastern Europe

Although the EU has never declared that its support for democracy is limited to any specific geographical areas, it is nevertheless clear that in practice the issue's weight varies from one case to another. To begin with, and as one writer points out, 'European policies aimed at promoting democracy and respect for human rights in Central and Eastern Europe is an integrated [sic] part of Europe's *foreign policy*, whereas the same aims are considered to be part of the *development policy* when the geographic focus is Africa, Latin America or Asia' (Olsen, 1998: 8; emphasis added). Concretely, this means that democracy in the CEECs is deemed to be sufficiently 'high politics' to be part of the emerging Common Foreign and Security Policy (CFSP) and entrusted to the Council. Knowing how difficult the inclusion of a particular issue in the CFSP may be, one can safely assume that only issues deemed to be non-controversial will be so included. However, the Council may have endorsed democracy in the Mediterranean and democracy in the CEECs for entirely opposite reasons. For the Mediterranean few members, if any, expected the policy to ever reach the stage of actual implementation, and endorsement would therefore be risk-free and politically rewarding, whereas in the second case of the CEECs endorsement indicates that most or all members want the policy to be implemented, and are even willing to back that up with money. Initially, the implementation of EU policy towards Eastern Europe was limited to two countries and was designed to support their transition to market economy, as the name of the aid programme indicates (Poland and Hungary Aid for the Reconstruction of the Economy or PHARE). But in 1992 PHARE was extended to other CEECs, and a special democracy programme with its own budgetary line was built into it. In the Mediterranean the EU set up the MEDA programme, but this has not been very successful; aside from having insufficient funds in relation to needs, the programme has suffered from so many other handicaps that the EU has had to undertake its complete overhaul.[6]

Of course EU policy of positive support of democracy in Eastern Europe is designed to prepare the CEECs for membership, but this form of positive conditionality to bring about democracy by convergence cannot be used in the Mediterranean, since no country on the southern shore can ever expect to become a member of the EU. However, one may still ask why the EU has not used *negative* conditionality as it did in parts of sub-Saharan Africa (e.g. Kenya in 1991 and Niger in 1996). It should be pointed out that the Lomé IV Convention does stipulate that respect for human rights and democratic principles constitutes an 'essential element' of the convention, a stipulation also found in the EMP agreements signed with Tunisia and Morocco; but Lomé further provides for a special fund to finance democratization programmes (Art. 224), and institutes negative conditionality whereby aid would be suspended for ACP countries that violate the 'essential element' clause – two stipulations that do not exist in EMP agreements.

It is clear that in the Mediterranean the EU uses neither the carrot method it uses in Eastern Europe, nor the method of the carrot and the stick that it uses in ACP countries. It does not even have an attitude of benign neglect that would allow MPCs to decide for themselves whether and how they want to institute democratic political systems. One cannot help but conclude that from the EU point of view, the stakes in ACP countries are sufficiently low to justify the risk of a proactive policy in support of democracy, whereas in MPCs the stakes are sufficiently high to justify the treatment of democracy as a serious threat.

Democracy as a Threat to Entrenched Interests

It is not my purpose here to partake in the ongoing debate on the definition of democracy. Instead, I propose to use the following indicators to determine whether or not a polity is democratic.

- All matters affecting one or more groups of citizens are submitted to an open and unrestricted debate leading to proposals for actions or decisions.
- Members of the group(s) agree on a method for choosing between proposals, and abide by the outcome of that method.
- Members of the group(s) agree on a method for mandating one or more individuals to implement the decisions, for monitoring the implementation process, for revising or abandoning adopted decisions, and for confirming or recalling mandated executives.

No particular claim is made about the value of this working definition of democracy other than the fact that it is based on the axiom that autocracy and democracy (and oligarchy) must be considered as mutually exclusive *attributes* or *qualities* of a polity to the same extent that gender is an attribute of a human being. Thus, a polity can at a given time only be *either* a democracy *or* an autocracy, and as long as it has not made the qualitative change from one category to the other, it can only be considered as still belonging to its original category. Therefore, the term 'democratization' ought to be avoided inasmuch as it may lead to the creation of categories of 'semi-authoritarian' and 'semi-democratic' polities, and especially to the belief that they are (functionally, politically, morally or otherwise) equivalent. The proposed indicators, on the other hand, even if they do not amount to an adequate definition of democracy, allow at least for the identification of polities that are *not* democratic.

Dearth of Democracy in the Southern Mediterranean

Whether one uses the proposed indicators, or any other yardstick, one could hardly deny that democracy in MPCs is about as present as water is in the deserts that dominate their landscapes. Few people contest the fact that the 'wave of democratization' that hit many parts of the authoritarian world in the 1990s has somehow failed to reach the northern shores of the African continent and adjacent areas. Because this part of the world happens to be made up of Arab Muslim states, many advanced the hypothesis (if not the certitude) of the existence of an Arab and/or Muslim 'exception', that is, democracy is incompatible with being an Arab or a Muslim. The self-appointed political juries that appeared on both sides of the Mediterranean to examine the question have already turned in their verdicts, and these are sufficiently well known to need no further presentation here.

As for the scientific juries, where they have been formed and entrusted with the case, they have not been nor will they any time soon be able to render a verdict, because they do not have sufficient evidence on which to base a decision. Even if one were to go beyond the eight Arab Muslim participants in the EMP process, and study all the other Arab and Muslim states, how many of them have carried out the democratic experiment in any meaningful way, and over a sufficiently long period of time, to allow a scientifically valid conclusion about the compatibility of democracy with Islam and/or with being Arab? In any case, existing evidence – as limited and unrepresentative as it may be – does not tend to support the hypothesis of incompatibility (e.g., Iran and Yemen).

Who is Afraid of Democracy?

If we do not know with any degree of certainty whether Arabs and Muslims are unfit for democracy, or are incapable of practising it, who would be opposed to finding a clear-cut answer to this question? Clearly and logically, opponents can only be those who suspect what the answer may be, and who are not willing to risk having their suspicion confirmed. The opponents of democracy are ruling regimes in the South, and northern governments defending national interests in the North.

Southern Opponents of Democracy Although MPCs have had decades to set up democratic systems, rare are those that have managed to do so. It is true that they had to tend to more urgent tasks: when they were not busy building the state, or socialism, or some other construct, they were fighting underdevelopment, imperialism, Israel and, most recently, the fundamentalists. However, part of the time has been put to good use. The rulers have accumulated power and wealth, and constituted with their allies an élite that has come to be identified with the state. This old guard presents itself as a bulwark against the traumatizing instability of democracy. When these rulers leave the scene, the clones who succeed them promise continuity, and they literally keep their promise – much to the chagrin of the concerned populations. Outside of the Middle East, new leaders who come to power through democratic means face the thankless task of allocating poverty, and when this leads to discontent, they have a choice between presiding over chaos, or declaring that a further period of 'democratization' is required. This scenario has been played over and again, most recently in Indonesia.

In some extreme cases, democracy has been used to quell mounting social and economic tensions: when people clamour for bread, they are offered elections; and when they refuse to play along, they are declared immature for democracy.

Those around the Mediterranean who oppose democracy point to the failure of the democratic experiments that have recently been attempted here and there, particularly in Africa. According to them the failure is due to an insufficient and inadequate transitional period, and hence there is no point in repeating an experiment that is doomed to failure, since peoples in MPCs are not prepared for democracy any better than their counterparts in Africa, and therefore require further education in this area.

It may be edifying to examine briefly how views regarding 'the people' shift according to circumstances and convenience. When the colonized countries were waging the battle of national liberation, no one was too young, or too old, or too ignorant to fight and die for the homeland and the noble cause of independence. Somehow, all those valorous citizens were able to assimilate such notions as imperialism, political rights to be claimed against the oppressor, cultural identity to be protected against assimilation, and the right of peoples to self-determination, as well as master the intricate art of war.

But as soon as independence was won, those who survived were declared unfit to participate in the running of the state that was built on the corpses of their comrades. Suddenly they had lost all the aptitudes they had only a short time earlier. Thus, whenever any of those countries faced political chaos or economic disintegration after independence, it was always the people's fault: they are too traditional, too religious, too ignorant; they do not save enough; they are not trained; they are not mobile, etc. Moreover, when it came to finding solutions to problems which affected those same people more than anyone else, or even to expressing an opinion on the solutions proposed by governments to solve such problems, then the people were once again deemed unqualified.

One may ask whether today's peasants living in Africa, or Bedouins living in the desert, are in fact less apt to understand and practise democracy than the French *sans-culottes* or the American settlers of the eighteenth century. In any case, what is certain is that they understand all too well that they do not have jobs, food, shelter and medical care, and they do have a fairly good idea about who is responsible for this situation. In this respect, they probably feel that they do not require very many lessons to acquire that body of knowledge.

More to the point is whether the self-appointed teachers (and, incidentally, their supervisors in Washington, Brussels and elsewhere, to whom we shall turn shortly) themselves need a refresher – if not an introductory – course in democracy. Will they willingly enrol for such a course? Will they sit for the final exam? Will they withdraw if they fail, or if they are expelled from class for disorderly conduct? And most of all, will they accept to have the people for a teacher? As a matter of fact, it is very likely that those who claim that 'they have no lesson to learn from anyone' on the subject of democracy are the very ones who need such a lesson most urgently.

Northern Opponents of Democracy   During the Cold War there was an ongoing competition between the opposing camps over allies; each one was constantly trying to attract as many 'supporters' as possible. Countries that were *de facto* or *de jure* members of one camp could expect the unconditional and unfailing support of the leader and 'senior members' of that camp, and those that were not could easily join and then proceed to claim full membership benefits.

When the Cold War came to an end, 'fifth wheelers' were left in disarray. Those that wanted to find their own path, and that presented no particular interest for the remaining camp, were left to their own devices; they could sink or swim. On the other hand, those that were unable or unwilling to stand alone tried to find ways of maintaining or attracting the attention and interest of the managers of the new world order. Finally, those that presented a particular interest in the eyes of those managers were offered the possibility of establishing, maintaining, or strengthening mutually beneficial friendly relations with those same managers. MPCs belong to this last group.

From the European point of view, the region is important mostly as a supplier of energy products. Trade is important, but hardly vital. Arms exports, on the other hand, are considered as politically vital as well as commercially important. The EU considers that some of its members face present or potential threats (see above) emanating from parts of the southern Mediterranean; this perception may be invalid, and one can try to correct it, but one cannot discard it as long as it is a basis of policy.

Each country has the right to define its interests and the duty to confront perceived threats; it is also free to define and use the means it deems necessary and appropriate for doing so. Clearly, such prerogatives may lead to abuses, and the international community has sought ways of limiting them. International law is one such way, but it has always been a last resort for the weak to invoke and an option for the strong to uphold. For this reason, it has not been a relevant tool in international relations. Consequently, one cannot realistically invoke it to challenge the EU for defending its interests. However, one can and should try to find other grounds on which to evaluate the approach used to define those interests, and the methods applied to achieve those interests.

Challenges Facing the EU in the Mediterranean

The main challenge that faces countries of the southern Mediterranean is to join the worldwide move to democracy. It is time for the Arab world to put an end to its status as the 'odd man out'. The impetus can and must come from the Arabs themselves. Any attempt by Europe or anyone else to impose a political change on the region will ultimately be counterproductive. However, Europe *must* also refrain from blocking a political change that the Arabs need and want. There are many positive measures that Europe can undertake to help the region operate a smooth transfer to democracy; they will be mentioned, but only as options that Europe may envisage, and will largely depend upon its goodwill. But there are other measures that are currently in use or contemplated, and which Europe urgently needs to discard not only as a matter of duty, but also out of enlightened interest.

Democracy as Equity

Assuming that Europe seeks peace, security and stability the fundamental question is whether a community can expect to achieve these goals when some members exploit and oppress other members. There is no doubt that large segments of Arab societies have been and continue to be oppressed, and many have begun to rise against their oppressors. Nor is there much doubt about the fact that a growing number of Arabs consider that the West (including Europe) is, directly or indirectly, to some extent or another, responsible for the inception, continuation and aggravation of the problems confronting them.

Recrimination may be sterile, but when it is skilfully manipulated, it does move people, and not always in the desired direction. The West cannot erase or change its past, but it can seek to convince people to set it aside. However, the attempt will surely fail if intentions are not buttressed by deeds. For years on end, the West has been telling 'the rest of us' that it wants cooperation and partnership in order to achieve a better world. But the question is: cooperation and partnership *with whom*? In the Mediterranean cooperation has been mostly with those who are perceived as the prime cause of the region's ongoing problems. In fact, this is the fundamental reason why the West is held in disrepute. The targets of popular resentment are well known; all Europe has to do is disassociate itself from them. It does not have to condemn or denounce them, or help their opponents (although it may), it can simply refrain from supporting them.

The word 'simply' may be inappropriate in this context, some might say, because nothing in international relations, and least of all in the Middle East, is simple. However, this leitmotiv repeated *ad nauseam* for decades has become a self-fulfilling prophecy: the longer a problem is left unattended, the less simple its eventual solution becomes. So, one is willing to grant that 'simply' is not the correct word: 'boldly' would be more appropriate.

Boldness is, in fact, what Europe needs to display in its oft-redirected Mediterranean policy, for it will take nothing less than boldness to face the fact that no policy will succeed unless it is based on *equity*. Even in the absence of opinion polls to prove this, one can state with little risk of error that the Mediterranean peoples want nothing more, and will accept nothing less, than equity in any relations with their northern neighbours.

From the South's perspective, equity does not preclude the North's right to protect what it considers to be its legitimate interests, but it does imply that the North concedes the South the same right. It is highly unlikely that interests will always converge; hence it is necessary for the parties to agree on some ground rules for dealing with potential conflicts. Ideally, violence in any form should neither be used nor considered as a recourse, even in the event of a deadlock. Short of that each party may defend its position as energetically as it can, while proceeding on the principle that 'you win some, and you lose some'.

At a game such as this, the South may not have many wins. Perhaps. But as all sportsmen know, one should never underestimate the opponent, nor over-estimate one's own aptitudes. No matter how high the stakes are, all teams should play a 'clean' game, consider that there will always be another game tomorrow, and keep in mind that no nation can expect to win all the medals in all disciplines all the time. Call this fairness, or equity, or just democracy: it is not the term that matters, it is the spirit. This spirit ought to prevail in all forms of interactions between Europe and MPCs, but particularly in the economic and political fields, inasmuch as the two can be separated.

Economic Democracy

It is rather ironic that democracy has traditionally been associated with capitalism, an economic system that is anything but democratic, and which does not even pretend to be democratic. Europeans, until recently, were well aware of this, or else they would not have adopted and practised social democracy or democratic socialism, or legislated a variety of social nets to protect citizens against the excesses of capitalism. Even the IMF had to admit, belatedly, that its neo-liberal (i.e. hard-core capitalist) SAPs can and do cause 'collateral' social damage.

Today, European governments are yielding to mounting social pressures, and are reconsidering, openly disavowing or surreptitiously disregarding some of the more damaging neo-liberal practices. The saga of the Multilateral Agreement on Investment (MAI), the calls for limiting the wild movement of capital around the globe, and the demonstrations that are organized at G-7 and WTO meetings illustrate the growing backlash against globalization and its pernicious effects.

Yet Europe insists on applying, and selectively at that, some of those principles in its economic relations with MPCs. The Mediterranean agreements that the EU signed with Tunisia and Morocco are a case in point. Without going into detail, it may be said that they are good examples of inequity, since they institute a 'free trade' that is rather lopsided: it applies to industrial goods for which the South is hardly competitive, but not to agricultural goods for which the North is at a disadvantage. In general, economic theory and practical experience show that this form of integration between unequally developed economies brings little benefit, and can cause major damage to the weaker partners.[7]

There are many other examples of the use of double standards. Take the rule of government non-intervention that is supposed to allow the undistorted free play of market forces. Currently, it is applied to governments in the South who are urged to do away with subsidies to basic goods and services (food, health, education, etc.), to refrain from salvaging inefficient firms and economic sectors, to dismantle tariffs, and to do away with restrictive practices (such as guaranteeing workers' rights or minimum wages). However, when governments in the North decide, individually or collectively, to spend billions on subsidizing their farmers, or to protect speculators against bankruptcy, or to act as guardians of private firms, this is not considered as interventionism.

One final point that needs to be raised relates to the relationship between ends and means. In principle, one is not allowed to use any means to reach one's ends, no matter how valid those ends may be. Thus, drugs allow peasants in Asia, traffickers in Colombia, and dealers in Europe to make a living, but most societies do not approve of the trade or use of drugs, because drugs kill, lead to deviance, etc. Yet some of those societies do not hesitate to manufacture, sell, use and allow others to use weapons, a type of product that is as deadly and anti-social as drugs. Worse yet, they find it quite normal to be on a constant lookout for newcomers to hook, to search for new products that would give those already addicted bigger and better 'highs', and even to turn their highest public officials into pushers who travel the world to sell their wares.

Regimes in the South have mismanaged their economies for decades; they have wasted scarce national resources, squandered public moneys, enriched themselves while drowning their societies in debt. They made disastrous decisions whose effects are either irreversible, or will continue to be felt for generations. As a result, the region depends on the outside world for income, food, machinery, science, technology and know-how. Little is being done to reduce the region's dependence on oil, or to stop – let alone reverse – the increasing marginalization of the Middle East in the world economy. Extreme income disparities exist between and within countries, and are on the increase. Yet despite it all, the Arab world is not a hopeless case, and just as its present situation could have been better, and its future brighter, had it had more dedicated managers, its future could be brighter if such managers were in charge of its destiny.

In some countries the economic situation has reached crisis proportions, and has led to sporadic outbursts or to complete disintegration; in others, efforts have been made to patch it up as well as possible. Most indicators point to the inefficiency of current policies. It may well be that alternative policies would not bring better results, or do not even exist; but the question should be examined and resolved by the citizens whose interests are at stake. The citizens ought to hear all sides, including those who believe that equality applies as much to the ballot box as it does to the pocket-book.

In this respect, it is worth remembering that Pericles thought that poor Athenians could not exercise their rights as citizens, and were in fact disenfranchised, because they could not afford to leave their work in order to participate in the activities of the *ecclesia* or the courts, and he therefore instituted the practice of compensating citizens who chose to exercise their civic rights. But even this measure proved insufficient, and democracy ultimately floundered, because Athens failed to extend citizenship and attendant rights to slaves. As one writer points out, 'the political equality which Athenian democracy had established for its citizens was, in the last instance, founded on economic inequality' (Fotopoulos, 1997: 186), and was therefore doomed to failure.

Finally, democracy cannot exist in a system where wealth is derived from power, and cannot sustain itself when power is derived from wealth alone. Consequently, democracy requires methods for preventing the distribution of political and economic power from becoming too skewed.

Political Democracy

The foregoing discussion implies, on the one hand, that democracy is indivisible, and on the other, that perfect democracy (i.e. perfect equality between citizens in all aspects of life) is impossible. This last statement may bring La Palice to mind, but it is meant to underline the idea that democracy is a *continuous* process tending towards that perfect state – a process that may well be called democratization. But until the process is effectively under way, democracy cannot be said to exist.

The Middle East today is not democratizing, let alone democratic. Citizens there have little opportunity to express themselves on matters affecting their lives. The contention made here is that Europe and the United States find this situation accommodating, and contribute to its perpetuation. As already suggested, western support of democracy is largely rhetorical, and opposition to autocracy is not a matter of principle. Democracy is unwelcome if its outcome is contrary to the interests of its actual or potential victims (e.g. Algeria). When autocrats become too embarrassing, they are advised to 'democratize' their regimes, to make 'progressive reforms', to get themselves elected and acquire as many of the democratic trappings as possible. When the advice is carried out, democracy is declared to exist. But can democracy be reduced to this? As Samir Amin states,

42

Contemporary interpretations, broadly typified by Anglo-American evolutionism and pragmatism, impoverish the debate by treating democracy as a set of narrowly defined rights and practices, *independent of the desired social outlook*. This democracy can then stabilize the society, by leaving 'evolution' to 'objective forces' *operating regardless of human will*. Furthermore, in the analysis of these objective forces the focus is on technical and scientific progress, while the realities that hide behind 'market forces' are systematically ignored. Finally, the democratic transformation of society is regarded as being largely the product of evolution; *hence the functional role of the revolutionary process in history can be played down*. (Amin, 1993: 75; emphasis added)

As soon as citizens attempt to play a meaningful role in managing their own affairs, established regimes and vested interests invariably treat this form of democracy, in Noam Chomsky's words, 'as a threat to be overcome, not as a prospect to be encouraged' (Chomsky, 1993: 80).

More and more thinkers are levelling similar criticism at western attitudes towards democracy, albeit in a more vivid language. Thus Robert D. Kaplan, referring to US policy, writes:

Of course, our post-Cold War mission to spread democracy is partly a pose. In Egypt and Saudi Arabia, America's most important allies in the energy-rich Muslim world, our worst nightmare would be free and fair elections, as it would be elsewhere in the Middle East. The Cold War has changed our attitude toward those authoritarian regimes that are not crucial to our interests – but not toward those that are. (Kaplan, 1997: 63)

Benjamin Barber, a political scientist and author of 'Jihad vs. McWorld', is blunter: 'Despots who slaughter their own populations are no problem, so long as they leave markets in place ... In trading partners, predictability is of more value than justice' (Barber, 1992: 9).

The Barcelona Declaration and the process that was designed to create a partnership between the northern and southern shores of the Mediterranean that encompasses not just economic but also political and social areas have not led to the expected results. The partners themselves admitted this failure at the Euro-Mediterranean Conference of Foreign Ministers held in Marseilles in November 2000 and promised renewed efforts to reinvigorate or relaunch the Barcelona Process. A detailed discussion of the Process and its perspectives cannot be presented here.[8] Suffice it to say that the EMP can succeed only if there is a greater correspondence between professed principles and proclaimed intentions on the one hand, and actual implementation and concrete measures, on the other. It should be remembered that the 1995 Barcelona Conference was mainly a European initiative, and that MPCs went along with it mostly because they perceived that there could be no danger in doing so. For a time, the EU focused on economic and financial issues, much to the satisfaction of all partners. But when the EU started to raise other issues such as democracy and human rights, the South reacted negatively.

At present, the Barcelona Process has come to a dead end. If the EU invokes southern commitment to institute democratic rule, the MPCs will invoke northern commitment not to interfere in the internal affairs of sovereign nations. If the South calls on the EU to open its borders to agricultural goods and migrants, the EU will argue that it made no commitments to that effect. If Europe pushes for the adoption of a charter for peace and stability, the Arabs contend that peace in the Middle East has to be achieved first.

This indicates that the EMP as it presently stands is unworkable. Its statutes may be revised to eliminate the contradictions they contain, but this would not be a useful exercise because what matters most in any contract is not so much the clauses as the disposition that the parties have towards the contract. If the signers want to fulfil the aim of the contract, they would not bicker about its wording, but if they did not want the contract in the first place or consider it as a mere formality, then they will use every excuse to prevent its implementation. In the case of the Barcelona Declaration, the South considers it as a non-binding document that does not have to be executed in its totality.

Consequently, a better strategy would be to revise the membership of the EMP. The current members hold different views concerning the parts of the Barcelona Declaration that have a priority. We find the same disagreement even in the case of the partnership agreements, which *are* binding. This is what usually happens whenever too many compromises are made in order to satisfy too many parties to an accord. The first concrete step that should be taken is to extend the EMP membership to all Arab countries. Despite all arguments to the contrary, the Arab world should still be treated as a unit and encouraged to behave as one. Furthermore, if the EMP is to deal with security issues, then Iran should also be invited to join. As for Israel, it will have to change its behaviour so as to be a constructive, and not a disruptive, member of the EMP.

The second step should be to encourage the MPCs to constitute a partnership among themselves. The League of Arab States would be a natural starting point for such an endeavour. All the Arab states need to start the effective implementation of the numerous integration agreements that have been in existence for decades. However, current regimes in the region are not likely to favour such a policy. That is why it is imperative that democratic rule be instituted in the region, so that the issue of Arab integration can be debated freely and publicly and the opinion of the concerned populations be ascertained. Only when southern countries are able to constitute a cohesive group similar to the EU can the EMP become a more balanced and effective project.

The EU can make a determined contribution towards the realization of this project. It has already called for greater horizontal cooperation among MPCs. This could be further supported by commitments to contribute to the construction of the material and institutional infrastructure needed to achieve regional integration among Southern partners. The EU can also make concessions that take into account the needs and circumstances of the South, such as opening its markets to agricultural products and delaying the implementation of the reciprocity rule in relation to trade of industrial goods. It can also adopt greater firmness against countries that refuse to introduce effective democratic reforms and indicate to them that they would not be associated to the new project if such reforms are not implemented.

Conclusion: Helping the Risk of Democracy Materialize

It is quite possible that Europe genuinely values democracy, and wishes to see it flourish everywhere. At the same time, it needs to protect its interests, whether by selling arms, winning markets for its products, protecting its producers against competition, or controlling immigration flows. As one author writes, 'promoters of democracy are inevitably in permanent competition with market reformers, environmentalists, drug enforcement agencies, and so on, for priority on the agendas of Western governments and international bureaucracies' (Whitehead, 1996: 269). Clearly, this is a problem that only Europe can solve.

At the same time, aspiring democrats (genuine or not) in the South may, for tactical or substantive reasons, call for profound changes in foreign policy, and reject previous 'givens' of the political structure, such as economic commitments, alliances, and alignments. They are also likely to denounce western ideas and policies, and promise the most dire punishment for those who will have stood in their way. Some movements in the South did show a propensity to make and act on such statements, but the North should go beyond using them as an excuse for blocking democracy and try instead to uncover the reasons for their emergence, just as it should abandon the casuistic argument that the South would be better off with potentially redeemable authoritarian rulers than with individuals who are *a priori* unrepentant dictators. In the current highly charged environment, excesses of all sorts are inevitable; nevertheless, 'a vital international dimension of many democratizations [*sic*] concerns the interactive process by which the external backers of the various contending political factions step (or are driven) back, relinquishing leverage over their protégés and lifting vetoes against competitors' (ibid.: 267).

The situation is quite clear: unmet social demands will maintain restlessness and instability. Present and contemplated policies are not likely to lead to satisfactory solutions. Governments in the South prefer repression to discussion, and governments in the North passively acquiesce. This situation mostly profits radical movements which, in reality, are more interested in gaining power than in solving problems. Various solutions have been proposed to break this deadlock:

45

- National élites should negotiate a series of pacts to resolve outstanding issues relating to the political, economic and social situation. They should proceed in a piecemeal manner, incrementally, and slowly, so as not to provoke internal and/or external opposition or rejection. In most countries this approach is unlikely to succeed because regimes have lost any legitimacy that they may have had, and anyone associating with them could hope for no credibility.
- Ruling élites should launch reforms designed to lead to democracy. This solution is unlikely to lead to a stable democracy, for he who gives can also take away, unless one is to assume that élites are willing to commit political hara-kiri.
- Opposition movements should mobilize the population and start a long-term, violent if necessary, uprising designed to wear down existing government. This solution may achieve the contemplated objective, although it is not certain whether there will be anyone to celebrate or be in the mood to celebrate the victory.

The only workable solution is for all spectators to leave the political field, and let the people and their leaders sort out their problems. Neither side should expect nor receive help in any form. If such a moratorium were to be effectively respected, a decision should not be long in coming; and whatever that decision is, it must be respected by the players and the outside world.

Ultimately, democracy can result from human will and action. The choice is ours: 'assume the worst, and it will surely arrive; commit oneself to the struggle for freedom and justice, and its cause may be advanced' (Chomsky, 1993: 99).

NOTES

1. House of Lords, Select Committee on the European Communities, Session 1994/95, *Relations between the EU and the Maghreb Countries*, London: HMSO Books, 1995, p. 48 (answer of the Tunisian ambassador) and p. 85 (answer of the Algerian ambassador).
2. The security issue and, in particular, the difference between 'soft' and 'hard' security are discussed in greater detail in Chourou (2000).
3. Commission of the European Communities, *Strengthening the Mediterranean Policy of the European Union: Establishing a Euro-Mediterranean Partnership*, COM(94)427 final, 19/10/1994, Annex II, p. 20.
4. SEC(92)40 final, 30 April 1992.
5. COM(93)375 final, 1 September 1993.
6. For a comprehensive evaluation of EU aid to the Mediterranean, see COWI Consulting Engineers and Planners (1998).
7. I published an early negative assessment of the 1995 Tunisia–EU free trade agreement; see Chourou (1997).
8. My views on the present state and future perspectives of the Barcelona Process are expressed in an unpublished paper presented at the workshop on the EU and the Mediterranean organized by the Geneva Centre for Security Policy and held in Geneva on 5–6 March 2001 (Chourou, 2001).

2

Democratization and the Arab World: Different Perspectives and Multiple Options

RODOLFO RAGIONIERI

Introduction

In recent years there has been much talk, both in academic and political circles, of democratic peace (Russett, 1993). According to this hypothesis, liberal democracies would have a remarkable inclination not to fight each other. It is well known, but it must nevertheless be remembered, that this theory does not maintain that democracies are more peaceful than other political regimes. It asserts that there is a kind of separate 'Kantian' peace among them. Taking this hypothesis as foreign policy advice, one has to take into consideration many connected questions and problems.

First is the desirability of democracy. In my chapter I assume that democracy can be preferred to other known political systems; however, I shall not discuss this value judgement. My view is, moreover, that democracy can be adapted to different cultural areas without basically disrupting its fundamental principles. This point is certainly not accepted by everybody, and I could be charged with flat political correctness and conventional wisdom. However, it should not be overlooked that this assumption has been criticized because it tends to enlarge too much the definition of democracy, and to make its conceptual determination too fuzzy.[1]

It is possible to add to these doubts, which are both political and theoretical, that it is by no means guaranteed that this programme can or should be implemented, or that its good intentions are not the same that pave the road to hell. For example, it is not beyond doubt that the purported beneficial effects of democracy can be imported, or that the whole process of democratization and stabilization is without risks of instability. On the contrary, historical experience shows that there is a conceptual and, unfortunately, an actual antithesis: crisis and consolidation.

Democracy and democratization in Arab countries provide a special problem. The issue is theoretically and politically challenging. For quite a long time there has been much talk of an Islamic or Arab exceptionalism. As Ghassan Salamé put it, the idea of an Arab and/or Islamic 'exceptionalism' has thus re-emerged among both western proponents of universal democracy and established orientalists, and this in turn has encouraged a great many local apologists of 'cultural authenticity' in their rejection of western models of government. (Salamé, 1995: 1)[2]

The idea of different exceptionalisms has characterized theorizing regarding democracy. At the beginning, during the 'first wave' of democratization, it was thought that only Protestant countries were a proper environment for this form of government. The second and, even more, the third wave disproved the hypothesis of the incompatibility of Catholicism and democracy. Moreover, the 'third wave' brought about democratization processes in Orthodox countries[3] (or countries with an Orthodox majority), such as Greece, Bulgaria, Russia, Romania, Macedonia and the Ukraine.[4] At the same time, analogous processes started in countries whose population and culture is predominantly Muslim. Thus, it seems hazardous to explain the difficulties of democratization in some countries assuming religion, in this case Islam, as the key variable: since imagined correlation between religion and democracy has been gradually disproved, any idea of exceptionalism could be considered as disqualified.

Two main complexes of problems must be addressed:

- democracy in Arab countries
- the feasibility and desirability of a 'democratic peace' approach as a tool for conflict prevention and the creation of a regional order in the area

In this connection, one has to take into consideration many problems:

1. the chances of democracy in Arab countries:
   - a look from the inside,
   - a look from the outside;
2. whether the development of democracy is a sensible policy; and
3. what possible role is there for an inter-Mediterranean dialogue

Democratization and the Arab World

The problem of democracy and democratization is increasingly perceived as a central issue in both domestic and regional Arab policy. As long as fair, multi-party elections were isolated events in Arab countries, this was only a matter of theoretical or academic debate. Now democratic processes are taking place in different countries, such as Jordan, Yemen, Morocco and the Palestinian areas. Thus, interest in the subject has recently become political as well. This is also proved by the number of articles appearing in newspapers and journals on the issues, often dealt with jointly, of democratization, human rights and civil society.[5]

The increasing importance of democracy has also been an occasion for self-critical revisions of many Arab intellectuals. For example, the Syrian Burhan Ghalioun already at the beginning at the 1980s acknowledged that, during the struggle for independence from colonialism and at the time of the foundation and formation of states, the problem of democracy was in a sense overlooked:

> In the first stage, like in other stages, the element of the revolt against the foreigner, in both cases of an occupation or of an economic domination, remained a constant factor; it was the main element in the ideology of the Arab ruling class. And the question was similar in the past; we did not stop to refuse democracy in name of the encompassing national unity against the outside and the foreigner. And in our view it was not important the party which supported the idea of democracy, beyond the fact that this idea was not well determined and signified little. (Ghalioun, 1995: 11)

In contrast, democracy is hotly discussed by today's Arab intellectuals (Al-Azmeh, 1994). The interesting fact is that self-criticism and the search for democracy do not characterize a single school of thought, but can be considered as more widely spread. As Salwa Ismail argues, Arab intellectuals seem to have made their way from *nahda* through revolution to democracy (Ismail, 1995). After the disillusionment of revolutionary nationalism, while a part of Arab public opinion seemed to lean towards radical Islam, a part of it started to look seriously at democracy, or rather at the lack of democracy, as one of the main problems of Arab societies. A further important point, which marks a difference with respect to past attitudes, is that democracy is in this context defined without adjectives. On the contrary, the use of adjectives (popular democracy, etc.) is seen as a trick to smuggle in dictatorship: 'democracy is the principle according founding authority on free popular choice and posing it under the continuous control of the public opinion' (Ismail, 1995: 127). Certainly this description cannot perhaps be compared with the more refined definitions of contemporary political science and political theory (Morlino, 1986: 83 ff; Sartori, 1993: 11 ff and 113 ff). It is, however, important in the context of the evolution of the Arab debate, and its transition from revolutionary nationalism to democracy.

Another part of this debate is the search for a legitimization in Islamic culture. The Arab word for democracy is the usual one of Greek origin, and this makes a difference with respect to many other expressions of the political vocabulary. This fact notwithstanding, there is a desire to find a source or an inspiration for democracy not in imported ideologies, but in an original history and political culture.[6] Such legitimization is found in the principle of *shura* (consultation), which can be found in the Koran and in the *Hadîth* of the Prophet Muhammad. First of all, it is important to remember that different positions with respect to the interpretation of the *shura* principle are possible. We could classify them as traditional, Islamic radical, Islamic reformist and 'liberal'.

The traditional position is very clear. The use of the principle of *shura* is a way of depreciating democracy as most people understand it. It can be simply a religious legitimization of traditional or tribal procedures: the consultation is understood simply as a tribal or almost-tribal council around the king, *amir* or sultan, as it is in the traditional oil monarchies of the Gulf. A typical example of this approach is the Saudi conception of the *majlis ash-shura*. Even though there was a reform of the composition and function of the *majlis*, it is clear that the function remains consultation rather than decision.

In the radical Islamic approach of the first generations, democracy is openly rejected, and *shura* is not considered as a justification or legitimization of democracy. If we take into consideration, for example, the work of Taqi ad-Din an-Nabhani (1907–77), a Palestinian Islamist ideologue, democracy is rejected and *shura* is interpreted in the framework of the caliphate. The rejection of democracy is based on the theory of the sovereignty of God (Nabhani, 1990: 27 ff): since sovereignty and the power to legislate is God's prerogative, the doctrine of popular sovereignty, which is the foundation of democratic and republican systems, makes these systems, according to Nabhani, incompatible with Islam. This incompatibility is made stronger by the fact that leadership is individual and not collective (ibid.: 122 ff), and by the character and prerogatives of the *majlis* (council). *Shura* is considered a right by Muslims, not a decision-making procedure (ibid.: 209 ff).

According to more recent Islamic political thinkers,[7] the concept of *khilafa* must be understood as collective vice-regency bestowed by God upon the whole community. Consequently, it makes sense to indicate a proper decision-making process, and this process is *shura* (Moten, 1996: 89 ff). This can be considered as a possible starting point for 'Islamic reformism'. Abdul Rashid Moten maintains that the principle of consultation is as important as the five pillars of Islam, and that '*shura* ensures not merely the participation of the people in public affairs but it acts as a check against tyrannical rule as well. *Shura* can be operationalised only if there prevails the two fundamental principles of freedom and equality' (ibid.: 90).

The difference between the Islamic principle and the current western democratic principle is made clearly and honestly by Abdelhadi Boutaleb, former minister and president of the Moroccan House of Representatives. He finds analogies and differences in seven different respects (Boutaleb, 1995: 111 ff):

1. democracy is a political system chosen by human beings for a given society, *shura* is a divine commandment revealed to the whole humankind;
2. democracy is a lay doctrine, *shura* aims at educating and integrating Muslims into a Muslim society;
3. democracy is a value-free system, *shura* is a way of life of the Islamic society;
4. in liberal democracies, usually representatives are elected for a given period, and for that period are free from popular control (within

constitutional limits), in the *shura* system the process starts with the summit, in such a fashion that leaders are always confronted with criticism;
5. individual and religious freedom is understood differently in a western society and in a Muslim society ruled according to the *shari'a*;
6. the source of sovereignty is people in democracy, God in an Islamic system; and
7. even though both systems want to control power, their methods are different and difficult to compare; their characteristics depend on historical circumstances.

Obviously, these considerations cannot be considered as the last word on the subject, but are nevertheless an interesting contribution to a clarification of the question.

A possible tentative conclusion is that (modern) democracy can be used or bent to the creation of a certain order. On the contrary *shura*, even at its best, if it is considered in its proper Islamic context, cannot be the base for a liberal democracy. This is not to say that it is better or worse, but simply to make some intellectual clarification. The main difference is that individual rights are in principle subordinated to the achievement of a certain given order, or at least of the *bonum commune*.[8]

However, and here we come to the 'liberals', *shura* can be considered not only as a reference to a divinely inspired and unchanging text, but also as a principle deriving from a religious source, and as a reference in the Islamic cultural tradition. It can be considered as a root of democracy that can be found independently of any foreign influence.

However, this attitude has its own values and problems. A first remark, which can be made without giving value judgements, is that this view expresses the will, on the Arab and Islamic side, to have democratic traditions independent of, if not even older than, the European one. Obviously the European–western tradition would be older if connected to the experience of the *polis* in ancient Greece, whereas the Islamic one is older if the European one goes back 'only' to the communal Middle Age tradition. If, on the contrary, the supporters of *shura* intend to legitimize democracy, a proper question is why the full implementation of the principle of *shura* was not possible in traditional Islamic societies, or why the Arab world was not able to transform the traditional *shura* into a more modern form of democracy.[9] This happened in Europe with the long and conflictual transformation of Middle Age 'states' assemblies' into modern representative bodies. This evolution was historically possible through the obliged passage of absolutism and the often violent destruction of allegiances deemed dangerous for the centralized state, as proved, for example, by the methods used by the United Kingdom to destroy the power of the clans in the Highlands.

After these necessary remarks on the issue of *shura* and democracy, it is useful to try to draw a tentative typology of different attitudes towards democracy in Arab countries. However, it is difficult even to build a proper typology. Usually social scientists like two-variable, two-value typologies, which are likely to be easily represented in a two-dimensional matrix. For example, Jean Leca proposes a typical fourfold typology of conservative Islamic, radical Islamic, democratic, authoritarian nationalist. Leca admits that his partition is rough, but it is nevertheless useful. This is undoubtedly true, but this typology has the limitation of including under the label 'democratic' different positions that are politically compatible but ideologically different, whereas other types look more homogeneous. A further problem is that religious positions are labelled as either conservative or fundamentalist: one would argue from this typology that *tertium non datur*. On the contrary, there are religiously inspired positions that are neither conservative nor fundamentalist, and that can be labelled reformist.

For example, liberal democrats such as Sa'd ad-Din Ibrahim are different from Islamic reformists such as al-Ashmawi, even though their political programmes can be considered as largely compatible, and both can be labelled as 'democratic'. A more refined classification would have the advantage of stressing the possible alliances between different groups or tendencies. To this purpose, one should take into consideration various dimensions: democratization, liberalization (social/political and economic), separation politics/religion, religious reformism, mobilization/participation. If one wants to take into account all these variables, 96 possible types could be conceived: every variable has two possible values (zero and one), with the exception of the mobilization/participation variable, which has three values, zero for neither mobilization nor participation, one for mobilization, and two for participation. The dimension of religious reformism has to be kept separated from the division between religion and politics, which is in turn different from the separation between state and church. In an Islamic context the problem of religious reformism relates to the interpretation of the texts and to the possibility of the reopening of the *ijtihad*.[10] This typology can be valid both for states and ideologies.

If we try to develop this typology we find many combinations in the multidimensional box. For example, the Saudi regime must be put with all the variables at the minimum, with only a certain amount of economic liberalization. Westernized thinkers such as Basam Tibi have a maximum of most variables, but one can find reformist Muslims such as al-Ashmawi with a relatively low separation religion/politics (cf. also many European Christian democrats), but with a certain degree of religious reformism, political and social liberalization and democracy. In this context the variables making the main distinction between traditional patrimonial regimes and radical Islam are those concerning the degree of mobilization and participation.[11] Ba'th would have zero for democratization and liberalization, but one for all other variables (but this is probably different in theory and in practice for the governments in Syria and Iraq).

An important aspect of the recent debate is the attempt to avoid or bypass the problem of secularism (Ghalioun, 1997). What is significant here is not the issue of the division between religion and politics, but the issue of democracy and freedom, which can be combined with an updating of religious conceptions (Ismail, 1995; Filali-Ansari, 1999). This implies that the strict separation between religion and politics is not always a watershed. Consequently, it is possible to have alliances or common position between people with different opinions in this respect; the basic problem in fact is what political use or interpretation of Islam is proposed.

It is possible to consider this stage of the political debate among Arab intellectuals as evidence for the unsolved problem of the legitimization of power. However, as it will be hinted at below, it could be paradoxical that a viable solution of the problem is found (or more probably suggested) just when the institutions of the territorial state are threatened by the crisis of sovereignty and by processes of deterritorialization and the different reconstruction of territories.[12]

Nevertheless, the complexity of the possible positions, which I have tried to make manifest by describing the multiplicity of dimensions of the problem, makes clear that the constellation of social and political forces necessary for a successful process of democratization is by no means assured. Those political forces or intellectual circles labelled as 'democratic' by Leca are often too weak or divided.

The West and Democracy Outside the West

There is a western attitude that democracy is contemporary 'white man's burden'. Even though this approach is declining among scholars in social sciences, it has a certain credibility first of all because of the opinions of traditional orientalists such as Bernard Lewis or Panos Vatikiotis (Vatikiotis, 1991). Moreover, there was a revival of geopolitics after the collapse of the bipolar international system,[13] especially in its civilizational varieties, such as Huntington's clash of civilizations (Huntington, 1998), or even more elaborate approaches (Cacciari, 1997, 1999; Santoro, 1998). However, it is not uncommon to find similar views spread among journalists or even scholars (Sartori, 1993: 269).

The first and more traditional type of approach points, as is well known, to a supposed incompatibility between Islam and political modernity, if not modernity *per se*. A first point made by those proposing this idea is manifold incompatibility:

1. the contradiction between the limited and particularistic territorial state on one side, and the non-territorial and universalistic idea of *umma*;
2. the irreconcilable struggle between the *dar al-islam/dar al-harb/dar as-sulh* partition of political space of classical Islamic thought and the

sovereignty of modern states;

3. the difficult conciliation of the plural allegiances to be found in Arab (and often in Islamic) societies with the unitary structure of the modern state; and

4. the relations of hierarchic tolerance of communities in traditional Islam, which, according to this school of thought, cannot be reformed or changed without a substantial (and in the short or medium run improbable) de-Islamization of societies.

This culturalist and determinist approach, both in its 'traditional orientalist' or 'politically correct' varieties, has been successfully criticized by scholars of older generations, such Maxime Rodinson (Rodinson, 1992: 115 ff), or by a *nouvelle vague* of 'orientalists', whose approach is closer to that of historical and social sciences, such as James Piscatori or John Esposito (Esposito and Voll, 1996). Nevertheless, as I mentioned before, it is still to be found among scholars of international relations and political science not specializing in the Middle East and North Africa, journalists and opinion-makers. Since criticism of this approach is well known, I shall not dwell on it. However, it is important to remember that the analysis of contemporary trends in terms of medieval texts or supposedly permanent characteristics would not be favourable even for Europe, where democracy was judged in negative terms until relatively recent times.

A second approach is related to geopolitics. The interesting point is that geopolitical theories, and the word 'geopolitics' itself, have become fashionable since the end of the Cold War and the subsequent search for paradigms or interpretations of international politics. It looks like the search for comfortable points of reference in an unknown landscape. In this context 'geocultural' theories, even though often more refined than Huntington's clash of civilizations, are now surprisingly frequent. A particular use of these theories is in an attempt to explain the lack of democracy in the 'East', and more specifically in Islamic countries. The idea that the border between Europe and the 'East' is at the same time the border between democracy and autocracy is old, and goes back to the Persian Wars. More precisely, it is this interpretation that has been given for centuries to the struggle for independence of some Hellenic *polis* against the powerful Persian land empire. For example, the Italian philosopher Massimo Cacciari in his two books on European identity worked out this argument (Cacciari, 1994: 52 ff; Cacciari, 1997: 13 ff and 117 ff). Here it is important to make two points. The first is related to Cacciari's elaborated arguments, and the second to their possible interpretations and political or ideological use. The complex and multiple correlations analysed by the Italian philosopher describe the way Europe has been taking conscience of its political and cultural identity as defined along and by means of a historic path. These connections are consequently not invariable borders (*limites*) defined once and for all. Moreover, this differentiation with respect to something is vital for Europe as seen by Cacciari, and at the same time this relation is not of exclusion or absolute enmity, but a relation of differentiation and reciprocal knowledge (Cacciari, 1999). In conclusion, his approach stresses the European origin of democracy, and even the coincidence of the differentiation Europe/Asia at the same time as the first appearance of the democratic idea, but it is also true that he rejects any idea of Europe as purely Frankish-Carolingian and isolated.

Other interpretations point at the Other, as seen in geopolitical terms, as the permanent enemy (Santoro, 1998). The West, and especially Europe, is seen as permanently threatened by Eurasian land powers, who through history have taken the form of the Achaemenid Empire, the Mongols, the Ottoman Empire, the Russian Empire and the Soviet Union. The opposition between 'Europe' and 'Eurasia' would be not only geopolitical, but cultural as well, including the dimension of democracy/autocracy (ibid.: 153 and 162). Whereas even a sober interpretation of the 'clash of civilization' paradigm implies an amount of dialogue between different cultural areas, in order to avoid dangerous military confrontation, this geopolitical approach only entails a policy of permanent confrontation between the same areas.

At the other extreme of the spectrum of interpretations, one can find analytical interpretations that try to look at even contradictory processes as symptoms of a generalized trend towards political participation. Esposito, for example, maintains that the development of political Islam is to be understood in terms of the contemporary trend towards the self-assertion of identity and democratization (Esposito and Voll, 1996). According to his hypothesis this development intends to act against the pressures both of globalization (as far as self-assertion of identity is concerned) and of local authoritarianism, both traditional and modernizing (as far as democratization is concerned). It is important to remind those analysing contemporary phenomena in terms of fourteenth-century jurists that elections were certainly not proposed as a method of selection in traditional Islam, and are now accepted by any regime in the area, with the only exception of traditional authoritarian states. More important, elections are requested, more or less instrumentally, by all the movements asking for more participation and empowerment.

The main divide is thus between those who support any kind of exceptionalism, and others who on the contrary try to understand the pitfalls and difficulties of democracy with the instruments of historical and social sciences.

At the end of this short review, it is important to remember that in recent years attempts to explain the developments and failure of democracy in Arab countries using the tools of modern social sciences are becoming more frequent than ideological approaches. In recent years theoretical and empirical research on this subject has substantially improved. These researches avoid the pitfalls of cultural and/or geopolitical determinism, and can be partially drawn back to different theories of democratization (Salamé, 1995; Brynen et al., 1995a). However, it is an interesting fact that one of the issues concerns the relevance of political culture as a variable. Discussion of the relevance of this concept for the Arab case can draw on two different, but perhaps interdependent, issues. On the one hand, we obviously have the lasting influence of the idea of an Arab cultural exception. On the other, especially in the last years and with respect to developing countries, there has been a revival of interest concerning the use of 'political culture' in comparative politics (Diamond, 1993). For example, Michael Hudson has argued that, with a certain degree of caution, it is necessary to take it into account (Hudson, 1995). His approach is, however, far from that of cultural determinism, since his first caveat is to avoid reductionist concepts and essentialist assumptions. Moreover, he argues that political cultures are multilayered and must be disaggregated, from the points of view both of different social classes and the different ways this culture surfaces (ideologies, opinions, attitudes, enduring values and orientations). It is apparent that this attitude is at the antipodes of the supporters of a cultural or anthropological Arab or Islamic exception. Just because of this complexity, in the same edited book, Lisa Anderson argues that the use of the concept of political culture requires too many specifications to be used usefully (Anderson, 1995).

Obviously many authors try to explain or to deny the difficult development of democracy in Arab countries using different theories of democratization, consolidation and crisis.[14] It is not possible here even to draw a rough typology of these studies. However some widespread tendencies can be hinted at. In order to do that I shall use David Potter's classification of democratization theories (Potter, 1997). Potter groups together different theories in three major types: the modernization approach, transition theories, and the structural approach. The first one, which is characterized by the use of general social and economic indicators that would make democracy possible, is usually not suitable for the Arab case, since the richest states are 'renter states'. The second approach, where the behaviour of élites is analysed in terms of rational behaviour, is most used for case studies. Finally the structural approach, which can be drawn back to the work of Barrington Moore (1966), is mostly used for general explanation and trends of the whole area.

However, if we take into consideration both Arab and Western 'scientific' (as opposed to 'ideological') studies, we can see that the relation between state, citizen, and democracy provides a recurrent (implicit or explicit) underlying theme. The weakness of democracy would be a consequence first of the weakness of the Arab state, that has not yet fully solved the problem of its legitimacy. Moreover, this same weakness affects the citizens. Intermediate allegiances make the whole game more difficult to solve.

Democratization as a Foreign Policy Tool?

First, one can question the assumption that fostering democracy is a good foreign policy. Second, it is well known that the EU's real policy has been to support economic opening rather than democratization or political liberalization.

I limit myself mainly to the first issue. As far as the second point is concerned, the Democracy Clause has never been properly implemented in bilateral economic agreements, and the request of respect of human rights has so far been more declaratory than real and effective (Feliu, 1997). In this respect it is possible to blame the EU's and other single countries' policies, or to accept this fact as a natural reaction of politics as it is against dangerous utopian ideas.

Coming back to the more general issue, one could reasonably argue that the use of democratization as a foreign policy tool could be subject to attack from many sides. As was recalled at the beginning of this chapter, the theory or hypothesis of democratic peace theoretically dictates this foreign policy. Consequently, a foreign policy of 'democratization' depends upon one's evaluation of this hypothesis. At the same time, the reverse is often true. The hypothesis is questioned because of its policy implications: some American scholars challenge it because, they purport, it supports a vague and idealist concept instead of defending more down-to earth 'American interests' in the world (Gowa, 1995).

Moreover, this hypothesis is often misinterpreted, and this misinterpretation can be really dangerous. For example, it can be considered as deterministic. Another common wrong interpretation is that democratic states could be at peace *only* with other democratic states. From the methodological point of view this is a trivial mistake, since it confuses a sufficient with a necessary condition. However, this is not only a mistake, it is also politically dangerous. For example, this is Ariel Sharon's interpretation, and his point that it is impossible to have real peace with Arab countries, since Arab countries are not democratic. By the way, he is not a genuine enthusiast of democracy, since he has written more than once that the national character of the state of Israel is much more important than its democratic system.

Independently of any misunderstanding, theory can be subjected to attack: as neo-realists and other theorists would argue, the argument is not relevant, since the structure of domestic political systems does not affect the anarchic environment. Another criticism of the theory was put forward by Raymond Cohen (Cohen, 1994). He maintains that the peaceful relations taken into consideration by scholars are not relevant (or the assumption is falsified) except in the case of the North Atlantic security community. This community was formed under the pressure of the Soviet threat, and democracy is not the proper explicative variable. This point is relevant, because it would be really unwise to foster the creation of an Arab security community by means of the creation of an external threat, or the creation of threat perceptions!

Another weak aspect is that the effect of democratic transition on the likelihood of violent conflict is not certain. Edward Mansfield and Jack Snyder claim that it is destabilizing (Mansfield and Snyder, 1995). Their first point is a statistical analysis. However, Kristion Gleditsch and Michael Ward claim that the probability of violent conflicts monotonically decreases with the increase of democracy coefficients (Gleditsch and Ward, 1998). Without daring to enter the minefield of statistical analysis, I want to take into consideration Mansfield and Snyder's theoretical argument. By means of an analysis of the foreign policy of four big powers (Great Britain, France, Germany and Japan) during a long process of democratization, they come to the conclusion that the internal dynamics between élites and pressure groups tend to stimulate aggressive foreign policy and a turn to war.

This is relevant to our case. The Middle East and North Africa are areas rich in actual and latent conflict. Thus, it would not be a wise policy to endanger what is commonly believed to be an unstable situation. Moreover, it is possible to see how in the past some leaderships in the area chose, perhaps with a conscious purpose, to wage war instead of initiate a process of liberalization. For example, if one looks at the recent history of the Middle East, it can be supposed that the choice of Saddam Hussein to go to war with Iran in 1980 was also dictated by the possible threat posed by a political opening in Iraqi society. This opening was made possible by the very social and economic successes of the regime. One could think of the Iran–Iraq war as a 'preventive war' against internal liberalization. Even within the current situation one cannot exclude the fact that threatened élites could use international conflict to divert internal tensions or menace.

Whereas the theoretical and empirical debate is open, with respect to policy-making issues one could draw on the constructivist explanation of democratic peace (Risse-Kappen, 1995). According to this point of view, democracies tend to be more peaceful in reciprocal relations because there is a process of learning in which democratic norms are used as communication devices. This common language is an important factor in the establishment of mutual perceptions. The same language and shared norms help actors to develop communications of peaceful intentions. This process can be especially relevant in an environment where a common culture and language is already established, such as the Arab world. Moreover, in this same environment an international institutional framework, the Arab League, has been working, with ups and downs, for decades, and this provides an arena for communication.

However, a further and more devastating point can be made, related to two important and debated theoretical (and not only theoretical) issues. These issues are the post-Weberian character of contemporary world politics, and the trajectory of the state in Arab countries. The first hypothesis stresses the fact that the territorial state is exercising its functions with a decreasing level of effectiveness. The second cluster of problems obviously refers to the unending debate about the future of the Arab state. One can find different and even opposite opinions in this respect. On one side, some scholars think that territorial states are consolidating through the multi-dimensional practice of sovereignty (Barnett, 1995). On the other side, the so-called neo-khaldunian (see Ghalioun's articles in the *Revue d'études palestiniennes* and the debate of the last years) thinks that the uncertain legitimacy of the Arab states is eroded by globalization on one side, and by internal and regional fragmentation on the other. The question could be conceptualized as follows: in an environment characterized by a double weakness of the state (globalization and traditional weaknesses), is the increasing complexity deriving from democratic processes a stabilizing or a destabilizing factor? Machiavelli, the imagined quintessential realist thinker, wrote in *The Prince* that decisions left to many people are more reliable than those left to individuals. However, the question is open.

In conclusion, if the hypothesis of democratic peace is uncertain, and if the state is of decreasing importance or strength, why bother about democracy? Three answers can be given.

1. The hypothesis of so-called democratic peace does not make much sense if taken from a pure dyadic perspective. Nevertheless, I think it makes sense, or must be taken into consideration in a wider framework and reconsidered from the point of view of communities of states where democracy is commonly thought to be a more reliable decision-making, conflict-prevention and management method.
2. The fact that the importance of the Weberian territorial state is declining does not mean that it is irrelevant. It means that it is a part of a picture where other elements contribute to determine the possible final outcomes.
3. The same can be maintained with respect to the Arab state.

Before concluding it is important to remind ourselves that not all constellations of political élites on both shores of the Mediterranean are favourable both to democratization processes in Arab countries and to the development of a consistent democratic peace policy on the European side. On one side of the Mediterranean the temptation to develop a closed and exclusive European identity (a wall-identity) in a 'European fortress' needs to be avoided. This identity would encourage Arab states to look at their neighbours as a dangerous threat to their civilizations or, in the best case, as a totally different and alien culture. On the other shore of the Mediterranean, it cannot be certain that the social and political alliances necessary for a stable process of democratization are guaranteed. In the worst case, a self-fulfilling prophecy could really bring about a clash of civilizations instead of trying to find a solution to an environment characterized by a multiplicity of cultures in each area.

To avoid these dangers, dialogue should be more related to the development of civil societies, and that cannot be thought of as related to democratization, but to the direct imposition of a *totally* determined political system. Rather, democratization is a part of a general strategy that aims to develop conflict management and resolution devices, where something different from a total victory is not perceived as a prelude to a catastrophic defeat.

NOTES

1. In a recent reflection on democracy, Katherine Fierlebeck wrote that 'the "western" conception of democracy itself is, and has been throughout its development, philosophically ambiguous and frequently contradictory. There is, simply, no monolithic account of what democracy is (or ought to be)' (Fierlebeck, 1998: 178).
2. Unfortunately the English version does not translate effectively the more polemical French original, where you can read of 'les thuriferaires globalistes de la démocratie autant que parmi les orientalistes patentés'.
3. For a definition of the three waves and considerations about the connection between religion and democracy, see Huntington (1993a).
4. The case is obviously different for Serbia, Montenegro and Bielarus.
5. See for example the contribution issued by various Arab intellectuals in *al-Mustaqbal al'Arabi*, 232 (October 1998).
6. This concept must here be understood in a wider meaning than the original one.
7. See for example Moten (1996).
8. The same, for example, could be said for the original, non-liberal idea of democracy, which can be connected to the values of republican *virtù* praised by Machiavelli in his *Discorsi*.
9. This point is also made by Ghalioun (1995).
10. The *ijtihad* is the effort of interpretation of the Koran and the *sunna*.
11. Theory and practice are in this case manifold and contradictory, since you can observe traditional theorists claiming that democracy cannot be reconciled with the theory of the sovereignty of God, other theorists purporting that the Koranic principle of *shura* is the basis of democracy, and the electoral practice of the Iranian regime.
12. For a treatment of this cluster of problems, readers are referred to the books by Bertrand Badie (1986, 1992, 1995).
13. For a critical review, see Ó Tuathail (1996: 225 ff). For a general historical geopolitical theory of international relations, see Santoro (1998).
14. For a definition of the conceptual dyad consolidation/crisis, see Morlino (1998: 12 ff).

The Foreign Policy of a Civilian Power?
The European Union in the Mediterranean

STELIOS STAVRIDIS and JUSTIN HUTCHENCE

Introduction

This chapter is about European Union (EU)–Mediterranean relations from the perspective of the 'civilian power' model. It is often a moot point whether a policy is successful or not. The reasons for assessing the EU's record in the Mediterranean stem from the fact that the Union is engaged in a particularly ambitious effort to create a new political and security system on the European continent and beyond. Such an effort has been made all the more difficult (but at the same time, all the more welcome and necessary) by the end of the Cold War. In other words, assessing the efficiency of the EU in the world is necessary because its impact is far too important to be ignored.

Why the 'civilian power' approach is used here as a testing ground follows from the fact that the existing literature appears to give it an *a priori* claim to be the 'obvious' concept to be applied to the EU (for more see Hill, 1990; Whitman, 1998; Zielonka, 1998; Smith, 2000).

Why the Mediterranean? First, because we need to test theories. Concepts such as that of 'civilian power Europe' do not mean much if they are not tested out with specific case studies, that is to say, empirical work. We are very much in favour of theorizing, but not just for the sake of it. Theories are useful only if they can help us understand the real world better (for more, see Chryssochoou, Tsinisizelis et al., 1999: 1–3). We hope that theories can also be useful for specific policy recommendations, although we think that the details are better left to the practitioners, be they diplomats or politicians. Indeed, we fully appreciate the limits of prediction in social sciences and the relative importance of a political role for academics (i.e. 'it is difficult to predict, especially about the future').

Second, we are using a number of case studies even if it unavoidably means less in-depth analysis. On balance, we think that the positive aspects of the comparative dimension outweigh the negatives. We will examine three case studies: the Middle East with an emphasis on the Middle East Peace Process (MEPP); North Africa, with an emphasis on the conflict in Algeria; and, finally, the Cyprus problem within the wider context of EU–Turkish relations. The case studies are taken from the Mediterranean, because:

- There has always been a Mediterranean dimension in European integration from the very start of the EC.
- The EC played an important role in the strengthening of the new southern democracies in the mid-1970s (Pridham, 1991).
- The Mediterranean has been identified as a zone of interest for Common Foreign and Security Policy (CFSP) joint actions by the June 1992 Lisbon European Council. The Lisbon presidency conclusions specified that a zone of interest existed as a result of geographical proximity and clear European interests in the region. In June 2000 the Feira European Council produced a CFSP common strategy on the Mediterranean, the third such instrument it has adopted since it was introduced in the Amsterdam Treaty reforms of 1999.
- Historically, the Mediterranean has been an area of concern in the EC's early efforts at foreign policy cooperation: the first European Political Cooperation (EPC) declaration in late 1970 mentioned the Arab–Israeli conflict. Examples of this are: the Euro-Arab dialogue (an attempt at a structured EC Mediterranean policy following the 1973 oil crisis) and the Renovated Mediterranean Policy.
- Earlier studies have identified the Mediterranean basin as an area of particular interest for European foreign policy, both geographically and thematically: Philippe De Schoutheete identified nine issue areas where *quelques résultats* in EPC collaboration could be identified that included Cyprus, the Middle East and human rights (De Schoutheete, 1986: 67–8). Gianni Jannuzzi pointed out at least seven areas where there has been a common stance, including again the Middle East and terrorism and human rights (Jannuzzi, 1988: 106).
- Importance is attached to the Middle East Peace Process by the EU, despite it being sidelined in the first instance but now 'emerging from the sidelines' (Peters, 1997).
- The economic and financial links between the two shores are important, especially with regard to the trade dependence on the EU of some Maghreb states (within a 60–70 per cent range for most Maghreb countries in either exports or imports or both, and high figures for the three applicant countries; see Table 3.1).
- The Barcelona Process (or Euro-Mediterranean Partnership)[1] is an effort not to forget the South while expanding the EU eastwards: the challenge of the new post-Cold War context has highlighted an East–South dimension within the EU's priorities at the turn of the millennium (Barbé, 1995, especially 15 ff; Tsakaloyannis, 1997). In addition, the EMP is seen as an attempt to remedy the failure of previous policies and the ensuing political and security instability in the region.

TABLE 3.1: EU SHARE OF MEDITERRANEAN COUNTRIES' EXTERNAL TRADE (%)

	Imports			Exports		
	1993	1995	1998	1993	1995	1998
Algeria	55.9	56.0	69.3	69.6	63.5	64.6
Morocco	54.5	53.1	76.9	62.4	61.3	81.6
Tunisia	72.3	69.1	75.0	78.3	79.0	80.1
Egypt	45.4	38.9	36.3	40.1	45.8	37.5
Jordan	40.0 (1992)	:	42.8	11.0 (1992)	:	38.7
Lebanon	42.3	43.6	63.2	16.7	15.8	39.1
Syria	36.8	31.7	45.9	60.7	56.7	74.0
Israel	51.5	52.4	48.5	30.6	32.3	30.8
Palestine	:	:	:	:	:	:
Cyprus	54.2	51.7	54.7	37.4	34.7	50.4
Malta	71.6	72.8	69.2	71.7	71.4	54.0
Turkey	44.0	47.2	52.4	47.5	51.2	50.0

Various sources, including Eurostat and FEMISE reports. Some figures have been rounded up or down. The main purpose of this table is to show the heavy dependence of most Mediterranean countries on the EU economy.

TABLE 3.2: COMPARATIVE DATA (DEFENCE, POPULATION AND ECONOMY)

	Defence budget	Active armed forces	Population	GDP $/GDP per head
USA	$ bn 267.6	1,401,600	277 m	8.1tr/29,300
EU 15	$ bn 144.3	1,890,281*	370 m	8.1tr/20,100
Russia	$ bn 64 (1997)	1,159,000 (est.)	147 m	1.1tr/6,800
Japan	$ bn 35.2	242,600	126 m	4.2tr/23,500
China	$ bn 36.6 (1997 est.)	2,820,000	1.2 bn	639bn/3,400

Source: *Military Balance 1998/99*, International Institute for Strategic Studies, 1998.

* France over 300,000; Germany over 300,000; UK over 200,000; Spain over 190,000. (Some figures have been rounded up/down.)

In other words, the Barcelona Process is an attempt to face the challenges of the emerging new international order and the new European architecture. Therefore, it aims to be a response to a number of threats, but not in the (in)famous Huntingtonian sense. It is not part of a clash of civilizations between the 'Christian West' and the 'Islamic East' (Huntington, 1993b). Rather, the Barcelona Process is a response to a complex variety of security problems in the region. This chapter can be seen as adding to 'the vast growing literature on the security challenges of the region' (Xenakis, 1999: 5).

Civilian Power Europe

International Actorness of the EU

While exact definitions are disputed, it is generally accepted that the EU is more than an international organization, but less than a state.[2] What we are addressing is the identity of the EU in terms of its international behaviour: is it just an 'international actor', a 'global power', an 'economic power/bloc', a 'civilian power', or a 'superpower in the making'?

Efforts to define the EC and the EU, especially with regard to its international role, were rare in the past but have tended to increase more recently. One such isolated effort was written 25 years ago by Johan Galtung, and was entitled *The European Community: A Superpower in the Making*.[3] A more recent one, though journalistic, was written by David Buchan in 1993; it concluded that the EC/EU was a 'strange superpower'. In early 1997, Christopher Piening's conclusion was that the EU was a 'global power' (Piening, 1997).[4] Richard Whitman argued that the EU is neither a civilian power nor a superpower in the making, but simply possesses a distinct international identity (Whitman, 1998). Finally, Jan Zielonka has argued that the EU should only be a civilian power and should not try to develop the characteristics of a superpower (Zielonka, 1998).

There is little doubt from the existing literature that the EU (and before it the EC) has now acquired an international role, even if its legal status remains unclear (Wessel, 1997; Whitman, 1998: 157–84). There is in fact general agreement that all EU institutions have acquired an international role of sorts. This is particularly true of the European Commission and the European Parliament (EP), but generally speaking this is due to the emergence of the EC/EU as an international actor.

Similarly, the Community/Union possesses observer status in many international organizations, such as the United Nations, and many non-member states have diplomatic relations and representation with the EC/EU. There are 147 foreign missions accredited to the EU in Brussels, which compares favourably to the 169 accredited to Washington – the highest in the world for a capital (Whitman, 1998: 132).

Civilian Power Europe

This term was first coined back in the 1970s,[5] at a time when economic and ideological power seemed to be more important in international affairs than traditional military power. This was illustrated by:

- the oil crises and the OPEC cartel;
- the end of the Vietnam War;
- the economic power of Japan and of West Germany;
- the non-military or low-level conflict with terrorism; and

- the beginning of the failure of the Soviet model and empire, especially in ideological terms, both in the Eastern Bloc and in western Europe in the form of Eurocommunism.

In Duchêne's own words a civilian power is: 'a civilian group of countries long on economic power and relatively short on armed force'; and 'a force for the international diffusion of civilian and democratic standards' (quoted in Ifestos, 1987: 62). Kenneth Twitchett also defines it as 'an international polity as yet possessing no military dimension, but able to exercise influence on states, global and regional organizations, international corporations and other transnational bodies through diplomatic, economic and legal factors' (ibid.: 62). That is to say, it is an entity with influence over a number of other international actors, though not through traditional military means. This definition must be contrasted with that of a 'superpower', which possesses power and influence and means to implement them in the following fields: ideology, politics, economics, finance and the military, especially in nuclear technology. There also usually exists a sphere of influence where the superpower has almost unlimited control or dominance (so-called 'back-yards').

In the existing literature on the subject there are two different approaches to 'civilian power Europe': the realists who deny the very existence of the concept itself, and the liberal view that tries to use it in a wider effort to understand what the EU actually is in world affairs, and by implication what its internal structure really is.

The realists argue that it amounts to nothing more than a 'contradiction in terms' (Bull, 1983). Panayotis Ifestos adds that 'the turbulences of the 1970s and first half of the 1980s ... [have] tended to discredit [the civilian power Europe approach]' (Ifestos, 1987: 68). Alfred Pijpers goes further in the late 1980s: 'EPC has some striking deficiencies in the field of security', and he stresses the lack of crisis management arrangements and the lack of coordination in the field of arms trade policy (Pijpers, 1988: 157).

The liberal view takes a more sympathetic approach. Reinhardt Rummel argues that 'When compared to the superpowers, Western Europe stresses moral persuasion, the "good example", and unconditional help and de-empha-sizes ideological warfare, the selections of proxies, and the "projection of power"' (Rummel, 1988: 130). Christopher Hill identifies several reasons for applying the phrase 'civilian power' to the EC (Hill, 1990: 43–4):

- International politics is not exclusively about military power.
- The use of military force to intervene in third countries has a dubious record.
- It is true to say that the record of civilian power in action is not insubstantial.
- Duchêne's original preoccupation was with the process of integration in

western Europe and in particular the reconciliation between France and Germany, which has been 'gloriously' successful (i.e. as the absence of the use or threat of force between member states testifies).

- A civilian power Europe is more desirable than a superpower Europe. In this respect Hill agrees with Duchêne's original view that the EC should not become a superpower, because such a development would go against its intrinsic nature.[6] One could suggest, too, that this would also be unlikely since it would imply a 'single finger' on a 'single European nuclear deterrent', a true European federation and a single European executive.

This concept of civilian power is useful, although there is no agreement as one can see over what it actually means and over whether this is the best definition for the EU in the early twenty-first century. To sum up:

- civilian power does not mean pacifism;
- civilian means usually refer to non-military means; and
- civilian principles and means come very close to democratic principles and means.

There is little doubt that the EU possesses significant financial and economic instruments as well as military capability if taken as a whole. We also include the second part of the Duchêne definition. Thus, a working definition for a 'civilian power Europe' is where non-military means are used to promote democratic principles and human rights in the world.

The Mediterranean

Each case study that follows starts with the positive signs of the existence of a civilian power Europe. The negative list is much longer than the positive one, which also contains several important qualifications. Our conclusion is therefore that despite a number of important civilian means, the EU is not acting like a civilian power, this is promoting democracy and human rights in the Mediterranean.

EU Relations with Cyprus and Turkey

This section (see also Stavridis, 2001a) considers in turn four areas:

- Cyprus;
- relations with Greece;
- human rights and democracy in Turkey (the role of the military and the impact of Islamic fundamentalism); and
- the Kurdish problem.

66

On Cyprus, on the *positive* side:

- There has been EC/EU verbal condemnation of the division of the island and support for relevant UN resolutions.
- The EU has appointed observers to act as its representatives 'on the ground' (Serge Abou, European observer for the Cyprus problem and Federico di Roberto, European coordinator for Cypriot affairs: 1994 and 1996).
- Enlargement negotiations have started but it is unclear as to when they may end and what the wider implications will be if the island's division is perpetuated.
- As is often the case, the EP is only occasionally active in blocking financial aid to Turkey. In protest at the civilian deaths in Cyprus in 1996 the EP blocked financial aid to Turkey under the recently agreed Customs Union Agreement.

On the *negative* side, it is fair to say that since 1974 the EC/EU has been hiding behind rhetorical support for UN resolutions and efforts at finding a solution regarding the two Cypriot communities.

The non-recognition of the 'Turkish Republic of Northern Cyprus' has not led to sanctions or prevented economic links with the occupied part of Cyprus.[7] Nor has the massive (in relative terms, due to the small size of the indigenous population) mainland Turkish immigration been condemned: most estimates mention a 2:1 ratio of Turkish Cypriots and Turks in the north of the island (100,000 Turkish migrants, mainly from Anatolia, plus 30–40,000 troops together with 70,000 Turkish Cypriots, i.e. as many Turkish Cypriots as there are in London: *Cyprus News*, 27 November 1997).

Even the 1994 European Court of Justice decision brought about by a Greek Cypriot has only led to most Turkish Cypriot produce not benefiting from special tax/customs exemption and has not led to an end to these exports. In comparison the European Commission has shown much more zeal in pursuing the Greek embargo over FYROM (Stavridis, 1997a).

The saga over the Russian S-300 missiles, which ended in early 1999 with a climb-down by Greek Cypriots, was not only significant for its outcome but for the fact that no EU state (except for Greece: Joint Defence Doctrine) accepted the right to self-defence of an already occupied state while arms sales to Turkey continued without any problem. France in particular was guilty of this (*Le Monde*, 19 March 1998), as was the UK. The latter returned to a traditional pro-Turkish policy after its six months of 'neutrality' because of its presidency of the EU Council in the first half of 1998.

It is significant in our view to contrast the then UK Defence Secretary George Robertson's vitriolic comments about the Cyprus decision to buy the Russian missiles when he argued that it is the privilege of any state to take decisions but that some decisions are worse than others (*NET/Nea Elliniki*

Teleorasi-TV News, 16 September 1998). A week later, he contested that it was acceptable for Britain to sell arms to Turkey as their use was for self-defence only: he added that he did not expect these weapons to be used for internal repression or external aggression (BBC 1, *Nine o'Clock News*, 22 September 1998).

On relations with Greece,[8] the Luxembourg European Council presidency conclusions (December 1997) developed a number of principles for better relations and also an acceptance of the role of international legal institutions in settling disputes (International Court of Justice or ICJ), which has been the traditional view of Athens. However, the EU did not produce any tangible policies to deal with international actors who will not comply with ICJ rulings. Over the years Greece has often been seen as the villain rather than the victim of Turkish aggressive policies, and has been penalized accordingly (WEU 1995 accession but simultaneous Turkish partner status and non-appliance of Article 5; refusal to extend territorial guarantees in Maastricht and Amsterdam despite the support of both the EC and EP – for more see Chryssochoou et al., 1999 – and the creation of the European citizenship with an international dimension).[9] One recent example was the lack of EU support over the Imia incident of 1996, mainly because of British reluctance (Valinakis and Pitsarou, 1996: 168).

Greek–Turkish relations further deteriorated with the Öcalan affair (the Kurdish problem) and the violent reaction sparked by the affair. The 22 February 1999 Council of Foreign Ministers declaration (Luxembourg) offered many carrots to Turkey if it behaved in a democratic manner, but only potential sticks if Öcalan were to be executed. Again very little action was taken by the EU while a violent conflict continues to take place in south-eastern Turkey and when being a Kurd means different treatment by the EU if you happen to be in northern Iraq or in southern Turkey. No attention is given to the fact that Öcalan had been refused entry by most EU states and that when he was under arrest in Rome, he was lucky to avoid extradition to Turkey on the grounds that the Italian Constitution does not allow the expulsion of a prisoner to a country that still permits the death penalty. Otherwise, it would not have been possible for the Italians to get off the hook so easily. But the fact remains that they did not consider the wider implications of throwing Öcalan out of Italy. In addition the Germans did not behave very well either when, despite an international warrant, Chancellor Schröder declared that he would not be requesting his extradition on political grounds (there are 2 million Turks and 600,000 Kurds on German soil). These responses do little for the EU's support for international law, Schengen and the common European justice area.

More recently, following earthquake diplomacy in late 1999 and the Helsinki European Council in December of that year to reiterate Turkey's 'candidacy status', relations with the EU have again improved. The Helsinki decision has been described as the 'final breakthrough' and led to euphoria in Turkey (Guney, 2001: 172). What remains remarkable however is that very little has changed in Turkey with regard to human rights, democracy, the treatment of Kurds, or over Cyprus. It is interesting to note that the November 2000 Commission Report on Turkey's accession is extremely critical on all these issues (Commission Report on Turkey 2000). The road to eventual membership has been confirmed all the same.

Not directly linked to the problem of Kurdistan, but still another example of this lack of consistency in favour of democracy and human rights (and a preference for commercial gains irrespective of these civilian principles) is the saga in France over the 1915 Armenian genocide, which is of course affecting EU–Turkey relations: first recognized by the Assemblée Nationale in 1998, it led to a loss of trade for several French goods (both military and civilian) as an informal ban was implemented by Turkey. In early 1999 the Sénat caved in to executive demands and dropped its discussion of the matter ('Le gouvernement refuse d'inscrire le "génocide arménien" à l'ordre du jour du Sénat', *Le Monde*, 12 March 1999). The decision taken by the French government not to pursue the matter further followed the reinstatement of Eurocopter (a Franco-German consortium) on Turkey's list of potential providers of combat helicopters worth \$4 billion (€3.6 billion). And when in late 2000/early 2001 the French Sénat came back with a vengeance and did finally pass a resolution condemning the Armenia genocide, both the French president and his prime minister (*Cohabitation*) rushed a joint communiqué arguing that this senate resolution had nothing to do with them. Turkey imposed 'sanctions' against French companies by not allowing them to bid for contracts. The EU still has no common policy on that particular issue, despite the existence of an EP resolution in the same direction in late 2000.

The same inaction by the EU applies to the overall lack of democracy in Turkey (the role of the military[10] and the way the state deals with Islamic extremists) and its appalling record on human rights according to Amnesty International (Amnesty International, 1996). When Ciller and the Customs Union were presented (see EP debates September to December 1995) as the only alternative to the Islamists in late 1995, the unrealistic character of this approach (which was also supported by the USA) was proved by the later arrival of Erbakan and his dismissal by the military a year later. To a large extent, the EU still appears not to have designed an alternative to this failed policy.

North Africa, Especially Algeria

On the *positive* side, there is some evidence of an emerging European interest in the conflict. Indeed, there is less tendency nowadays to allow France to think of Algeria as its own *domaine réservé*. In 1998 (note that this was six years into the civil war) there were a junior foreign minister EU troika visit and an EP members' visit. This increased interest has had positive though limited outcomes, such as occasionally critical minority reports (Cohn-Bendit and

Rieu, 1998), or has referred to other states such as Morocco in 1987 (over political prisoners) and in February 1992 (over the non-implementation of UN resolutions over the western Sahara), where some financial penalties did materialize.

But, on the *negative* side, most observers were critical of reports by the EP and the troika and the UN fact-finding mission (Spencer, 1998b; see also Cohn-Bendit and Rieu, 1998: 5). The EP report was very limited in its criticisms of the Algerian regime and fell short of tackling the key issue of who was mainly responsible for the violence visited upon the Algerian population. It is also fair to argue that the troika visit (1998) almost gave a clean bill of health to a regime that (together with the violent Islamic terrorists) has led to about 60,000 dead (1992–98). A rather sickening thought for a civilian power in the wake of the most violent Ramadan in years (December 1997–January 1998).

Continuing on the negative theme, when other EU states made efforts to go beyond the French-led *de facto* support of the current regime (like Italy's 1995 effort to organize a meeting in Rome of non-violent opposition movements), these were quickly scuppered by the French. Some argue there is an EU split between those who are more amenable to a negotiated solution (northern states) and those further to the south who are more concerned about the implications of a collapse of the present regime and the coming to power of the extremist FIS government (especially if these states also have or produce migrants) (Rich and Joseph, 1997: 17). We will leave this debate here, but simply note the importance of domestic sources of foreign policy (for more on the existence or otherwise of a 'southern' lobby in the EU see Tsakaloyannis, 1997 and Gillespie, 1997b). There are those member states within the EU that are relieved that the military and not a radical Islamist government in the shape of the FIS are in power in Algeria. They perceive that an FIS-led Algeria would be a greater security threat to their states (Blunden, 1994: 144–5).

Due to the historic ties France has with Algeria, most EU states tend to follow this country's lead in this area. France, while it claims that it does not wish to be involved in Algeria's domestic politics, finds it difficult to stay out of them because 1 million out of 3 million French Islamic citizens have dual passports with Algeria or are of Algerian descent. Thus, French domestic policy is strongly influenced by its foreign policy towards Algeria and vice versa (Spencer, 1996: 132). In spite of Algeria's political reluctance for outside intervention (which it perceives as interference in internal affairs), Algeria is willing to accept France's efforts to get its international debt rescheduled. France also contributed $1 billion in annual aid in 1995 and $6 billion in credit (Rich and Joseph, 1997: 16).

As most of Algeria's gas and oil go to the EU, there are no sanctions (despite EMP rhetoric) and EU companies continue to work and prosper (note that the violence is in the littoral where most Algerians live, whereas oil and gas resources are in the southern desert). Trade in gas between Algeria and the

EU amounts to 20 per cent of the EU's imports in gas. The EU is Algeria's largest trading partner (*The Economist*, 10 January 1998). The EU is in the midst of renegotiating an association agreement with Algeria. There is an existing agreement whereby Algeria benefits from EU aid and loans. Between 1996 and 1998 Algeria received over 60,000 MECUs out of a total committed aid of just over 231,000 MECUs (European Commission, 1999a).

As for the *de jure* recognition, the current EMP framework offers a political legitimization of the regime in Algiers. The same applies to the current negotiations for a new EU agreement with Algeria.

In brief, we can argue that while there have been statements, declarations and even *démarches* condemning the violence in Algeria, little that is tangible has been done in the way of pursuing the EU's stated aims. The EU has not attached any political conditionality to the aid, trade and financial relations it already has with Algeria, even though there are very strong links in these areas that it could exploit.

The Middle East, with Emphasis on the Middle East Peace Process

Here, we tend to offer a less negative assessment than with Algeria as we can identify more *positive* aspects in the EU's role:

- The EC/EU has been active in promoting a settlement of the situation for some considerable time. Its most notable policy statement was the 1980 Venice Declaration. However, the EC/EU did not have any real practical role in the peace process until after the 1993 Oslo accords, when the EU became involved in the multilateral dimension of the MEPP (Peters, 1997), and especially its involvement in the Regional Economic Development Working Group (REDWG). As a CFSP joint action, the EU also sent monitors to the Palestinian elections in 1996.
- Since 1996 the EU has had a special envoy (Miguel Angel Moratinos) whose background as the former Spanish ambassador to Israel and diplomatic skills have helped to gain the respect of all parties involved. (His role is also important in institutional terms for the CFSP as he is a kind of 'mini-Mr PESC' for the MEPP, and the role of special representative has now been codified by the Amsterdam Treaty.)

There are, however, *negative* aspects: first, there is little or no conditionality, although there has been some foot-dragging when the peace negotiations were going badly and when they have improved the EU has allowed the trade agreement with Israel to move forward (Hollis, 1997: 19–20). The EU–Israel Association Agreement ratification was slowed down by the French parliament. In other words, again it was not a collective EU civilian action. However, due to an interim agreement, the economic aspects of the agreement had already come into force (Ahlswede, 1999), thus rendering even the French action only symbolic.

Second, the now publicly acknowledged corruption of the Arafat regime has not led to any 'sanctions' despite the fact that the EU is currently the single largest funder of the Palestine authority (Hollis, 1997: 17). Indeed, the EU has funded the Palestinians between 1993 and 1997 to the tune of €700.95 million, including EIB assistance and support for UNRWA (COM[97]715 final).

Third, nothing is being done by the EU to encourage Israel to implement the UN resolutions concerning its illegal occupation of territories. This is in sharp contrast to EU policies over the Iraqi invasion of Kuwait. The EU's inaction has more in common with its attitude to the illegal occupation of northern Cyprus. While the EU condemns such abuses of international law, it is not as willing to use its economic weight to enforce its views.

Fourth, the EU's role is simply that of financier (especially with regard to the Palestinian authority) and not one of mediator (USA). This is the view of a number of observers and practitioners alike and confirms that the civilian means that the EU currently possesses do not translate into actual civilian power (M. Marin, European Commission Vice-President, *El País*, 14 April 1997).

Fifth, 'the efforts to increase the profile of the EU in relationship to the Peace Process have had the effect of raising expectations. These expectations continue to be unmatched by the EU's capabilities within the Middle East, the EU remains restricted by the lack of leverage it has with Israel and Syria and overshadowed by the strategic power of the United States' (Hutchence, 2001).

Conclusions

The case studies can be summed up as follows:

- The EU's approach to the connected issues of Cyprus and Turkey highlights the double standards that appear within the EU's foreign policy. A lack of consistency in the EU's foreign policy goals can be held responsible for this.
- Conflicting internal interests contribute significantly to the 'EU's impotence' in dealing with Algeria (Walker, 1998).
- The EU's willingness to fit in behind US foreign policy otherwise described more accurately as *la diplomatie du créneau*[11] (Charillon, 1998) typifies the EU's policy towards the Middle East.

In other words, there is no consistency between the pillars but also within the pillars. Which points to more substantial causes than institutional concerns, however legitimate these might be (contrast Monar, 1998, to Stavridis, 1997b). It is necessary to return to the two definitions of a civilian power that were used by Duchêne and especially the latter of the two: 'a civilian group of countries long on economic power and relatively short on armed force'; 'a force for the international diffusion of civilian and democratic standards'. The second definition is better suited in our view to assessing the record of the EU in the Mediterranean. This is not to say that the first definition is not relevant but simply that as a definition it is one that describes a situation by default: i.e. something is missing from the EU and therefore it is just a civilian power. Whether correct or not, this approach fails to embrace the full implications of what the foreign policy of a civilian power Europe would (and should) be. Otherwise one runs the (unwelcome) risk of thinking that 'civilian power Europe' was only useful as a concept during the Cold War (Allen and Smith, 1998: 50).

With regard to EU relations with the Mediterranean Basin, we have argued that on balance a civilian power Europe has not materialized despite the availability of many economic, financial, diplomatic and other political means.

This is not the place to consider the military dimension of the EU and how it affects the civilian power Europe concept (see Smith, 2000; Stavridis, 2001b). However, how can a civilian power project itself, if it does not have the means, including military, to achieve its stated objectives? It seems to us that from the three case studies it is clear that the EU has no clearly defined objectives, nor the intention to consistently and coherently project them to the Mediterranean beyond mere rhetoric about the benefits of democracy, peace, human rights and economic prosperity.

In other words, the foreign policy of a civilian power would be that of projecting democratic principles abroad, by whatever means, provided they did not affect the principles they were meant to put forward. But military force could be used if it is:

1. for military interventions of a humanitarian kind or peace-keeping/making (the so-called WEU Petersberg tasks, which have been included in the Amsterdam Treaty)

or

2. to prevent genocide; that is to say, an ethical and democratic policy

Assuming we are right, what can the EU do in the Mediterranean to be seen to be acting as a real civilian power? It needs consistency in fighting the lack of democracy and the abuses of human rights. Economic and financial means are vital but the 2010 objective of a MEFTA should in our own view be geared towards democratization (the promotion of democracy) and not just at stabilizing the status quo (for a similar view, see Kienle, 1998 and Romeo, 1998).

But this would mean finding a way to end the existing double standards. Perhaps, then, 'a strengthening of democracy and respect for human rights, sustainable and balanced economic and social development, measures to combat poverty and promotion of greater understanding between cultures' (Barcelona Declaration, 1995) will materialize and the EU could get some credit for such a necessary development. It would also mean that at long last the EU is acting like a civilian power.

NOTES

An earlier draft of this chapter was presented by Stelios Stavridis at the international workshop 'The Euro-Mediterranean Partnership in Social, Cultural and Human Affairs: the Human Dimension of Security as the Key to Stability and Prosperity' (organized by Dr Stefania Panebianco) held in Malta, 13–16 May 1999. The authors would like to thank the organizer and the other participants for useful comments. The usual proviso about responsibility applies here too.

1. For details, see Gillespie (1997a); for more on the foreign policies of the EU's Mediterranean states, see Stavridis et al. (1999).
2. This section draws from Chryssochoou et al. (1999: 137–42).
3. Galtung (1973).
4. Piening uses a regional approach first taken by Edwards and Regelsberger (1990).
5. For references to Shonfield and Duchêne, see Bull (1983: 149).
6. For a similar view, see Zielonka (1998).
7. Mrs Thatcher's response in the 1980s to the fact that a semi-official 'TRNC' travel office was operating from Pall Mall (in the heart of London and next to Whitehall and Parliament) was that it was a matter for private enterprise. The same applies to all the existing tourism, academic and other links between the UK and the 'TRNC', which have been flourishing over the years.
8. For a more optimistic assessment than the one that follows, see Georgiades (2000).
9. It is surprising that none of the abrasive statements by leading Turkish politicians is totally ignored by the media of other EU states. Equally, most EU countries refuse to even consider offering an automatic territorial guarantee to Greece but pretend at the same time that there is no Turkish threat and hence that such a guarantee is not needed!
10. For more on the role of the military, see Turan (1997).
11. In French *faire le créneau* means to reverse into a parking space between two cars.

Part II:

TOWARDS A DYNAMIC ROLE FOR CIVIL SOCIETY

Part II

TOWARDS A DYNAMIC ROLE FOR
CIVIL SOCIETY

4

Civil Society in the Euro-Mediterranean Arena

FIFI BENABOUD

If there is a single socio-political notion that has enjoyed widespread popularity, it is undoubtedly that of civil society. Paradoxically, however, the frequent use of this term does not always correspond to a precise idea of its meaning. One certitude alone seems to prevail: the flexibility of its definition, if indeed it can be said to have a definition. We can agree that civil society represents what is outside politics and the state, that civil society mediates between the political centre and the society it serves; but these definitions are above all descriptive, and cannot reveal the rich and complex nature of the concept. In point of fact, civil society has a definite composition, a complex and heterogeneous structure, and a distinct function, and above all, there are certain conditions that allow it to emerge.

How should we orient our reflections on civil society? Is it possible to define civil society in such a way as to grant it the status of a concept and hence that of a scientific analytical instrument? Or is it rather a notion inextricably linked to systems of political organization (in which case there would be several models of civil society)? In this chapter, I will subscribe to the latter position in order to give an overview of civil society in countries located on the southern shore of the Mediterranean. In doing so, I hope to define its role in the construction of the Euro-Mediterranean Partnership consecrated by the Barcelona Conference of November 1995.

The topic of civil society in Mediterranean countries is complex, so it is necessary to define the players clearly in order to promote objectives other than those pursued by commercial companies. One must first decide whether one wants to adopt a broad or a restricted definition of civil society. In the broader sense, civil society includes political parties, cooperatives, unions, formal and informal associations, etc. In the restricted sense, the principal players are associations, non-governmental organizations and unions.

Faced with regimes in crisis, civil societies on the southern shore of the Mediterranean show a marked tendency to distinguish themselves from political society, especially since the latter has a propensity to invade and permanently to occupy state institutions. Civil societies on the northern and southern shores of the Mediterranean have four characteristic elements in common:

- the emergence of the individual as the subject of the law;
- action that is freely organized on the basis of solidarity and existing affinities within a complex and heterogeneous social fabric;
- the autonomy of this action with respect to the state; and
- the state nevertheless remains the legal point of reference for the organized actions of various groups in civil society.

Civil society is thus characterized by a context either of dialogue or of confrontation with state institutions.

For a number of years, the concept of civil society has been in great favour in southern Mediterranean countries, but its new orientation frequently leads to erroneous interpretations and consequently raises a number of questions:

- Should we make a radical distinction between civil society and the state?
- Should we think of civil society in terms of mediation between society as such and the state?
- Should we necessarily think of civil society as being in opposition to the state?

My intention is not to respond directly to these questions, but they do deserve to be asked and debated, especially since the responses will allow us, if not to zero in on a clear definition, at least to outline the contours of this concept, which remains a complex and heterogeneous phenomenon.

This chapter is principally devoted to the role of associations. The idea of organization and association is not foreign to traditional societies of the southern Mediterranean. The existence of common law already offers examples of this type of traditional community organization.

At the end of the last century, Charles de Foucault observed that in the Maghreb 'each group governs itself apart, as they choose, by means of an assembly where each family is represented'. In Arabic this assembly is called *djemaa* and in Berber *anfaliz*. Before colonization and even at the outset of colonization, in both the towns and the countryside, organized groups based on Muslim law and Berber common law were typically used as a tool for collective action in areas such as agriculture and religious education. Many traditions of this sort remain in effect today. These organizations – which are called informal because they have no judicial status and, for the most part, elude state jurisdiction – represent local efforts organized by a community of believers to respond to the needs of its citizens.

The Muslim associative tradition is not fundamentally opposed to the state, although it does maintain a certain degree of autonomy with respect to the state. This tradition forms a community space for social and religious bonding, and it is based on the interaction between faith and social life. Accordingly, in Arabic there is a difference between *al mujtama' al ahli*, or civil society, and *al mujtama' al madani*, or civic society. The first concept encompasses the whole of civil society, integrating components of the traditional, tribal and confessional modes, while the second refers to modern concepts such as citizenship, secularism and the relation of the individual to the law.

As for international law, the Universal Declaration of Human Rights stipulates: 'All persons have the right to freedom of assembly and peaceful association. None can be obliged to take part in an association.' In the southern Mediterranean region, however, a number of limitations are placed on free assembly. As a result, setbacks can be observed in three areas: lack of legal recognition for associations; dissolution of associations; and the imposition of sanctions on their founders or their leaders. Today, associative activities are in fact carried on within a context of restrictive legislation.

At the same time, the state and political parties maintain close relations with associations that are active in 'sensitive' areas. This close contact has the effect of blocking action and discouraging the autonomy of these associations. Frequently viewed as instrumental, they do not fully participate in the rules for developing the democratic process. These groups often assume the guise of institutions acting on behalf of the state; when they do, they meet with more tolerance, as long as their avowed goals betray no intent to significantly alter political orientation and decision-making in their spheres of action. In this case, associations mainly act as regulatory mechanisms in the service of both the state and political parties, as a means of supervising the population and recruiting new members while orienting associative activities in a direction favourable to the party line.

Despite legislative problems that limit their room for manoeuvre and their effectiveness, and despite restrictive pressures that are often very strong, associations have become highly visible on the political scene of southern Mediterranean countries over the past few years. The principal areas in which civil society has been organizing and strengthening itself are cultural development, human rights, women's rights and environmental protection.

I should also stress the important role played by women's organizations in improving the judicial status of women. Previously, the condition of women was viewed as a social question; today, owing to organized action by these associations, it is perceived as a human rights issue. This is considered a great step forward, in view of the growing attention focused on human rights by both the state and civil society. By demanding egalitarian treatment in ever-increasing numbers, women's organizations have placed the question of women's rights at the centre of the political debate, despite social resistance that holds on to patriarchal traditions dating back thousands of years. This move is critical for making the transition to democracy, since in Arab countries women play a pivotal role in society. The condition of women lies at the core of debates concerning the establishment of a state of law and the principles of democracy, equality and non-discrimination.

Since the 1980s Arab societies have been undergoing change at several levels: moral, cultural and ideological. In practice, this evolution amounts to raising the collective consciousness on human rights, environmental protection and so on. In theory, the evolution of civic awareness and of the collective consciousness in southern societies should necessarily lead to change, because the citizen is increasingly attentive to the preservation of his or her rights and liberties.

Certain societies in the southern Mediterranean region are 'frozen' owing to a difficult social and institutional environment, which in turn is largely due to rigid state monopolies. The state's excessive intervention undermines the liberty and autonomy of civil society, whereas a democratic process would imply not only the openly expressed determination of its citizens to control the political, economic and social system, but also their full participation in all aspects of national life. These countries are in the process of development, and their populations have for the past 20 years been undergoing social mutations in a political context where the ruling élite has maintained power without offering any prospect of change. This dysfunction has gradually given rise to socio-political fissures between the dominant élite and the rest of society, and here the generational factor becomes an overriding concern: the under-30 age group, which constitutes two-thirds of the population, suffers the consequences of a deficient educational system and social exclusion. All this has led to a new dynamic of questioning established systems.

The inactivity of civil society is the main reason for these countries' failure to achieve democratic transition. The fact is that the transformation from an authoritarian regime to a democratic regime does not depend only upon the will of the 'Prince'; it also calls for the mobilization of a civil society dedicated to the principles of liberty and human rights, and committed to effective participation in elaborating rules and implementing political, economic, social and cultural projects. We are witnessing the development of increasingly powerful middle and professional classes, which aspire to greater participation and real representation in politics. The crisis of legitimacy that afflicts these states is unprecedented, but unfortunately civil society does not seem to be capable at this point of demanding a political space and thereby counterbalancing the state structure.

This analysis must take into account the social evolution that is occurring in the southern Mediterranean countries, the processes that have forged this society and the contexts in which it has developed. On the one hand, there is indeed a primarily middle-class sector of civil society, the members of which have had access to a good education and professional integration. It is in this 'modern urban' sector that associations defending human rights, women's rights, the environment and political parties will be formed.

On the other hand, economic restrictions, structural adjustment policies and the *infitah* (the opening up to economic liberalism) have accentuated the exclusion and marginalization of a large portion of the population, composed largely of young people. This segment of the population constitutes a considerable social force, characterized by rejection of the educational system, very low purchasing power and a virtually non-existent professional future. Moreover, it strongly rejects 'modernity' and the socio-political system from which it is excluded.

In this area, Islamic movements will provide both the cohesiveness and the impetus needed by organizations promoting social solidarity in medicine, education, training, etc. It should be noted that these Islamic organizations do successfully compensate for deficiencies of the welfare state. It is not my intention to affirm that they solicit only the underprivileged class of society – far from it. However, an analysis of Islamic movements as an inescapable element of civil society in Arab countries would stray too far from the subject and would require a long and complex development which space does not permit.

It can be stressed, however, that the moderate Islamic movements today seem to represent an undeniable social force capable of organizing a strong civil society when confronted with states in crisis, which become more fragile daily, both politically and economically, and which face increasingly sharp social opposition. These movements constitute a genuine challenge for the future evolution of these societies. This dynamic is linked, in large part, to the relationship between religion and modernity in the social structure, to cultural values and to a sustained desire for legitimacy and political participation.

The problem for these societies is locating the 'middle ground' that will enlist these new players in the transition to democracy. The solutions brought to this problem will ultimately determine the geopolitical future of the region.

The Barcelona Conference introduced a new development in this Euro-Mediterranean arena. On the margins of the official intergovernmental conference, a series of civil fora were held that attested to the need for, and demands of, civil society. The final document, signed by 27 governments, assigns an important role to civil society and stresses that its participation is indispensable if a partnership in the Euro-Mediterranean space is to be established. The Barcelona Declaration insists on the 'necessity of facilitating exchanges between civil societies on both shores of the Mediterranean, giving priority to culture, youth, education, training and the condition of migrants'. It also affirms that the potential contribution of civil society is vital for trans-Mediterranean interdependence and cooperation. For this reason, it was decided to encourage decentralized cooperative programmes that support exchanges between different components of civil society, such as cultural activity, universities, researchers, media, associations, public and private enterprise, and so on. The Barcelona Declaration is innovative with respect to civil society in that it goes beyond the simple framework of predominantly economic partnership and underscores the need for political reforms that could start up the process of democratization, which in turn is likely to ensure economic development and regional stability.

In this Euro-Mediterranean space one goal is essential: to reassert the value of the enormous human capital that Mediterranean nations possess, especially on the southern shores. No proposed partnership will promote any real political or economic advancement if it is not accompanied by a plan to mobilize this human potential. Without question, the civil societies of these countries, on both shores of the Mediterranean, are destined to play a decisive role in ensuring the success of the Euro-Mediterranean Partnership and the effective integration of the North and South in this space. Within this framework, civil society can make a vital economic contribution to the entire region, but above all must create and reinforce the cultural basis of cooperation. Civil society can lay the foundation for knowledge, understanding and mutual confidence, which are vital for the construction and survival of a common Euro-Mediterranean space in both the medium and the long terms. In this space, linkages and networks between civil societies of the northern and southern shores will serve as a basis for economic, social and cultural development; there will be clear awareness of what separates but also of what unites; and the Mediterranean will be recognized as a great common resource with considerable potential.

Neither the state alone nor the market economy can create this common space. All elements of civil society must participate by contributing all of their resources and capacities. If the economies of the southern Mediterranean states are to take off and regional instability to cease, the contract between the state and its citizens must be renewed, for the existing contract is obsolete.

To conclude, I can affirm that civil society in the southern Mediterranean countries exists within a historical perspective linked to the evolution of these societies, including both the Arab Muslim tradition and modern secular traditions.

The existing political systems place definite constraints on positive organized action by the civil societies in these countries. Consequently, these civil societies are not yet solid and productive social forces. One can be sure, however, that the transition to democracy cannot come about through the efforts of civil society alone, especially since civil society is weak and subject to pressure.

The transition to democracy cannot occur in opposition to the state, but only in cooperation with the state. Confrontation between civil society and the state will not allow for the construction of viable social and political projects. Only by means of a consensual pact between the components of civil society and the state will the southern Mediterranean countries be able to build their future. A stronger civil society is essential in order to ensure that this pact will be well balanced, and education is the decisive element that will permit civil society to emerge.

The profound transformations occurring in these societies must take on an institutional form if they are to result in solid social cohesion and a dynamic oriented towards the future. At the same time, there must be cooperation between northern and southern civil societies, not in the form of 'assistance' or the imposition of a universal western model, but as a real partnership enlisting the southern civil societies in the decision-making process and in the realization of their projects, taking into account their specificities and their values.

NOTE

This chapter previously appeared in A. Bernard, H. Helmich and P. B. Lehning (eds), *Civil Society and International Development*, Paris: North–South Centre of the Council of Europe, Development Centre of the OECD, 1998.

5

The EuroMed Civil Forum:
Critical 'Watchdog' and Intercultural Mediator

ANNETTE JÜNEMANN

Civil Society in the Euro-Mediterranean Partnership

The Euro-Mediterranean Partnership (EMP) is based on the assumption that the deepening of interregional relations cannot be achieved through governmental agreements alone; to bring the partnership to life it needs the participation of the people. Therefore, the 27 signatories of the Barcelona Declaration agreed that they 'recognize the essential contribution civil society can make in the process of development of the Euro-Mediterranean Partnership and as an essential factor for greater understanding and closeness between the people' (Barcelona Declaration, 1995).

Chapter 3 of the Barcelona Declaration, Partnership in Social, Cultural and Human Affairs, is the most important one in this context, as it comprises specific instruments for the support of civil society. Most important are the MED-Programmes,[1] MEDA Democracy,[2] EuroMed Heritage,[3] EuroMed Audiovisual[4] and the EuroMed Youth Action Programme.[5]

While all these activities take place *within* the framework of the EMP, there are other activities on the level of civil society complementing the EMP from *outside*. Subject to this article are the latter, the civil society conferences that accompany all Euro-Mediterranean conferences on ministerial level since 1995, summarized under the notion EuroMed Civil Forum.

The relevance of the EuroMed Civil Forum for the EMP has increased, since various of the Chapter 3 programmes mentioned above have been suspended due to the crisis of the European Commission.[6] The role of the EuroMed Civil Forum can be defined by four different functions.

1. *Intercultural dialogue between the South and the North.* Against the background of mutual prejudices and misperceptions, cooperation in the framework of the EuroMed Civil Forum contributes to intercultural understanding between the South and the North. Intercultural under-

standing can be encouraged either directly, for example through a religious dialogue conference, or indirectly, through the cooperation in any project of common interest.

2. *Reconciliation between societies in conflict.* The conflict lines in the EMP are not only running between the North and the South, but also between societies within southern and northern regions respectively (examples are Israelis–Palestinians, Greeks–Turks, Turks–Kurds). The reconciliation of societies in conflict can, again, be supported either by directly addressing the conflict, or indirectly through technical cooperation.

3. *Critical observation of the EMP.* It is the task of a vivid civil society to scrutinize the construction of the EMP and to elaborate concepts for its improvement. Deficits that are addressed in this context are, among other things, the lack of a social dimension and the neglect of environmental considerations. A major reproach against the EMP concerns the unbalanced interdependence of the Mediterranean Partner Countries (MPCs) and the EU, favouring the latter.[7]

4. *Political challenge of authoritarian regimes.* Civil engagement, no matter in which field, undermines the authoritarian structures of non-democratic countries and is thus a first step towards political liberalization. Authoritarian regimes feel threatened by civil engagement, as it can lead to the development of opposition movements or opposing political parties pushing for political change.

The first function of the EuroMed Civil Forum, intercultural dialogue between the South and the North, is consistent with the common goal shared by all participating countries of the EMP, to create a region of peace and stability. The second function, reconciliation between societies in conflict, is less consensual, due to the intensification of conflict, especially in the Middle East. When Arab countries refuse to cooperate with Israel because of Israel's negative stand towards the Middle East Peace Process,[8] cooperation at civil society level is often hampered too. The third function, critical observation of the EMP, concerns mainly the EU and its member states, because of Europe's often criticized dominance within the EMP. In contrast to that, the fourth function, political challenge of authoritarian regimes, provokes especially the many non-democratic regimes among the MPCs.[9] Yet, due to deficits in European migration politics, accusations of insufficient respect for human rights also concern the EU and its member states, though to a much lesser degree.[10] In sum, civil engagement is a double-edged sword for all participants of the EMP and explains the political relevance that is attached to the EuroMed Civil Forum.

While authoritarian MPCs either openly oppose the EuroMed Civil Forum or try to undermine it through various strategies that will be explained later on, the position of the EU towards the EuroMed Civil Forum is generally speaking supportive, but somewhat ambivalent if one looks at the extent of this support. The general support of civil society is part of a new strategy adopted after the end of the Cold War, to promote democratization as an essential goal of Europe's foreign relations.[11] This new strategy is based on the assumption that there is a causality between civil society, democratization and development:

> A viable civil society creates favourable conditions for the development of democracy, and the existence of democracy enhances a country's development potential ... There is irrefutable evidence today, gathered from a broad range of cross-cultural and ideologically diverse political experience, that links the existence of democratic politics, policies and practices with social and economic development. (Entelis, 1995: 47)[12]

Yet, in the given context of the EMP, the goal of democratization can get into conflict with the prior goal of stabilization, at least for certain periods of transition. The reason for this is that in most of the MPCs the process of democratization will most probably lead to an extremely unstable period of transition, bearing the risk of violent upheavals or even civil wars (Jünemann, 1998b). As the initiative of the EMP goes back to Europe's overriding interest in stabilizing this turbulent region, the EU promotes democratization only to a degree that does not challenge the survival of the governments in power, no matter how authoritarian they are.[13]

This chapter focuses on the politically extremely sensitive fourth function of civil society within the EMP, the political challenge of authoritarian regimes. Since this function contradicts the national interests of many countries participating in the EMP, it was determinant for the development of the EuroMed Civil Forum since its inception in 1995. The EuroMed Civil Forum was founded against strong pressure from some MPCs to either exclude civil society from the EMP altogether, or at least to reduce its role to its consensual function of promoting intercultural dialogue between the South and the North. The genesis of the EuroMed Civil Forum and its follow-up illustrate how much political impact is attributed to it, allowing the thesis that the EuroMed Civil Forum has a potential to outgrow the modest role it plays so far in Euro-Mediterranean relations.

The Genesis of the EuroMed Civil Forum

The first EuroMed Civil Forum took place in Barcelona on 29 and 30 November 1995, immediately after the Euro-Mediterranean Interministerial Conference that gave birth to the EMP. Its coming into being was the result of a political strategy to avoid the setting up of an alternative NGO conference that would have radically challenged the ministerial Euro-Mediterranean summit. During the preparations for this summit, the Spanish presidency was informed about the intentions of several NGOs to organize just such an alternative conference at non-governmental level. The European Commission shared the worries of the Spanish presidency that an alternative conference of NGOs might overshadow the main event, as had happened before at the big international conferences in Rio, Cairo and Beijing. To prevent this from happening, they decided to initiate a non-governmental conference themselves, thus allowing them to influence the selection of the participants and the agenda.[14] In terms of credibility, this task was transferred to the Institut Català Mediterrània, a research institute belonging to the regional government of Catalonia, the Generalitat de Catalunja.

The idea corresponded with the interests of the European Commission to have the ministerial conference undisturbed and to enhance the civil image of the EU. Spain's national interest was to gain the reputation of pursuing an especially active Mediterranean policy. Besides that, it has to be taken into account that Spain's socialist government on a national level was, towards the end of 1995, rather weak, and thus depended to a large extent on the support of governments at regional level. The decision to have the Euro-Mediterranean Conference in Barcelona instead of Madrid was presumably taken to repay the Catalan regional government for its political support.[15] To let it also have the civil society event can be explained by the same pattern, as it is one of the major interests of the Catalans in the context of Spanish regionalism, to present themselves as active players also in the field of foreign relations (Sabá, 1996: 200 f.). The Generalitat de Catalunja sponsored the EuroMed Civil Forum with a considerable amount of money, which was generously supplemented by the European Commission.

The Institut Català Mediterrània shared the intention of the European Commission, the Spanish government and the Catalan regional government to avoid a conference that would radically challenge the participants of the ministerial Euro-Mediterranean summit. Thus, instead of stressing civil society's 'watchdog' function, emphasis was put on the promotion of interregional and intraregional dialogue. This task was successfully fulfilled by bringing together more than a thousand people from both shores of the Mediterranean. Nevertheless, criticism from various sides has to be taken into consideration before coming to a final evaluation of the first EuroMed Civil Forum.

One controversial point was the ambitious effort of the Institut Català Mediterrània to institutionalize the EuroMed Civil Forum under its own roof. Although the institute has definitely proved its qualification for such a task, it has also provoked suspicion that it might want to *instrumentalize* the EuroMed Civil Forum to enhance Catalonia's and/or Spain's international reputation as a leading power in the Mediterranean. Such suspicion was especially strong within the European Commission, since the goal of institutionalizing the EuroMed Civil Forum contradicted the philosophy adopted at the ministerial summit, to keep the administration of Euro-Mediterranean cooperation light (and cheap). Having co-financed the EuroMed Civil Forum in the beginning, the European Commission pulled out as soon as it was over, refusing to support its follow-up. After having abandoned the project of the EuroMed Civil Forum, the European Commission was harshly criticized by many of the affected NGOs.

Despite the understandable disappointment of these NGOs, there are arguments of principle against institutionalization that should be taken into consideration. First of all, there is the general assumption that institutionalization contradicts the *procedural* and *heterogeneous* character of civil society. New issues on the political agenda permanently generate new groups and new forms of civil society. It can be doubted that any institution would be flexible enough to integrate all the new groups and networks that arise and to drop others that for one reason or another should be excluded.[16] Furthermore, it cannot be denied that institutionalization generates power games and competition between *insiders* and *outsiders*, leading to a waste of energies and resources. Last but not least, institutionalization reinforces the serious problem of legitimization that civil society already suffers from. A lack of democratic legitimization is due to the fact that NGOs only represent segments of society and that their members are not elected. This deficit can only be compensated for through structures that are extremely open, giving room for as many NGOs as possible representing contradicting interests.[17]

Another aspect that gave rise to criticism was the conception of the EuroMed Civil Forum. Instead of being an independent *alternative* summit, it followed an approach to *incorporate* civil society into the EMP. Although it is undoubtedly a positive signal that the EMP opened itself to the demands of civil society, the incorporation of the EuroMed Civil Forum also had ambivalent effects. Being co-financed by the European Commission and organized in agreement with the government of the country hosting the ministerial Euro-Mediterranean summit, the first EuroMed Civil Forum was too close to the EMP to fulfil a critical 'watchdog' function. Yet, due to the lack of binding structures connecting the EuroMed Civil Forum with the EMP, it was too far away to influence it from within.

Theoretical Reflections on Civil Society

The controversy about the conception of the EuroMed Civil Forum has a theoretical background, concerning the vague definition of the term 'civil society'. Originally, civil society was a European model that referred to Enlightenment concepts of reason and rationality, presuming basic tensions between (civil) society, economy and the state.[18] Yet there never existed a generally accepted definition of the term 'civil society', not even within the western world. The

88

difficulties of finding a clear-cut and universally acceptable definition can be explained, among other things, by the fact that civil society is a normative and value-laden concept:

> The values involved are those relating to liberty, to civilised or civilising behaviour, and to a set of ethics relating to work, social relationships, respect for human rights and so on. The emphasis on one or another aspect may vary from definition to definition, yet liberty must always be at the centre. Descriptive definitions which focus on pluralism or on a realm that is simply distinct from the State miss the point. There are pluralistic societies in which civil society does not exist; they are little more than fragmented societies if liberty does not transcend the various groups. (Mabro, 1999: 46)

Based on these normative values, certain criteria became consensual for describing (rather than defining) civil society.[19] According to these criteria, an individual or association that claims to be part of civil society:

- participates in the political and social development of the country;
- is tolerant and rejects violence; and
- is democratic in its internal structures.[20]

Within the framework of these consensual criteria, there is a wide range of different forms of civil society, depending on the historical, cultural and religious background of a society but also – and particularly – on the political system.[21] Consequently, there are other criteria besides the three consensual ones mentioned above that are highly controversial:

- independence from the state;
- independence from private business; and
- independence from primordial structures.

Due to the scientific character of the Institut Català Mediterrània, there was theoretical reflection on the definition of civil society in the run up to the EuroMed Civil Forum, although it would be exaggerated to claim that the organization of the EuroMed Civil Forum was based on an elaborate theoretical concept. A certain amount of pragmatism seemed to be adequate for the difficult task of organizing such a big civil society conference. The European Commission's attitude towards civil society is even more pragmatic, focusing mainly on the *efficiency* of civil society projects. Yet, no matter how pragmatic the approach of the practitioners dealing with civil society might be, the three controversial criteria have to be coped with in one way or another, as they have political implications that should not be ignored.

Independence from the State

The most controversial point concerning the first EuroMed Civil Forum was the question of its independence from the state. Being linked to the Generalitat de Catalunja, the Institut Català Mediterrània itself is – strictly speaking – not an NGO. Accordingly, it rejected the narrow, *dichotomic* definition of civil society that considers complete independence from the state to be an essential criterion of civil society and defines the relationship between civil society and the state as contrastive and polarized.[22] In opposition to that, an *integral* concept was favoured that perceives civil society as part of the political system.[23] The function of civil society according to the integral concept is not only to control the state, but also to contribute to its legitimization through civil participation. In the context of the EMP the integral concept is not unproblematic, because it is based on the theoretical assumption of a *democratic* political system while in reality most of the MPCs have authoritarian regimes. Nevertheless, the Institut Català Mediterrània decided to have a EuroMed Civil Forum representing the integral concept of civil society, in accordance with the short-term interest of the EU, to avoid too much embarrassment of the ministerial Euro-Mediterranean summit, and its long-term interest to support no more than a carefully controlled process of gradual political reform.

Independence from Private Business

With regard to the theoretical question whether private business is part of civil society or whether it should be regarded as a separate sphere beside society and the state,[24] the Institut Català Mediterrània decided to invite entrepreneurs to the EuroMed Civil Forum, thus acknowledging the affiliation of private business with civil society. There are two reasons why the inclusion of private business makes sense in the context of the EMP. First, because private trade accelerates interregional and intraregional rapprochement, thus being consistent with the first two functions of civil society, promoting intercultural dialogue between the South and the North and promoting the reconciliation between societies in conflict. Second, as private business reduces the dominant role of the state sector, it can play a positive role in the context of the fourth function of civil society, the political challenge of authoritarian regimes. Yet the arguments against the inclusion of private business into civil society are also worth discussing, especially with regard to the high priority that the EU gives to privatization in the context of Chapter 2 of the Barcelona Declaration. Some theorists warn that Europe's focus on privatization, 'which has a rationale of its own (greater efficiency) … may increase the power of groups in society that are connected to the political establishment' (Mabro, 1999: 47), contradicting the cause of freedom and democratization in authoritarian-led countries. Since entrepreneurs depend on stable political structures to run their business, they have no interest in directly challenging the state. Thus, entrepreneurs tend to rather side with the state, even if it is authoritarian, than with the democratic forces of civil society:

> If we wish to treat civil society as that realm which stands against the political despotism of the State, then we should ... leave the economy out, because entrepreneurs, merchants and firms will not fight the State politically but only in defence of their economic interests, and the pursuit of these interests may well lead to alliances with the State that reinforce its political authority and its despotic tendencies. (Mabro, 1999: 39)[25]

With regard to all pros and cons concerning the relation between private business and civil society discussed above, it can be concluded that entrepreneurs may be acknowledged as parts of civil society, but only if they stand for political and social goals that go beyond their private economic interests. Thus, contrary to what many officials at European and national level like to believe, the encouragement of privatization alone is not sufficient to promote political change in the MPCs. Privatization is a necessary request in the context of economic development, but detached from the values of civil society it has little to do with the support of democratization.

Independence from Primordial Structures

Likewise, it is difficult to answer the question as to whether groups that are organized according to *primordial* structures of society like family, clan, or tribe are part of civil society. The politically sensitive aspect of this question concerns the problem of how to deal with associations from the very heterogeneous spectrum of political Islam, as religious institutions also belong to the category of primordialism. Do Islamist associations meet the theoretical categories defining civil society?

Some Islamist thinkers reject the concept of civil society (*al-mutjama al-madani*) because of its western roots. They argue that the acceptance of the term already implies the acceptance of a western model of society. Instead they have developed the alternative concept of citizen society (*al-mutjama al-ahli*), meaning primordial structures of society such as family, clan and especially religious institutions. These are not seen as (second-best) equivalents to civil society, but as authentic structures in the context of a Muslim state (Ferhad, 1995: 39).[26] For the question discussed here it is important to note that the values of citizen society do not necessarily contradict the values that constitute civil society.

Many intellectuals in the Arab world, especially those from the *secular* sphere of society, do not agree with this view, as their understanding of civil society is based on the liberty of *individuals*, not groups or clans. They insist that primordial institutions should not be accepted as parts of civil society, as they are not based on the free and rational will of their individual participants. Some of them also reject the idea that political Islam can be tolerant. Against the background of Algeria's civil war, they draw the decisive conflict line not between society and the state, but between secularism and Islamism (Ferhad, 1995: 28).[27]

To avoid conflict with the mainly secular NGOs, on the one hand, and with the governments of the MPCs (especially Tunisia, Algeria and Turkey) on the other, the Institut Català Mediterrània pragmatically decided to exclude primordial associations from the EuroMed Civil Forum. Other institutions in charge of organizing civil society conferences in the years that followed solved the problem with similar pragmatism, restricting the invitations to networks and NGOs that already had some kind of working relation with the host institute or the European Commission. The result was the same; the participants coming from the MPCs belonged mainly to the rather small spectrum of secular intellectuals. Although it is much easier for Europeans to cooperate with secular partners, there is a growing awareness that the problem of how to integrate the Islamists has to be solved, because the secular segments of civil society are rather élitist and little representative for the societies in the MPCs.[28] In contrast to them, most Islamist associations are deeply rooted in society through their charitable engagement, filling the vacuum left by incompetent or corrupt governments. The difficulty in choosing dialogue partners within the spectrum of political Islam lies in the inscrutable links that often exist between radical and moderate groups.[29] Yet it would be a severe misperception to equate Islamism with terrorism, as some secularist intellectuals especially in the Maghreb countries do.[30] Political Islam and democracy are not necessarily incompatible and not all Islamists are intolerant and violent:

> So long as religious based parties and associations accept the principle of pluralism and observe a modicum of civility in behaviour toward the different 'other', then they can expect to be integral parts of civil society. In this respect, even the Islamists may evolve into something akin to the Christian Democrats in the West or the religious parties in Israel. There is nothing intrinsically Islamic that contradicts with the codes of civil society or democratic principles. (Ibrahim, 1995: 38)

The integration of such moderate Islamist associations into civil society networks such as the EuroMed Civil Forum could contribute to the reconciliation of torn societies (Algeria or Turkey), would be helpful for a better understanding between Muslims and non-Muslims within Europe or across the Mediterranean, and, last but not least, is a necessity to gain a broader legitimization of the EuroMed Civil Forum itself.

Coming back to the first EuroMed Civil Forum in Barcelona in 1995, the controversy was not so much about the inclusion or exclusion of private business or political Islam – there seemed to be unspoken consensus about that – but about the relation between civil society and the state. Critics of the EuroMed Civil Forum claimed that civil society should be strictly independent from the state, according to the dichotomic concept. Yet, in practice, the division line between the dichotomic and the integral concept of civil society is not as clear-cut as it is in the theoretical model. Since there is no such thing as a complete democracy, the classification of a political system cannot be more than gradual and procedural. This applies even to authoritarian regimes, provided they have entered a process of political transformation. Consequently, civil society is in practice situated somewhere *between* the two poles of (dichotomic) anti-system opposition and (integral) mediation between society and the state. An association belonging to civil society can develop, moving from one pole to the other (in both directions), and it can coexist with other associations that situate themselves differently. If they cooperate, they sometimes even generate effects of synergy, as the development of the EuroMed Civil Forum between 1995 and 1999 proves.

The Alternative Mediterranean Conference (AMC)

Unsatisfied with the conception of the EuroMed Civil Forum, those who had planned an alternative summit did not give up their original idea and organized a strictly non-governmental Alternative Mediterranean Conference (AMC) that took place from 24 to 28 November 1995. Although this event competed with the EuroMed Civil Forum for the attention of the mass media, the organizers cooperated, generating effects of synergy. Since both events were located in Barcelona, the organizers gave interested NGOs the chance to visit both.[31] The AMC focused on the 'watchdog' function of civil society, especially on the critical observation of the EMP. Since the EMP is a European initiative, northern countries in particular were exposed to the cross-fire of an extremely critical discussion. By pointing out the structural deficits of the EMP, the AMC managed successfully to pour some water into the sweet wine of partnership rhetoric. Compared to that, the work on the fourth function of civil society, the political challenge of authoritarian regimes, was rather secondary. Patriarchal cultures and structures of domination affecting especially women's rights were denounced,[32] but this was the only reference to the issue of democracy and human rights, reducing the merit at least of the written output of the AMC.

In contrast to the AMC, the EuroMed Civil Forum welcomed the establishment of the EMP and concentrated its work on selected issues within the given framework of the EMP. Eleven panels dealt with the following issues:

- trade without frontiers;
- investment;

- tourism;
- technology and cooperation;
- transport and territory;
- university and research;
- cultural dialogue;
- media cooperation spaces;
- the role of women;
- migrations; and
- environmental and energy challenges.[33]

Yet due to the underlying concept of civil society as an *integral* part of the political system, the conference suffered from the negative impact of governmental interference. Various southern NGOs reported that their governments had successfully prevented them from being invited to the EuroMed Civil Forum. Instead, so-called governmental NGOs were sent to Barcelona. These are organizations installed by the governments themselves to keep civil activities under control and to fulfil western requests for participatory democracies.[34] Furthermore, criticism was expressed among the participating 'authentic' NGOs that they had not been able to push some politically sensitive issues on to the agenda. In sum, the EuroMed Civil Forum did a lot of noteworthy and constructive work in many fields of civil participation, contributing thereby to the task of interregional and intraregional understanding. Yet many issues that were politically sensitive were excluded, leading to discussions less critical than those at the AMC.

Despite the deficits of both conferences specified above, taken together, the AMC and the EuroMed Civil Forum complemented each other, producing noteworthy results. The AMC offered the framework for an open and critical dialogue harshly challenging the governments (especially of the North). Yet being completely independent of the official level, it did not gain any practical influence on the development of the EMP. In contrast to that, it was the achievement of the less critical EuroMed Civil Forum to give civil society a strong voice, thus enhancing the awareness of public opinion towards the needs of civil society. The attention the EuroMed Civil Forum gained in the international mass media generated growing pressure for a permanent follow-up. Due to this success, the concept of having completely independent *alternative* civil society summits was dropped, while the concept of a EuroMed Civil Forum partly integrated into the EMP became the model for similar events in the years that followed. Yet this follow-up did not develop progressively, but rather in 'zig zag' fashion. The crucial question that determined this process was, and still is, to what extent the EuroMed Civil Forum should interfere in politically sensitive issues.

Intercultural Dialogue in the Mediterranean: EuroMed Civil Forum II and III

Although the European Commission prevented the institutionalization of the EuroMed Civil Forum, it supported a similar conference called EuroMed Civil Forum II on the occasion of the second Euro-Mediterranean Conference of Foreign Ministers in Malta in April 1997. This time the organization was delegated to a number of institutions, presumably to distribute the financial burden[35] of such an event on several shoulders, but perhaps also to avoid any one-sided domination or instrumentalization. Leading was the Mediterranean Academy of Diplomatic Studies in Malta and, to guarantee a certain degree of continuity, the Institut Català Mediterrània.[36] The task of the EuroMed Civil Forum II was obviously the same as it was two years before: to bring civil society together without creating too much embarrassment at the ministerial conference. Yet there were also differences between EuroMed Civil Forum I and EuroMed Civil Forum II, most noticeably in size – EuroMed Civil Forum II was much smaller[37] – but also in concept.

The organizers of EuroMed Civil Forum II invited no entrepreneurs and no governmental officials, but exclusively NGOs. Nevertheless it was less political – and less *dichotomic* – than EuroMed Civil Forum I, because the agenda was limited to an intercultural dialogue in the Mediterranean. Furthermore, there was no complementary AMC this time to address politically sensitive issues. Thus, while a lot of constructive work was done in terms of creating and strengthening Euro-Mediterranean networks at the cultural level,[38] EuroMed Civil Forum II had moved further away from the original idea of a politically challenging *alternative* summit. In contrast to that, the approach of the Malta conference aimed at bringing the EuroMed Civil Forum more closely in line with the EMP, to give it a stronger voice *within* this framework. Two achievements were made in this context. First, in Malta the EuroMed Civil Forum met before and not after the ministerial Euro-Mediterranean conference, thus improving the chances of making its voice heard. Second, in contrast to the Barcelona meeting it was agreed that the work of the EuroMed Civil Forum should in future be integrated into the follow-up of Chapter 3 of the Barcelona Declaration, the Partnership in Social, Cultural and Human Affairs.[39] Having agreed to that, the European Commission gave a signal that it had changed its negative attitude towards the EuroMed Civil Forum. Since the EuroMed Civil Forum of Malta, the European Commission has given the impression that it has gradually opened itself to the needs of civil society in the Mediterranean.[40]

In December 1997, Naples was hosting a third Euro-Mediterranean conference on civil society level organized by the Fondazione Laboratorio Mediterraneo, again in cooperation with the Institut Català Mediterrània. It was supported by the EC, the EP and the region of Campania. This EuroMed

Civil Forum was not connected with a ministerial Euro-Mediterranean summit, and it gained little attention in the media. Nevertheless, the Naples civil society conference had more in common with the Barcelona EuroMed Civil Forum than with the Malta EuroMed Civil Forum, as it went back to the broader definition of civil society, and included also governmental officials and entrepreneurs. Furthermore, it went beyond cultural issues, picking up most of the subjects that were discussed in Barcelona two years before. This is why it is argued that the Naples meeting was much more in line with the EuroMed Civil Forum I in Barcelona, and is accordingly labelled EuroMed Civil Forum II (Fondazione Laboratorio Mediterraneo, 1998).

The confusion in labelling and numbering the various Euro-Mediterranean conferences on civil society level throws light on two facts. First, the term EuroMed Civil Forum does not really stand for a continuous process, but for separate events following more or less homogeneous concepts. Second, the decision to incorporate the EuroMed Civil Forum into the follow-up of Chapter 3 has so far not been converted into practice. Yet being neither independent, nor incorporated into the formal structures of the EMP, it is almost impossible for civil society to take an active part in the Barcelona process, especially if its political demands go beyond the accepted limits of cultural or technical cooperation.

Civil Society at the Stuttgart Summit: A New Approach

When the third Euro-Mediterranean ministerial conference in Stuttgart was in preparation, the issue of organizing a EuroMed Civil Forum arose again. As before, it was the (informal) task of the host country, this time Germany, to find an adequate institution willing to organize the event. While institutions in southern countries were almost competing to get the job, it was rather difficult to find someone in Germany. Although it cannot be denied that these difficulties had something to do with Germany's low profile in the interregional cooperation of Chapter 3,[41] the decisive reason was the corruption scandal of the European Commission caused, among other things, by the mismanagement of the MEDA Programmes. Until the very last minute it was completely unclear whether the European Commission would be allowed to co-finance the EuroMed Civil Forum or not. As a result, one German institute that had already arranged with the former Kohl government to organize the EuroMed Civil Forum cancelled its commitment in late 1998, and new partners had to be found quickly.

The problem was solved through the introduction of a new concept. Similar to EuroMed Civil Forum II (Malta), the task (and the financial risk) of organizing a EuroMed Civil Forum was divided between several institutions. But in contrast to the former EuroMed Civil Forum, they were asked to organize five independent conferences instead of organizing just one big event. The Friedrich Ebert Foundation, an institution close to the Social Democrat Party in power, was responsible for two conferences: a Euro-Mediterranean human rights conference and a conference bringing together social partners from both shores of the Mediterranean. The Heinrich Böll Foundation, an institution close to the smaller coalition partner Bündnis 90/Die Grünen, chaired an environmental civil forum. The German–French Institute held a Euro-Mediterranean symposium on education, research and culture, and the Chamber of Industry and Commerce in Stuttgart[42] organized a Euro-Mediterranean economic conference. Taken together, the five conferences built the framework for a civil society dialogue that was, according to people who had been participating in all the previous EuroMed Civil Fora, much more critical, putting much more weight on the 'watchdog' function of civil society. This success was due to the separation of the five conferences, taking into account that some of them are much more challenging for the governments than others.

Considering the fact that since 1995 human rights conditions in the Euro-Mediterranean region have increasingly given rise to grave concern, it is only natural that the human rights conference was the most challenging event in Stuttgart. Human rights NGOs stand as per their definition in a *dichotomic* relationship, that is in direct opposition, to authoritarian regimes based on the violation of human rights. Their antagonism against these regimes is so strong that it leaves little room for an *integrative* concept of civil society. Knowing that, some of the MPCs tried to prevent the coming into being of a human rights conference in Stuttgart. Yet having signed the Barcelona Declaration and thus a commitment to the principles of human rights and democracy, they could not openly do so.[43] Behind the scenes, they put a lot of pressure on the organizers, and tried to undermine the conference or at least to influence the composition of its participants. To protect participants from governmental pressure, the Friedrich Ebert Foundation tried to exclude the governmental sphere as much as possible, inviting only trustworthy NGOs.[44] Despite this precaution, they could not prevent the appearance of a few NGOs that turned out to be disguised envoys from various governments.[45] However, this was not completely unexpected, because wherever civil society meetings are held, authoritarian governments try to smuggle in a few people, either secretly to collect information, or openly to intimidate the participants, as Tunisia did in Stuttgart. The conclusion that should be drawn from this experience is to keep human rights conferences at working level as small as possible, while the big human rights conferences, that are held to gain public attention and support, can be staffed with activists in exile or Europeans who are less vulnerable.

In contrast to the human rights conference, there was much less resistance to the other four conferences. Environmental NGOs, trade unions and intellectuals working in the sphere of education, research and culture find it much easier to be both critical 'watchdogs' and integral mediators. As long as they do not openly question the political system as such, they can push political reforms forward *within* the given system, using a mixed strategy of political pressure and professional consultancy. Governments that open themselves towards civil society gain in return an increase in democratic legitimization, thus contributing to internal stability, which is a precondition for economic development. Beyond that, democratic legitimization becomes more and more important for southern countries to be accepted as partners of the EU. Thus, MPCs have a positive incentive to cooperate with civil society at least to a certain extent. For this reason, the environmental forum, the social partner conference and the symposium on education, research and culture were organized as fora for an open dialogue between civil society, governmental representatives and the public in general.

Yet the political impact of *integrated* civil engagement should not be underestimated either, as it is not as harmless as issues such as ecology or social dialogue might seem to be at first sight. During the transformation process of Eastern and Central European countries, it could be observed that environmental NGOs and trade unions were the door-openers for the rising process of democratization. Viewed in long-term perspective, civil society's permanent demand for transparency and its constant interference in governmental decision-making helps to undermine authoritarian structures of regimes and societies. Such a pioneer role of environmental NGOs was proved in Stuttgart, when some of them succeeded in being received by the official German delegation before the ministerial conference started. As a result of this meeting some of the demands made by the environmental NGOs were included in the official conclusion of the ministerial Euro-Mediterranean conference, documenting the participation of civil society in the governmental decision-making process.[46]

Finally, the economic conference has to be mentioned. This was the least problematic for the MPCs. As all MPCs have opted for integration into the world market, including the precondition of economic liberalization, the relationship between private business and their respective regimes is one of, though unbalanced, interdependence. Thus, it was rather less problematic that many of the southern country delegations were led by their ministers of economy or finance. The obvious harmony between entrepreneurs and governmental officials confirms the theoretical thesis brought forward previously in this chapter, that entrepreneurs share certain interests with their governments, no matter whether they are democratic or not. Yet, despite this politically dubious coalition, the economic conference had a fruitful impact on the EMP, as it focused on the third function of civil society, the critical observation of the EMP. The economic conference mainly discussed Chapter 2 of the EMP, and came to very sceptical conclusions concerning the planned free trade area.[47] Worries of the MPCs were confirmed that under the present conditions of European protectionism the free trade area implies too many risks for economically backward countries.[48]

To sum up, it can be stated that the innovation of separate fora has proved to be an adequate concept considering the heterogeneous forms and different tasks of civil society. Yet despite all the differences between them, there was common awareness that democracy and respect for human rights are indispensable preconditions for a vivid participation of civil society in *all* political and social fields. Any civil engagement depends on free information, the right of free expression and the right to freely assemble.[49] Thus, there was an impressive coherence among the five different fora in their commitment to the basic values of civil society.

This coherence was also demonstrated in a final and joint session of all five conferences together with governmental representatives. Here civil society was given the opportunity to carry forward its demands directly to officials from Germany, Morocco, Egypt and the European Commission.[50] This top-level event was an innovation of high symbolic value, as it gave a clear political signal that the demands of civil society are taken seriously. Of course it would be naïve to believe that the declarations of good intention made by governmental representatives in response to the five reports will change anything in the short run. Yet the indirect effect of such declarations should not be underestimated. We know from the CSCE process that the declaratory acknowledgement of democracy and human rights was the first step of their future enforcement.[51] Official declarations, no matter how sincere they are, set new standards that can hardly be ignored afterwards. They are helpful preconditions to develop a dynamic and irreversible discourse on democracy and human rights.

Reflections on the Future Development of the EuroMed Civil Forum

Since EuroMed Civil Forum I in Barcelona there have been repeated demands to give the Euro-Mediterranean civil society dialogue stable structures instead of having disconnected events every two years. This demand was also expressed during the final joint session of the five civil society conferences in Stuttgart. People who had been in Barcelona, Malta, Naples and Stuttgart complained at having a strong feeling of *déjà vu*, since many of the discussions had been merely repeated without any progress. A second argument in the discussion concerning the future of the EuroMed Civil Forum is that continuous work *in between* EuroMed Civil Forum conferences is needed. Contin-uous grass-roots work should be performed by as many NGOs as possible, dealing with all the social and political issues concerning the EMP. Yet considering the bad experiences of governmental interference in the past, politically sensitive subjects such as human rights would need to be treated with the discretion that only very small circles can guarantee. In contrast to that, the EuroMed Civil Forum could serve as a representative civil society summit, presenting the results of all the grass-roots work that has been done in between. To take full advantage of the chances these EuroMed Civil Forum summits offer to mobilize public opinion regarding the needs of civil society, well-organized umbrella organizations should coordinate the manifold demands coming from the various NGO networks and help prepare them for presentation. Yet no matter how well organized a EuroMed Civil Forum might be, a contradiction between the political ambition to present civil society as a strong and solid force on the one hand, and the heterogeneous character of civil society on the other, will remain. As long as there is consensus on the democratic values transcending civil society, varying viewpoints will have to be accepted, including those of political Islam.

Umbrella organizations qualified to help prepare such summits already work in numerous fields of civil activity. Exemplary have been (and only those that have demonstrated their professionalism at the Stuttgart conferences are mentioned here): in the sphere of environmental policy, the very efficient Comité de Suivi,[52] in the sphere of migration policy, Migration-Développement,[53] and regarding human rights, the Euro-Mediterranean Human Rights Network (EMHRN).[54] To fulfil the demanding task of co-ordinating the manifold grass-roots activities, such umbrella organizations, and the institutions that finally host a EuroMed Civil Forum, need to be given stable and reliable structures within Chapter 3 of the EMP. Therefore, the decision to organize a EuroMed Civil Forum should not be left with the government of the country hosting the ministerial summit any more.[55] Instead, the EuroMed Civil Forum should become a regular event, guaranteed by the EC.[56] While the European Commission would provide stable structures,[57] the selection of participants and the development of the agenda would have to remain with the networks and the institution hosting the EuroMed Civil Forum, to guarantee the independence of civil society.[58]

With regard to the Stuttgart EuroMed Civil Forum, two innovations are worth maintaining for the future. One is the separation of the EuroMed Civil Forum into several conferences to provide adequate working conditions for the varying, sometimes incompatible tasks of civil society. Only in the long term is it imaginable to join them together, provided that authoritarian MPCs enter a credible process of democratization, allowing all parts of civil society to become *integral intermediators* between society and the state. Second, the final session of the EuroMed Civil Forum together with representatives of the governments was a success, as it up-valued the political role of civil society. Yet the symbolic value of such a high-level dialogue forum could be raised in the future by joining together representatives from *all* governments participating in the EMP.

Concerning the relationship between the EuroMed Civil Forum and the official level of the EMP, suggestions were made in Stuttgart to establish regular exchanges between civil society and the Euro-Med Committee (which manages the follow-up of the Barcelona Process),[59] and to strengthen contacts between civil society and the European Parliament.[60] While regular contacts with the Euro-Med Committee are important to enhance civil society's influence within the EMP, the importance of closer contacts with the European Parliament goes beyond questions of efficiency, which leads me at the end of this chapter to some theoretical reflections on civil society's role in the process of democratization.

This chapter has focused on civil society's fourth function, political challenge of authoritarian regimes. Some authoritarian regimes counter this challenge by admitting controlled civil activity, while denying the development of a truly representative democracy. It is often overlooked, especially by the advocates of civil society, that political repression can easily be relaxed without expanding political participation. 'Indeed, far from automatically preceding or accompanying democratization, such partial liberalization can be intended to stave off democratic pressures' (Brynen et al., 1995b: 4). To assess civil society's role in the transformation process of a country, it is therefore necessary to differentiate between political liberalization and political democratization:

> *Political liberalization* involves the expansion of public space through the recognition and protection of civil and political liberties, particularly those bearing upon the ability of citizens to engage in free political discourse and to freely organize in pursuit of common interests. *Political democratization* entails an expansion of political participation in such a way as to provide citizens with a degree of real and meaningful collective control over public policy. (ibid.: 3)

Thus, political liberalization is only a step towards democratization when it is combined with *institutional* reforms. These institutional reforms have to go beyond the establishment of so-called 'low-intensity democracies',[61] guaranteeing the accountability of the government to public control, broad possibilities of public participation, the rule of law and, of course, full respect for human rights. The core of institutional reform has to be a strong parliament that derives from democratic elections, and that is also equipped with constitutionally guaranteed political powers.

Yet institutional reform by itself is not sufficient either; it needs a vivid civil society to bring democracy to life. Political liberalization and political democratization should therefore be acknowledged as interdependent and inseparable. Both processes need equal promotion from the EU, if the development of truly representative democracies is to be the long-term goal of European policy in the Mediterranean.

Epilogue

None of the ideas born in Stuttgart to shape the future of the EuroMed Civil Forum as an active player within the EMP has materialized so far. How can this stalemate be explained? The most decisive factor is presumably the paradigmatic change of the regional and the international environment, which had far-reaching implications for Euro-Mediterranean civil society cooperation. However, all changes at the external level have to be analysed in the context of other factors, such as diverging interests and structural weaknesses within civil society.

The first decisive event was the outbreak of the Al Aksa *intifada* in September 2000 and Israel's incredibly harsh reactions. These events had direct effects on the EuroMed Civil Forum of Marseilles, which accompanied the fourth Euro-Mediterranean Ministerial Conference. During the EuroMed Civil Forum of Marseilles, solidarity with the Palestinian cause was the overarching issue. However, against the dramatic background of the escalating Middle East conflict, neither Palestinian nor Israeli civil society re-presentatives seemed to be able to distinguish between the realm of civil society and the realm of governments. Therefore, the EuroMed Civil Forum of Marseilles dealt to a much lesser extent (compared to previous EuroMed Civil Fora) with the conflicting relations between civil societies and their governments. Instead, the focus of Marseilles was on the *general* confrontation between 'Israel' and 'Palestine'.

Although understandable against the background of the acute crisis, this development had negative effects on the EuroMed Civil Forum as a genuine institution to strengthen civil society. It shed light on the often neglected fact that NGOs compete *against* each other for attention, resources and influence. In Marseilles, the Palestinians had been rather successful in marginalizing the multitude of no less important issues raised by NGOs coming from other countries. Furthermore, the blurring of the boundary line between the realm of civil society and the realm of governments resulted in an uncritical attitude of Palestinian and Israeli NGOs with regard to their respective governments. The silence of the majority of Israeli NGOs intensified the negative impression that Israel's civil society is siding with its government.[62] However, Palestinian NGOs were not much better in terms of credibility when they refused to address human rights violations by the Palestinian Authorities; an issue which had been discussed without taboos in Stuttgart. Taken together, these developments weakened the credibility of the EuroMed Civil Forum and with it the role of civil society as an active player within the EMP.

A second decisive factor for the development of civil society's role within the EMP was – and is – the growing tendency to securitize Mediterranean politics. Chapter 3 of the Barcelona Declaration, which was originally dedicated to cooperation in social, cultural and human affairs, is gradually being transformed into something like the third pillar of the EU Treaty, dealing predominantly with justice and home affairs (JHA). The positive attempt to include the wide range of policy and secret service operations in the fight against terrorism is thus being overshadowed by a negative tendency to marginalize the participation of civil society in the EMP. Since the sensitivity of JHA is similar to that of hard security issues, JHA is exclusively object of intergovernmental cooperation. This given, the EMP's third chapter risks becoming another domain of predominantly intergovernmental cooperation, at the expense of civil society representation.

The tendency to securitize Mediterranean Politics and especially Euro-Mediterranean cooperation on civil society level has already been observed in Marseilles, where the French government also exercised considerable control over the EuroMed Civil Forum. Sensitive issues such as human rights were marginalized not only by the Middle East conflict, but also by the organizers of the forum; NGOs close to the French government that shared the official interest in saving North African governments from embarrassment when coming to Marseilles.

The decisive role of the organizing NGOs brings back into our minds that the development of the EuroMed Civil Forum is not determined by external factors alone. A complex network of interests on local, regional, national and supranational levels, including the interests of (competing) NGOs, has to be taken into consideration. Plans made in Stuttgart to strengthen the EuroMed Civil Forum through a loose form of institutionalization have not materialized due to the lack of political will on the part of the EU and its member states, but also due to the inability of civil society to organize itself on a transnational level. Therefore, no final conclusion can be drawn with regard to the future development of the EuroMed Civil Forum. Against the background of an ongoing tendency to securitize the EMP, general conditions for civil society to make its voice heard have clearly worsened. This, however, can also be taken as an incentive to overcome weaknesses and conflicting interests within civil society. Perhaps the challenge is powerful enough to reunite all civil forces in their efforts to strengthen the badly neglected normative dimension of the EMP.

NOTES

1. The MED Programmes promote networks of universities (MED-Campus), the media sector (MED-Media) and local communities (MED-Urbs). They were suspended in 1996 because of mismanagement (European Commission, 1996).

2. MEDA Democracy 'grants subsidies to non-profit-making associations, universities, centres of research and to public bodies to implement projects which aim to promote democracy, the rule of law, freedom of expression, of meeting and of association, to protect target groups (women, youth, minorities) and to increase the awareness of socio-economic rights' (European Commission, 1997). In 1998 all MEDA Democracy projects were stalled due to a ruling of the European Court of Justice. The legal problems were solved in 1999, so that projects could be relaunched. In 2000, the administration of all democracy projects in the Mediterranean was transferred to a new Democracy and Human Rights Department in the Commission and has been subject to an unsettling ongoing process of reform.

3. EuroMed Heritage is a regional programme for the protection of cultural heritage. A special conference on this issue took place in Bologna in April 1996 (European Commission, 1999b).

4. EuroMed Audiovisual is a regional cooperation programme that has become especially important since the suspension of MED-Media (European Commission, 1999b).

5. The EuroMed Youth Action Programme was launched at the end of 1998 and aims at acting both as a bridge across the Mediterranean and as a link between the southern partners of the EMP (European Commission, 1999b).

6. When the European Commission was forced to withdraw in spring 1999, most civil Euro-Mediterranean projects were stopped. Not even granted funds will be paid out until all accusations of corruption are removed.

7. The EMP is the result of a European initiative. Therefore the relationship between the EU and the MPCs is not really an equal partnership, but rather an unbalanced interdependence favouring the EU. For a comprehensive analysis of the EMP see Jünemann (1998a) and the introduction to this volume.

8. The second Euro-Mediterranean conference, which took place in Malta in April 1997, was almost blocked by the crisis of the MEPP (Jünemann, 1997).

9. The political systems of the MPCs are all very specific and cannot be generalized. Yet, despite the differences between them, most share deficits concerning democratic standards and the respect for human rights, justifying the notion *authoritarian*, although to different degrees (Kamrava, 1998: 63).

10. For a critical discussion of Europe's migration policy see Jünemann (1999).

11. For the Common Foreign and Security Policy (CFSP) see Article 11 of the Treaty of Amsterdam (Art. J.1, Paragraph 2 of the old Maastricht Treaty). For Europe's development policy see Article 177 of the Treaty of Amsterdam (Art. 130u, Paragraph 2 of the old Maastricht Treaty).

12. For the interdependence between democratization and development see also Boeck (1992).

13. Besides that, the EU is bound by the treaties made with the MPC's *governments*. In the case of an unbridgeable conflict between civil society and a government, the EU has to side with its official partner, the government.

14. This version of a Spanish official was confirmed by others who had been involved in the decision-making process. None of the interviewed partners wants to be quoted. Confidential interviews were made in Brussels in March 1996 and in Barcelona and Madrid in November 1998.

15. Interview with Professor Esther Barbé Izuel (1998).

16. Groups do not belong in civil society if they become violent or if they adopt programmes contradicting democratic goals and values. Others might disappear along with the solution of the political problem they had been working on. For the definition of civil society see the third section of this chapter.

17. The lack of legitimization and other problems arising from the heterogeneity of civil society are discussed by White (1996).

18. For an in-depth reflection on civil society in European thought see Taylor (1989).

19. For the problem of defining civil society see Cohen and Arato (1995).

20. This criterion obviously concerns associations and not individuals. Experience shows that in non-democratic countries civil engagement requires especially strict and efficient structures of its associations to enable them to resist repression and persecution. The internal organization of NGOs therefore often reflects the authoritarian structures of the regime they oppose; European standards of internal democracy can thus not simply be transferred to the MPCs. For the sometimes problematic internal structure of civil society associations, see Merkel and Lauth (1998).

21. For a contemporary discussion of civil society in the Arab world see Ferhad and Wedel (1995), Norton (1995), Schwedler (1995a).
22. According to the *dichotomic* concept, civil society is completely independent of the state. Its primary function is to control the state, which implies the legitimization of civil society to overthrow an *authoritarian* regime. This concept goes back to the political thought of John Locke (Richter, 1997: 38 f.).
23. According to the *integral* concept, civil society is part of the *democratic* political system. There is no clear-cut division line between the state and society; civil society functions as a *corps intermédiaire*. This concept goes back to Charles Montesquieu (Richter, 1997: 38 f.).
24. For the role of private business see also Schwedler (1995b).
25. See also the rather polemic article of Fülberth (1991).
26. In contrast to Ferhad, Helmich and Lemmers translate *al-mutjama al-madani* with *civic* society and *al-mutjama al-ahli* with *civil* society (Helmich and Lemmers, 1999: 19). For the Islamist discourse on civil society see also Moussali (1995).
27. Concerning the difficult relationship between Algeria's cultural élite and the traditional representatives of Algerian society see also Maougal (1997).
28. The necessity to integrate political Islamism into Euro-Arab intercultural relations was one of the results of the Third German–Arab Media Dialogue. This was organized by the Institut für Auslandsbeziehungen by account of the Presse- und Informationsamt der Bundesregierung Deutschland (Rabat, 8–9 June 1999).
29. Radical groups are often also engaged in social welfare, so that charitable activities are not a sufficient criterion for choosing a partner organization.
30. To reduce Islamism to its radical segments is understandable from the personal perspective of people being pursued by Islamist terrorists. Nevertheless it is an inadmissible simplification, ignoring the manifold non-violent segments of political Islam. Within this very heterogeneous spectrum there are noteworthy attempts to redefine Muslim society in terms that are compatible with western concepts of democracy. To give only one example, a growing number of Islamist feminists legitimate their emancipatory demands with a new interpretation of the Koran (Pinn and Wehner, 1995).
31. As the AMC was lacking funds, the Institut Català Mediterrània even helped out by financing parts of the travelling costs. The Generalitat de Catalunja is mentioned as a supporter of the conference. The documentation of the AMC can be found on the website of the Institut Català Mediterrània.
32. See *Project Outline of the Conférence Méditerranéenne Alternative* on http//www.pangea.org/events/cma95/eng/about/html
33. The results of these panels are documented in Institut Català Mediterrània (1996).
34. Governmental NGOs are not necessarily new foundations. A less conspicuous strategy of authoritarian regimes to get civil society under control is to co-opt authentic NGOs by infiltrating them with loyal people.
35. The organization of a conference with participants coming from 27 countries is extremely expensive, due to high travelling costs and the need for many translators. At the EuroMed Civil Forum in Malta there was no sponsor comparable to the Generalitat de Catalunja.
36. The other institutions were the Foundation for International Studies, University of Malta, the North–South Centre of the Council of Europe, the University of the Mediterranean (UNIMED) and the European Cultural Agency/Mediterranean Programme (UNESCO).
37. Due to its modest funding, EuroMed Civil Forum II was restricted to 130 participants compared with over 1,000 two years before, at EuroMed Civil Forum I. See *Agénce Europe*, 17 April 1997, p.14.
38. One workshop concentrated on cultural tourism, another one on youth, education and media and a third one on university training, research and culture. For the results of the second EuroMed Civil Forum see Foundation for International Studies (1997).
39. During EuroMed Civil Forum II, there was a strong demand for improvements of the third chapter and suggestions for its follow-up.
40. See the promising presentation by Jaques Giraudon of the European Commission at the opening of EuroMed Civil Forum II in Malta (Foundation for International Studies, 1997).

41. Despite its general interest in Euro-Mediterranean cooperation, Germany's profile in cultural cooperation within the framework of Chapter 3 is rather low. For an in-depth analysis see Jünemann (1998c).

42. The Chamber of Industry and Commerce organized the conference together with the Bund Deutscher Industrieller, the Deutscher Industrie und Handelstag and the Ministry of Economics of Baden Württemberg.

43. The essential importance of democracy and human rights is stressed in Article 2 of all Euro-Mediterranean Association Agreements and in the Barcelona Declaration itself.

44. The Friedrich Ebert Foundation functioned as host and coordinator, delegating the task of choosing the participants to two trustworthy partner organizations, the Euro-Mediterranean Human Rights Network and the Forum des Citoyens de la Méditerranée.

45. Human rights activists from several MPCs reported having been threatened by these people during their stay in Stuttgart, and the organizers had to withhold the list of participants to prevent it from getting into the wrong hands.

46. The demand to ensure environmental policy integration into all policies and activities of the EMP appeared in the formal conclusions made by Joschka Fischer, who stated that the indicative programmes should be based, among other things, on an environmental review of the respective country (Heinrich Böll Foundation, 1999; German Foreign Ministry, 1999).

47. See the resolution of the Stuttgart Conference on Economic Development, Industrial Relations and the Role of Trade Unions, which is available on http://www.euromed/net/activities/conferences/stuttgart/civil_forum.htm

48. For the risks of the planned free trade area see Nienhaus (1999).

49. To stress this point, the environmental forum invited two representatives from human rights NGOs to give presentations.

50. The final declarations of the Stuttgart EuroMed Civil Forum are available on http://www.euromed.net/activities/conferences/stuttgart/civil_forum.htm

51. For the effects of the CSCE human rights regime see Rhode-Liebenau (1996).

52. Members of the Comité de Suivi are the Arab Network for Environment and Development (RAED), European Environmental Bureau (EEB), Friends of the Earth (FoE), Med-Forum, Mediterranean Information Office (MIO-ECSDE) and the WWF Mediterranean Programme (WWF/MEDPO).

53. This network was founded in 1996 in the context of a Euro-Moroccan conference in Tangier. Migration issues are at the top of the political agenda in the Maghreb countries and Turkey, less in the other MPCs.

54. The EMHRN was founded in 1997 in response to the Barcelona Declaration and is situated in Copenhagen. It delivers regular reports, most importantly giving information on human rights conditions in the area. It is transparent concerning its own work.

55. Host countries of Euro-Mediterranean governmental summits could (and should) support the realization of the EuroMed Civil Forum. Yet governments opposing the idea of civil participation in the EMP could not prevent the EuroMed Civil Forum from coming into being; they could at most hamper its organization.

56. The weakest point of all five civil society conferences in Stuttgart was the short time that was given to their organization. If the EuroMed Civil Forum had already been integrated as a regular event into the EMP, the networks could have started preparing themselves in time.

57. This includes a regular financial commitment that organizers can rely upon.

58. Without interfering in the selection of participants, the European Commission could support the building of civil society networks through the EU delegations working in all MPCs, as these are in permanent contact with many NGOs participating for example in the MEDA-funded programmes.

59. The Euro-Med Committee meets on a quarterly basis at ambassadorial level. It is chaired by the EU presidency, and consists of the troika, MED partners, Council Secretariat and Commission representatives (member states not in the troika participate as observers). The Committee gives its opinion concerning activities to be financed in accordance with the Regional Indicative Programme, and prepares for ministerial meetings, *ad hoc* conferences of ministers of various portfolios, and of senior officials, experts and representatives of civil society.

60. The EMHRN for example announced that it would make contacts with 'country rapporteurs, members of the Sub-committee on Human Rights, the Sub-committee on Foreign Affairs, Security and Defence Policy, the Delegation to the EU–Turkey Joint Parliamentary Committee, the Delegations for relations with the Maghreb countries and in the Arab Maghreb Union, the Delegation for relations with the Mashrek countries and the Gulf States, the Delegation for relations with Israel and the Delegation for relations with the Palestinian Legislative Council' (EMHRN, 1998: 24).

61. The terms 'low-intensity democracy' or 'formal democracy' stand for political systems that fulfil only a minimum of the formal criteria defining democracy, without allowing political participation and public control over the government. The EU has often been criticized for contenting itself with the establishment of such low-intensity democracies in the Mediterranean, instead of insisting on real democratization.

62. The only Israeli NGO raising its voice against Israel's government was B'Tselem.

6

Civil Society, God and Cousins: The Case of the Middle East

YOUSSEF MOUAWAD

Introduction

It is very fashionable in today's Arab East to invoke civil society: a ready-made concept that fits any given speech. This trend reached its climax in terms of literary production in the middle of the 1990s (Barakat, 1985: 171; Kawtharani, 1988: 47–66; Kawtharani, 1992: 119–31; Ghalioun, 1992: 733–55; Messarra, 1995; Ibrahim, 1996; Ya'qub, 1997: 40–68; Bishara, 1998). Although some may consider it as a passing fancy, it is not going to fade away easily, for some people built their careers on promoting it, on networking its NGOs, and last but not least, made a living out of it.[1]

Those who most quote civil society nowadays are those who summoned the popular masses (*al-jamahir al-sha'biyya*) to uprising in the 1960s and the 1970s. As if by magic, those same intellectuals and militants who were advocating violence as a legitimate means of political action have renounced it, and have changed both their vocabulary and phraseology. Today, it is not politically correct to mention class struggle or the revolutionary avant-garde. So, the keyword is nothing more bourgeois than civil society, and thus Mother Theresa has replaced Che Guevara as a model for future generations.

This chapter contends that although Middle Eastern, and more generally Arab Islamic, civil society is rooted in the past, it is still inconclusive, if we pass judgement by 'alien' western standards, for primordial allegiances hinder the development of an assertive citizenship. Primordial allegiances as a term will be used hereafter in the widest sense, as suggested by Al-Khatib, 'to include ties of fealty, religion, kinship and such congruities of blood, sacred and personal relations' (Al-Khatib, 1994: 117–18). In terms of format, this chapter will provide relevant historical examples and interpretations.

The *'asabiyya (esprit de corps)* is the cement of group cohesion, whether in the case of primary identity acquired at birth, such as family, neighbourhood or religious community (Lewis, 1998: 4–5), or in the case of a different level of identity acquired by voluntary choice and through 'ideological' commitment. This second level is no more legitimate than the first one, although the former may lack the 'civic' ingredient.

Review of the Literature

Civil society is 'straightforwardly society' and the adjective 'civil' does not endow the term with content (Kukathas, 1998: 37–8). It is, according to Lesrek Kolakovki, 'a whole mass of conflicting individual and group aspirations, empirical daily life with all its conflicts and struggles, the realm of private desires and private endeavours' (ibid.: 39). Nevertheless, both as a concept and an object of analysis, it is a commodity of a recent importation to the East.

Thus a question might be raised to see whether it is relevant to seek in the Arab Islamic past something resembling a civil society? The answer is positive. The fact that Karl Marx only elaborated the concept of class struggle in the nineteenth century does not mean that one cannot use it in an attempt to understand the eighteenth century. But is it absolutely necessary to find civil society anywhere and in any place? Is it indispensable to take liberties with this flexible concept and to impose it upon any event? It is not enough to prove the existence of a brotherhood or the establishment of a religious endowment (*waqf*) somewhere in history to deduce the existence of civil society. This would lead us to pretend that any group or any short-lived popular protest, whether violent or not, constitutes some form of civil society.

Besides, the concept of civil society was elaborated in the West; trying to interpret Arab history from this perspective might prove hazardous. Arab authors may be inclined to make unfounded statements on the grounds that the West has nothing to teach the East. They would try to prove with many details that Arab civil society is as deeply rooted in the past as other civil societies in the world. But, once more, they forget that while making this comparison, the western model remains their epitome and example. And when Arab civil society does not fit in with the European or American model, they try to explain it by eastern specificity or by minor momentary setbacks.

Civil society is always presented as the opposite pole of the state, whether in the Mashreq or in the Maghreb (Heinz, 1995; Heinz, n.d.). We are warned against the replacement of economic and social factors with bureaucracy planning, the dictating of individuals' rules of conduct, especially in Third World countries where the way to modernity is usually decided by rulers. In contradistinction to this, civil society is hailed as a bastion of democratic values and as the last resort in thwarting those oppressive plans attributed to ruling authorities, which are always trying to invalidate the role of grass-roots organizations.

One should always keep in mind that even from a liberal perspective, where the state is considered a necessary evil, it is not an absolute evil. We still need the state and the state has the advantage, at least in theory, of being impartial, whereas on the other hand civil society represents contradictory interests and usually opposing pressure groups. Just as the state is not the absolute evil, so civil society is not the supreme ideal.

Asserting that civil society is a buffer zone between individuals and the state is not very accurate, for such a contention would eliminate the existence of a political society or a political sphere that stands between civil society and the state. It is in this sphere, in a spirit of healthy democracy, that the political debate takes place, for it is a mediation zone between the state and civil society (Touraine, 1994: 71–8). A totalitarian state may reduce the political sphere, it may confiscate it, but it cannot dismiss civil society's role, even though it can forbid its manifestations that we call associations and NGOs. Whatever an oppressive state may do, a civil society, though dumb and chained up, keeps its capacity to reproduce itself.

Edward Shils expressed his caution concerning the problematic interaction of the state, the political space and civil society, before civil war in Lebanon confirmed his doubts and apprehensions. What he means hereafter by civil society refers to civism:

> Lebanon is not a civil society. It has many of the requisite qualities, but it lacks an essential one: the politically relevant members of Lebanese society are not inclined to allow the obligations which arise from their membership of the society to supervene when they feel that interests which they regard as vital are threatened ... It lacks the attachment to the national society as a whole, that sense of identity. (Shils, 1966: 1–11)

The multiple identities in the East have certainly created different levels within civil society, as well as within personal commitment. Augustus Norton raised relevant questions when he wondered whether democracy was at home in the Middle East and whether Middle East society is civil, that is, civic (Norton, 1993: 211). Since the question is asked, one might dare say that a civil society is not necessarily a 'civic' one. It is neither 'civility' nor ethics but autonomy that makes civil society. In any case, how does one check this civility? Is the object clause of an NGO substantiating evidence? As I shall show below when discussing 'primordial ties', a civil society in the East, as certainly in other areas, may be constituted around other themes than that of responsible citizenship. Civil society, although proclaiming its ideals, may have its negative sides. Norton did not fail to note that 'self-interest, prejudice and hatred cohabit with altruism, fairness and compassion, sometimes making unrestrained free play of civil society a chilling thought, not a warm and fuzzy one' (ibid.: 211). All the same, Ralph Dahrendorf scoffed at a candid approach in these words: 'values are thought to "emerge" somehow, by freeing people from constraints, encouraging them to be their best selves, bringing them together for discourse and communication. Somehow like geysers out of Iceland, i.e. soil, truth, goodness and beauty will arise' (Dahrendorf, 1997: 65). One should avoid certain pitfalls inherent in idealizing civil society, for, as mentioned above, it may have a negative side.

Historical Evidence

Researchers usually give examples of civil society in Islamic history without caring to say in what sense the mentioned groups or institutions had the proper elements or ingredients to be recognized as such. Of course, it would be in vain to search for today's western standards in medieval history. One could not ask Abbasid society to cultivate civic virtues under Harun al-Rashid. Once again, the question to ask is not how far our civil society was civic, but how far it was autonomous *vis-à-vis* the ruling authorities? Did given examples such as *futuwwa*, guilds, religious brotherhoods and religious *waqfs* (Kawtharani, 1988: 47–52; Kawtharani, 1992: 127; Kandil, 1995: 27–33) constitute a sort of precocious civil society in their respective periods? One should be very cautious when it comes to extrapolation, and the famous sentence by the orientalist Louis Massignon – 'What is interesting in Islam is that the municipal life is independent from the sovereign' (Massignon, 1963: 373) – is misleading. In my quest for autonomy, I shall examine two usually mentioned groups, the *ahdath* and the guilds, to assess how far they were free from the tutelage of official organizations; then I will examine how far Freemason lodges contributed to the promotion of democratic values.

Al-Ahdath in Damascus from the Tenth to the Twelfth Centuries[2]

The traditional pejorative western view is that people in Arab cities were passive. The example of *ahdath* in Damascus in the tenth and twelfth centuries may shed a new light on the subject. *Al-Ahdath* were more or less militias constituted of young men who joined forces against the ruling authorities. These groups left a mythical image to the extent that some writers conferred upon their action the attributes of proletarian claims (Al-Najjar, 1981: 161–2), not taking into consideration the fact that the *ahdath* played the role of police *shurta*. Actually, the institution of the *ahdath* would evolve over passing time into an official institution: its chief became the chief of the city, and sometimes his descendants inherited his title and office. So, the status of the *ahdath* was to become strictly official, even though at one time one could have contrasted the official *ahdath* to the popular *ahdath* who sometimes consisted of the mob, who led a communal life and engaged in anti-aristocratic activity (Cahen, *Futuwwa*, EI). The real difference between the *ahdath* and the classical police is not to be found at the level of functions, but at the level of recruitment. The *ahdath* are city dwellers affiliated to professions but not actually professionals. They constituted a militia, a 'national guard' (Cahen, 1958: 245). They translated the feelings of the population, and they did actually use their military capacities in opposing foreign lords who tried to rule the city.

Did *al-ahdath* represent the urban population in its entirety or only certain elements that were opposing each other? It seems that in certain cases the *ahdath* regrouped around chiefs belonging to the wealthy bourgeoisie or around a *sharif* who may have adopted, for personal reasons, demagogic or democratic attitudes. On the other hand, the *ahdath* may also have represented the opinion of a social stratum. Occasionally, we notice conflicts between popular elements within the *ahdath* and moderate bourgeois elements less autonomous than one would believe, for autonomy may have put them at the mercy of the deprived classes (Cahen, 1958: 246). In fact, the important characteristic of the *ahdath* institution is the expression of a conscious specificity of cities or of urban agglomerations in the face of lords, princes or military regimes that were felt to be alien (Cahen, 1959a: 250).

Roughly, the *ahdath* represented the dynamic element of municipal opposition (Cahen, *Ahdath*, EI), an example illustrating the fact that Syrian cities were not as passive as some would have liked them to be (ibid.). Nevertheless, this autonomy of sorts is not the accomplished type, although the participation of the deprived classes was obvious.

Guilds and Craftsmen in Cairo in the Seventeenth and Eighteenth Centuries[3]

When it comes to professional organizations, it is advisable to refer to the distinction made by Claude Cahen (1959b: 26) between:

1. Organizations that are established and run by the state without any real autonomy. That is the example of Roman Byzantine colleges. In this case, whatever the economic role of the professional organization, it only plays a minor role in social structuring. Efficient popular associations in social life would try to constitute themselves outside these colleges.
2. Associations that are relatively autonomous as were the corporations of the late European Middle Ages. In this case, professional corporational life may be the principal form of an autonomous collective life.

According to Cahen, the professional associations in the Arab world in the first centuries of its evolution remain within the ambit of the Roman Byzantine tradition and it is outside this ambit that a role in the social and political life is played (ibid.: 26–7). But that was in the first centuries of Islam. What about merchants and craftsmen corporations in Egypt before Bonaparte's guns introduced modernity to the East? Were guilds subservient to the ruler (Ayubi, 1999: 398), or were they quite autonomous?

In the seventeenth and eighteenth centuries, Egypt's society was twofold: on the one hand were the ruling authorities, i.e. pashas, beys, janissaries and mameluks; on the other were the *ra'aya* or subjects, a category to which belonged craftsmen and traders. One can easily imagine the socio-economic role these guilds played in Cairo and its suburbs; but did they play a political role or were they as subjects subservient to the rulers? The first impression they give is that they were fragmented. There were about thirty groups of corporations. An observer mentioned that merchants and traders also formed corporations 'according to their country, the species of their commerce, and their religious worship' (Raymond, 1973–74: 523). These guilds assumed administrative, fiscal and economic functions, as well as providing assistance and mutual support to their members. They had their own public ceremonies, their corporative ideology, the *futuwwa* introduced to Egypt by the Ottomans, and their rituals. As far as hierarchy was concerned, there were apprentices and masters of each trade, and chiefs of corporation, as well as an assembly of corporation.

Any person of the *ra'aya* could belong to one or more of these groups, which were more or less structured according to his area of residence, his guild or his religious brotherhood. All these elements favour autonomy. However, there are other arguments that would qualify this opinion. The corporations were relatively closed to outsiders. Heredity constituted a fundamental element in the socio-professional organization. It forbade the access of deprived elements to mastership, for there were social cleavages within the organization of the guilds.

Besides, one could not ignore the fact that the guilds were affiliated to the ruling military class. The interpenetration between the two classes was accelerated in the last third of the seventeenth century when traders and craftsmen introduced their emancipated mameluks to the military class, in order to exert a certain influence by way of their intermediary, while at the same time the militias directed some of their people into economic activities (ibid.: 677–9). In the long run close relations were established between the military and the subjects. In short, there was no insurmountable gap between the two levels, the ruling authorities and *ra'aya*. The demarcation line was porous.

However, at the beginning of the eighteenth century, when the prevailing order started to degenerate, sub-corporations developed without restraint. This flexibility denotes that the system was neither strictly organized nor rigidly centralized. Could we still speak of an autonomous society in this case, or of a class-conscious population? There was certainly a municipal civil society that was trying to express itself, and eventually did so when, after three centuries, the political and social system broke into sherds within a period of weeks. The vacuum gave *ulama*, craftsmen and traders the opportunity to participate in the political events taking place in Cairo (ibid.: 819). That happened in 1805, when Muhammad Ali took power in Egypt with the support of a coalition of traders and *ulama*, who helped him crush the mameluk rule. In his bid for power, he counted on the butchers' sheikh and the vegetable merchants' corporations (Monteil, 1987: 100).

Al-Ahdath and guilds are two historical examples of civil society that took place before European intervention on the scene of the Middle East and the adoption of western models. The society was then traditional, closer to the 'historical model' where the Law bestowed upon the faithful by God was in the custody of the community, and where the sovereign, who assumed responsibility for its implementation, was neither its source nor its guarantor. In that period the state was not considered as a superstructure with which the population felt no solidarity (Cahen, 1959b: 26), as may have been the case in Europe. So in our quest for groups somehow autonomous from the state, we should always keep in mind that the state then meant something other than the European model, and consequently, society reacted differently towards it. It is only when one moves to a later period, when the nation-state model, constitutionalism, freedom and other western elaborated values were imported to the East, that a comparison may become relevant.

Freemasonry: A Semi-neutral Society at the End of the Nineteenth and Beginning of the Twentieth Centuries[4]

The impact of western influence through education, military might, trade, travel, etc., introduced liberal ideas to the Middle East and brought the mimetic establishment of Freemason lodges in the Arab lands of the Ottoman Empire. As Zeine N. Zeine puts it, people of the Near East 'were slowly waking up to a new world of progress and power which was taking shape in the West, in sharp contrast to the state of ignorance and weakness' that prevailed in the East (Zeine, 1973: 33). In spite of all the accusations and conspiracy theories that surround Freemasonry, the lodges became the meeting-places of the social and intellectual élites of the era: reformers, military officers, civil servants, journalists, writers, and even men of religion such as Jamal al-Din al-Afghani (Sulayman, 1993: 586). To say that all these people had the same convictions is a hasty generalization. However, these were people who were breaking partially or fully with the prevailing state of things, with the 'old regime', and who gathered around ideas that were somehow subversive in a traditional society. Of course, Freemasonry was not a model of an open society. However, what is interesting is the fact that its members came from different backgrounds, different classes and religious confessions. For the first time, there grew in the East a new sociability more or less influenced by the ideas of the demiurgic West. As Antun Saadah, a prominent member of the lodges, summarized it when submitting his resignation:

> The organization of Freemasons was founded for those who think freely in the world; its aim is twofold: liberating people from the chains of despotism and freeing the human mind from the slavery of superstitions and illusions. The struggle the Freemasons led against absolute oppressive power is evidence of its action, and the French Revolution is an example of it. All the same, the national campaign against superstition and clerical myths in the world testifies to its program. The achievements

114

of Freemasonry in this field are numerous. Therefore, I add to the organization of Freemasons the word *madrasa* (educational institution). (Saadah, 1978: 2)

One has to note the undoubted anti-clericalism, secularism and universalism of this quotation.

The fact is that from the end of the nineteenth century onwards, a real change in mentalities took place in certain spheres of the cultivated bourgeoisie. Social relations between Christians and Muslims were occurring spontaneously due to a larger open-mindedness. It meant social recognition of others: people separated traditionally by religious cleavages started meeting in fields that were not exclusively those of business (Katz, 1984: 49). Associations that had ethical, social or charitable objectives grew in number. Gathering in order to pursue a common, intellectual and educational goal presupposes a certain higher degree of commitment (ibid.: 50). In Freemasonry, men would meet on the basis of a minimum religious common denominator: a religion of reason (ibid.: 52). The deistic constitution of lodges did not necessarily suppress all traces of its members' religious practices (ibid.: 53). But the fact is that by the end of the nineteenth century, a new climate prevailed in certain open-minded spheres of society, where religious zeal had somehow regressed. Tolerance became a virtue under the influence of rationalism and the Enlightenment. However, in spite of these apparently tolerant declarations, it seems that the Freemasons only constituted a semi-neutral society outside the scope of traditional hierarchies (ibid.: 54).

The authors, mainly Christians, who triggered the Arab Renaissance (*nahda*), started writing for a wider Arab and oriental public instead of addressing exclusively the readers of their own community. In so doing, they transcended the boundaries of their minority communities to integrate into a larger environment. Clubs and societies of different affiliations were meeting-places for the exchange of ideas among learned people. Being admitted into these circles meant that one was recognized socially in a society that used to be exclusive and discriminating (ibid.: 62). By this time, society was showing its willingness to liberate itself from the weight of tradition and to erase reciprocal exclusions based on religious antagonism. Although the integration of Christians into Muslim society remained incomplete, the partial crossing of barriers between Christians and Muslims appeared as an important social revolution, as if all segregation between them had vanished, a feeling that contributed to the belief that change in all sectors of society was imminent: a form of social Utopia. Although these changes only reached privileged social strata, they may have been the first seeds of civism in the East. The ideals of the French Revolution were the slogan of Freemasons. Their writings called for a separation of state and religion. Candidly, they tried to shape a new man, but society at large was not ready for a drastic change. And modernity was to remain the privilege of those rulers who tried to impose it on their subjects.

Before going further, we should wonder why the Arab East that had known in the past a 'proto-civil' society and was later exposed to the winds of change, did not give birth to a 'civic' society? Why is Arab Islamic civic society nowadays still unaccomplished?

The Quandary of Civil Society

The reasons why Arab Islamic society did not grow into a civic one are numerous; they could be classified under the heading of underdevelopment. Some insist on the economic aspects, others on the cultural or social ones. Some argue that the Middle Eastern city, throughout history, was an *urbs*, that is a physical agglomeration rather than a *civitas*, a space for collective debate and action (Ayubi, 1999: 398). The answer depends on whether the explanation is Marxist, Weberian or otherwise. Hassan Hanafi pretends that in the case of Egypt, it is due to the adoption of Ashaarite doctrine (Hanafi, 1990: 101–4). Mehdi Mozaffari, following Krämer, believes that the problem stems from the fact that Arab Islamic political thought has followed Plato rather than Aristotle (Mozaffari, 1998: 36).

In this race for arguments, I would like to suggest and stress two socio-cultural causes that are in my opinion obstacles to the emergence of the individual and therefore to the constitution of a real civic society. I shall first give an example from the Arab Maghreb rather than from its Mashreq. The novel by Fouad Laroui, *Méfiez-vous des Parachutistes* (1999), illustrates the situation of a Moroccan engineer who returns home after years in Europe, where he has adopted western ways. The story revolves around a question and an obsession: how to be recognized as an individual nowadays in an Arab country, where one is invaded by family and neighbours? Episodes of his life back home and violations of his privacy bring the engineer to the verge of committing suicide. He is saved by finding refuge in the Koran, which teaches that life and death belong to God (Sura 6–162). As Nazih Ayubi notes, life in Muslim and some Mediterranean societies is often 'lived in public', family is not yet an 'island of privacy', and matters of personal conduct are usually regarded as public morals to be 'enforced collectively' (Ayubi, 1999: 439). In the novel by Laroui we find the ingredients of the fatal opposition between the freedom of the individual as promoted in western civilization and the alliance to God's order and family solidarity as perpetuated in oriental cultures. How could the concept of individualism emerge when God and family are omnipresent?

Problems derive from the fact that certain societies did not emancipate themselves and are still under tutelage. The individual had not yet emerged fully as a value, contrary to what took place in western Europe where, since Renaissance times, a change in mentalities developed around the idea of man. The individual, then, started thinking of himself as a free and autonomous subject who could impose his will upon his environment. The individuality of man became a value in itself (Burckhardt, 1958: 204–10). Looking at the world and society with new eyes, the promotion of the idea of liberation in the west brought individuals to break with old habits and traditions, which were inculcated in their minds by the various groups to which they belonged. According to Robert Klein, this exacerbated individualism was not going to lead to singularity, but rather gave access to universality and boosted liberty of thought (ibid., 1958: 11–55). By the eighteenth century, European Enlightenment was openly challenging established beliefs. Rationalism put in question the foundation of the Christian mental universe and proposed new perspectives as a substitute for the old ones (Chaunu, 1970: 520). The way was paved for man to assert his individuality more and more, to the point where Nietzsche, a century later, could proclaim the death of God and consequently the advent of the *Übermensch*.

Nothing of the kind happened in the Arab Islamic world, and Ira Lapidus may still maintain that there are in Islam 'two fundamental, original, and persisting structures', on the one hand the family, the clan, the tribe, and on the other, 'unities of culture, religion and empire on an ever-larger scale' (Lapidus, 1988: 3). Contrary to the modern West, where the nation-state is the apex of political loyalty, 'throughout Islam the small group and the great faith have been the principal foci of loyalty and commitment' (Huntington, 1998: 174–5). They may also have been the main, although not exclusive, obstacles hindering the radical valorization of man. Two socio-cultural faultlines, the relation to God (a belated and inconclusive secularization) and tribal allegiances, which involve blood ties, kinship and extend to clientelism (the society of cousins) most probably prevented Middle Eastern society from developing into a model of modern occidentality.

A Belated and Inconclusive Secularization

Edward Said was right in warning against western prejudice in the study of Islamic societies. It is obvious that some orientalists envisage Islam as a monolith and tend to explain today's Middle East by quoting medieval writers or *'ulama*, as if Islamic culture were fossilized in its pre-modern formulation (Mayer, 1995: 10). Being cautioned against such distortions, we have to admit nevertheless that Islam as a revelation is not contingent upon history. And whether or not we admit that social attitudes are explained by the intrinsic and permanent character of religious belief rather than by temporary and historico-political external circumstances (Weber, 1967: 37), it is clear that the individual did not emerge in Arab countries because God and not man is the supreme value. In any case, history tells us that an early secularization of mentalities is a typical western vintage, although not proper to all Christian areas. In the Byzantine Russian realm, for instance, the tradition of the emperor-priest hindered the development of an autonomous, responsible civil society and the establishment of a system of counter-powers that would act as checks and balances to the reign of arbitrary rule (Badie, 1997a: 67).

Islamic society did not develop an intellectual climate that would have enhanced the idea of the individual (Mayer, 1995: 40). Although the Muslim East introduced many western concepts into the intellectual and political environment, it did not adopt those trends of modernity that dismiss God from the public sphere. At this stage, there is a culture-based resistance to affirming man as supreme value, and rulers until today, however secular, are not in a position to transgress the rule. Most constitutions in the Arab Islamic world refer to God and to religious law. The Universal Islamic Declaration of Human Rights (1981) relies more extensively and explicitly than the Iranian Constitution (1979) does on Islamic criteria to limit rights (ibid.: 73). And more recently, the Cairo Declaration on Human Rights in Islam (1990) stressed the inferiority of humans *vis-à-vis* their Creator (ibid.: 57). Whereas the Universal Declaration of Human Rights (1948), while guaranteeing religious freedom, does not make any reference to God, all charters of Islamic inspiration have set a prerequisite: the religious law.

Up until today, the Muslim East has not been able to divorce faith and reason by adopting the Spinozan distinction according to which the aim of philosophy is the truth and that of faith is exclusively obedience and piety. It is not true that Islam is inherently incapable of accommodating principles of individualism; it is more accurate to say that individualism could not spread in a traditional society that is not willing to pay the price of a breach with God, a price so high that it may involve an utter change in this life and external damnation in the other. One cannot deny the fact that in the Arab East, God is over-present in the public sphere, for on the sociological level confessional affiliation is usually dictating people's political loyalties and solidarities. Besides, in any traditional society, individuals are envisaged as part of a group and Islam, which bestows on believers a strong feeling of identity, refuses to consider the *umma* (community) as an accumulation of the faithful.

The 'Society of Cousins': Solidarity Versus Individual Freedom

In the Arab East a person's status in society is widely characterized by the 'concrete and lasting tie' of kinship, which is attributable to one's accident of birth regardless of individual qualities or merit (Al-Khatib, 1994: 120). Family patterns dictate such strict rules of behaviour that it certainly hinders the development of individual freedom. In the Arab East personality traits that reinforce group cohesion are encouraged from childhood, whereas those that are detrimental to the group are censured (Patai, 1983: 78). How far did Arab Islamic culture remain communal, collectivist and organic, and how far did it readily adopt solidaristic and corporatist influences from Europe rather than liberal ones (Ayubi, 1999: 398)?

Family, clan, kinship and clientelism as a whole (Johnson, 1986) provide a feeling of solidarity that one is deprived of in the West, where the individual, although enjoying his freedom, is lonely and therefore weak, because he lacks a sense of security that the society of cousins provides so naturally. In this sense, contrasting a society of citizens with a society of cousins may cast light on the subject, although both societies deserve the appellation of civil society. A society of cousins is a society of arrangements and accommodation, a society of hidden, selfish and exclusive solidarities, a society based on what has survived from the old die-hard clanic framework (Maspéro, 1997: 63). It confers a strong sense of identity, for it is an innate fact of 'primordial culture'; it is a general atmosphere that conditions its members, who are nurtured in the common womb of the tribe (Maffesoli, 1988: 243).

In contradistinction to such a society of cousins is the society of citizens, which implies a 'shared sense of identity', by means of at least a 'tacit agreement over the rough boundaries of the political unit', and a 'sense of citizenship, with associated rights and responsibilities' (Norton, 1993: 213). That would be called the 'secondary culture', to which individuals would aggregate by voluntary choice, and usually, but not necessarily, after repudiating their 'primordial culture' (Maffesoli, 1988: 243).

At this level, civic society 'refers to a quality – civility – without which the milieu consists of feuding factions, cliques and cabals. Civility implies tolerance, the willingness of individuals to accept disparate political views and social attitudes' (Norton, 1993: 215). But a society of cousins where the 'I' is kept in subjugation to the 'we' (Elias, 1991: 282), and where nepotism and the trading of favours blossom, is not always the utmost evil. A clanic society may find in blood ties and kinship a place of safety in facing an oppressive state that tries to annihilate all traces of opposition by confiscating civil society. The clan or tribe may serve a good purpose in preventing the state from establishing absolute power. The example of Albania under Enver Hoxha is significant: due to its network of solidarities, it produces a counter-society to resist state encroachments. Therefore, the primordial community may play a positive role as long as it is on the defensive.

On the other side of the coin, clan solidarity may prove dangerous. Imagine a clan taking power in a country: the case of Saddam Hussein and his Tikrit people in Iraq. A clan would infiltrate the state apparatus, structure the power machine according to its interests and govern according to its whims, thereby excluding the participation of others. If Arab society is so much a 'society of cousins', then how can one reconcile it with the nation-state, this western concept that requires from citizens a higher level of common dependencies? There is certainly a gap between what the western model state requires in terms of citizenship and the gregarious 'we' that identifies with kinship. The permanence of tribal allegiances perpetuates ancestral weights that hinder the individual freedom of initiative and the capacity to adapt to change (ibid.: 258).

Islamic society has changed, but repudiated neither God nor cousins. Arabs today do not talk as much by maxims and proverbs (*hikam*) as their fathers did.

But the fact that they quote verses from the Koran in many circumstances, apart from illustrating and showing outwardly their feelings and beliefs (Guillaume, 1990: 75), cements hereditary transmissions and group cohesion, for the word of God stresses unity, terminates disputes and differences of opinion and provides serenity. Besides, Arab society will, according to tradition, stick to a façade conformism, by decency and a sense of propriety – a question of urbanity, but mostly the price of maintaining cohesion (Gardet, 1961: 234). Arab cities have succeeded in allying their conformism with its counterpart, a rebellious spirit, that questions authority, a feature that is so typical of Muslim agglomerations (ibid.).

To illustrate in architectural terms, one could say that the oriental mansion has a ceiling that is religion and lateral walls that are cousins. This mansion may be considered either like a house of splendour, a refuge, a haven, or on the contrary, as a prison that prevents the individual from moving away and assuming his total freedom. Some people have chosen to remain in the old house and to root themselves there. Others have decided to flee, but often after years of wandering in the world they come back to the old mansion like Ulysses, to heal their wounds. However, most people hesitate, do not take a decision and try to reconcile freedom with their ancestral chains.

Postscript

Ever since the West appeared on the oriental stage, Middle Easterners have been constantly questioning themselves: how much authenticity (*asala*) should they maintain, and how far should they adapt to modernity (*hadatha*)? These questions have also been raised with regard to civil society.

Wajih Kawtharani drew a distinction between modern civil society (*al-mujtama' al-madani*) and traditional kinship society (*al-mujtama' al-ahli*) (Kawtharani, 1992: 120). He did not deny the fact that the latter served a purpose in its own time. He noted, however, that nowadays it may sow the seeds of division (ibid.: 130). On the other hand, Burhan Ghalioun believes that contrasting *al-mujtama' al-ahli* with *al-mujtama' al-madani* is a political attempt to counter Islamic fundamentalism and its traditional values as opposed to modern values promoted by *al-mujtama' al-madani*, consisting of political parties, trade unions and women's associations (Ghalioun, 1992: 734).

According to Saad Eddin Ibrahim's legalist definition, conditions have to be met to constitute *al-mujtama' al-madani* and kinship society (*al-jamaa al-qarabiyya*) fails to qualify on two grounds (Messarra, 1995: 5–6). First, civil society is a body of organizations constituted freely by members who joined on the basis of an agreement, and kinship society lacks this fundamental characteristic. This definition is quite restrictive: what of civil society that established itself spontaneously? The drafting of by-laws and the registration of statutes are certainly not the foundation acts of *al-mujtama' al-madani*.

Formalism is a legal requirement to adduce evidence, and civil society existed without the need to materialize in duly registered NGOs. Why should civil society take the formal structure of an association? The second ground for refusing the qualification civil society to a kinship group, according to Ibrahim, is that the free-will act that is required on joining *al-mujtama' al-madani* is not required on being born into a family or a tribe. Again, the definition is quite restrictive and the demarcation line is certainly blurred between kinship society and many NGOs that reproduce primordial ties and duplicate the identity and solidarity of the natural environment. What about the Lebanese lady who joins a charity organization, who takes care of the orphans of her own specific religious confession, and what about the southern Iraqi nurse who is helping through an informal association the deprived people of the tribe she was born in? Of course, this sort of action does not require a breach with the natural environment and people joining these associations do not feel they are betraying their 'society of cousins', but should we disregard this kind of civil society on the grounds that it is an extension of the 'primordial culture', whether tribal, sectarian or religious? Opposing the 'traditional' NGO is the 'ideological' one that implies a breach with religious, clanic or tribal solidarity. It is at this level that individuals transcend tradition and communal solidarities, choose a certain destiny and share with others a common myth (Foreseen, 1997: 37–8). A typical example is that of a Turkish lawyer who militates within an NGO in defence of Kurdish prisoners of opinion. She is taking risks, she has broken with her natural environment, which might provoke hostility. Between the 'traditional' and the 'ideological' NGO types lies civil society, with varying degrees of commitment. Both types are legitimate, even though the 'ideological' type requires or presupposes a hard choice, a conversion, and maybe a social price to pay. But that should not devalue the traditional elements of civil society, for these may be, as mentioned above, the last obstacles to an overwhelming Leviathan state.

In order to have a real civic society (not just a civil one), it is not enough just to have a religious brotherhood, a *waqf*, a syndicate, or even political parties and women's associations. It is not enough to have façade NGOism. Besides 'civility', effervescence is a must in a healthy 'civic' society, where associations should multiply like human cells. In his classic, *De la Démocratie en Amérique*, Alexis de Tocqueville wondered about the American way of life that consisted in associating without end:

> Les Américains de tous les âges, de toutes les conditions, de tous les esprits, s'unissent sans cesse. Non seulement ils ont des associations commerciales et industrielles auxquelles tous prennent part, mais ils en ont encore mille autres espèces: de religieuses, de morales, de graves, de futiles, de fort générales et de très particulières, d'immenses et de fort petites; les Américains s'associent pour donner des fêtes, fonder des séminaires, bâtir des auberges, élever des églises, répandre des livres, envoyer des missionnaires aux antipodes. (Tocqueville, 1981: 137)

But that was the New World, where people did not strain under the weight of tradition. In the Middle East, on the other hand, in spite of a noted pressure for change (Ibrahim, 1993: 304–5), the individual is still impeached, and it is not paradoxical to assert that traditional civil society, which has developed into a 'proto-civic' one, has already reached its most accomplished form.

NOTES

1. The author of this chapter is one of them.
2. The section on *Ahdath* relies mainly, if not exclusively, on Claude Cahen's contributions (see references).
3. This section on guilds and craftsmen owes a lot to the work by Professor André Raymond (see Bibliography), and also to a long and most rewarding conversation with him.
4. This section on Freemasons owes much to Jacob Katz's book *Hors du ghetto*, especially pages 35 to 63, where I found room for extrapolation.

Part III:

HUMAN RIGHTS: MEETING UNIVERSAL STANDARDS?

7

Human Rights and Democracy in the European Legal Order: The Euro-Mediterranean Partnership

JAMILA HOUFAIDI SETTAR

The Introduction of Human Rights and Democracy in European Foreign Policy

The introduction of human rights and democracy in European foreign policy was not an easy task. The difficulties encountered were first due to the divergences that emerged among the member states as to the importance to be assigned to human rights in the European Community's relationship with Mediterranean Partner Countries (MPCs) and, secondly, to the resistance MPCs put up to the inclusion of even the slightest reference to human rights in the agreements binding them to the European Community (EC) (Buirette-Maurau, 1985: 475).

Nevertheless, due to the pressure exerted by public opinion (both in Europe and in MPCs) and particularly by the European Parliament (EP), some progress was made in the form of a compromise between the positions of the parties concerned. This is how the first mention of human rights came to be included in the preamble of the Third Lomé Convention (1986). This provision was not legally binding. However, it enjoyed the assurances of the EC that it could lead to automatic suspension of development aid in case of violation of human rights.

The signing of the Fourth Lomé Convention (1989) was a further encouraging step, especially since clear reference to the United Nations Charter was made in the convention.[1] However, although this provision provided an undeniable legal foundation for the taking into consideration of human rights issues, it did not provide for the suspension of cooperation in the event of any significant breach. In fact, the EC gave a rather limited effect to this article. First, it did not really ensure that this provision was being adhered to in all circumstances, as it preferred to examine each situation in the light of a given situation. Second, Europe gave priority to democratization at the expense of human rights. In other words, it seemed that the EC was satisfied with the belief that a semblance of democracy existed in its African partners. In effect, the launching of the democratization process was more than enough to discharge oneself of one's moral duty. Even when such a process was brought to a halt, sanctions were lifted on a mere declaration that the democratization process had been resumed.

Moreover, the European Parliament, which adopted the same approach, distinguished between

- fundamental rights of human integrity and dignity, established by Articles 3 and 5 of the Universal Declaration of Human Rights. For this category, the EC does not tolerate any violation for whatever reason;
- economic and social rights that have a general value but whose implementation does not necessarily depend on factors within the control of the states; and
- civil and political rights that are, according to the Union, a matter of time (considering that it took Europe centuries before securing them): however, the EC offered to help in attaining these rights by linking them to development aid.

By splitting up these various aspects of human rights, the EC secured for itself a wide margin of appreciation, enabling it to assess every case on its own merits. As a matter of fact, cooperation was actually suspended only in cases of serious breaches of human rights. In less serious cases, it only froze some ongoing projects and launched a dialogue with a view to convincing governments to review their policies. At that time, security was defined in terms of absence of war. The European Union was mainly concerned with the stability of the African regimes, whereas respect for human rights was merely a political and ethical consideration.

The fall of communism in Eastern Europe had great repercussions on international law in general and human rights in particular and, due to these tremendous changes, the European Union introduced decisively in its foreign relations the obligation of respect for democracy and human rights. It is to be noted that, although the European Union did not pioneer these principles, it nevertheless contributed significantly to their affirmation in the international legal order prior to introducing them in its partnership relations.

The International Legal Order

While during the Cold War the law was excluded from standard rhetoric used to justify the situation, in the 'new world order' it made a comeback not only through the affirmation of the necessity to observe the law, but also through its use as criterion to determine legitimacy (Corten, 1996: 103).

Following the fall of the Berlin Wall, law represented an alternative method of legitimatization as opposed to the political justifications of the past. Therefore, the principles of international law were upgraded and came to be used as the source of any necessary justification. Any violation of human rights was thus construed as a threat to international peace, and the concept of peace became multi-dimensional. In addition to conventional military threats, this notion combines political, economic, cultural, social, environmental and technological elements. Moreover, the notion of multi-dimensional peace is flexible and changing. The quest for peace is directly linked to the protection of human rights, of the right to self-determination, to fighting terrorism, racism, fundamentalism and pollution.

Now, this new dimension of peace and security places human rights at the very centre of international relations, thus reinforcing Article 1 of the UN Charter, which sets forth, among the objectives of the organization, the 'respect for human rights and fundamental freedoms'. The new world order has brought about the universal acceptance of democracy and the necessity for all countries to abide by the same rules.

New Legal Instruments

The instruments under scrutiny in this paragraph do not hold the same legal value, however, they do confirm current trends in democracy and human rights issues that are contained in international legal instruments.

In 1990 the United Nations General Assembly adopted, for the first time, a resolution (45/150, Dec. 1990) calling for 'the reinforcement of the effectiveness of the principle of regular and fair elections' and providing some elements of definition for the notions of human rights and democracy. Moreover, the United Nations agreed to monitor and supervise electoral processes in a number of countries.[2] These trends are being affirmed in many other international fora.

At the Vienna meeting of the Conference for Security and Co-operation in Europe (CSCE) (before becoming the Organization for Security and Co-operation in Europe – OSCE) in January 1989, the participants declared that democracy is an inherent element to the notion of rule of law. They committed themselves to a democratic system based on free elections and rule of law and recognized the paramount importance of political pluralism. At CSCE level, the Copenhagen Declaration of 29 June 1990 and that of the Paris Conference of 21 November 1991 asserted the human dimension of the cooperation process of the organization under the three principles of human rights, political pluralism and rule of law. In the Paris Charter the European governments considered that democracy is the only acceptable system of government for CSCE member states. They described this *acquis démocratique* as irreversible. By adopting this charter, CSCE member states pledged to build, sustain, consolidate and reinforce democracy as the only system of government for their nations. This commitment was reiterated in Moscow in October 1991, when the member states declared that democracy should be the cornerstone of the international community. In Helsinki in 1992 the CSCE officially and formally declared that human rights concern all states and do not fall within the exclusive remit of domestic affairs.

The preamble of the Paris Agreement of 1990 providing for the setting-up of the European Bank for Reconstruction and Development referred to democracy, political pluralism, democratic institutions, human rights and rule of law. According to the first article of the agreement, the Bank is to contribute 'to the progress and reconstruction of the countries of Eastern and Central Europe who pledge to respect and implement the principles of political pluralism, democracy and market economy'.

In a similar way, the declaration adopted in Vienna on 25 June 1993 by the World Conference on Human Rights refers to democracy that is 'based on the freely expressed will of the people to determine their own political, economic, social and cultural system and fully participate in all aspects of community life'.

This approach reminds us of the prescriptions of European Court case law (in the Handyside case), which consider that

> a society is democratic when pluralism, tolerance and open-mindedness are effectively translated in its institutional regime, when the latter is submitted to the principle of supremacy of law, when it contains essentially an efficient control mechanism of the executive power implemented, without prejudice to parliamentary control and scrutiny, by an independent judiciary and when it ensures the respect of the human being.[3]

Therefore, in the 1990s the concept of democracy challenged the state's functions of protection of individuals' and peoples' rights and has acquired a universal dimension that is shared by all human beings and which justifies and legitimates the intervention of one and all in matters that concern the whole of humankind. This new concept is being given greater consideration by international law.

Traditional Principles of International Law

The post-communist era gave a new lease of life to human rights in the principles of international law. A brief analysis of these principles is provided here to stress this evolution.

Sovereignty When analysing the Universal Declaration of Human Rights, Virally wrote in 1983 that 'international law homes in straight into the shrine of sovereignty' (Virally, 1983: 123). For this author 'sovereignty is determined by rights belonging to subjects of law other than the states: international law evolves then from an inter-state law, drawn up according to the interests of the states, to supranational law, with the aim of ensuring, in the name of the common and supreme values of states, the protection of interests within the states themselves (those of the individuals living under the national authority)' (ibid.).

Ultimately, the logic behind these developments should theoretically lead to a new definition of international law that would affirm the legal monism propounded by Georges Scelle, according to which man is a subject of both international and national laws (Sudre, 1997: 46). International law shall be no longer defined as the law of the community of states but as the law of the universal human community and shall include two main parts: on the one hand, the fundamental status of man within diverse state entities, and, on the other, the laws governing inter-state relations.

These revolutionary changes had already had a practical effect on the European continent due to European instruments and mechanisms protecting human rights. Now they affect the international community as a whole. Gone are the days when Nicolas Politis said 'the sovereign state was like an iron cage for its subjects, who could have no legal contacts outside its perimeter except through very narrow bars' (Politis, 1927: 91).

The new international order opens doors wide for new stakeholders. Today, beyond the rhetoric that confirms the role of the state as the guardian of human rights, there is 'the duty of the international community, namely, universal, international or regional organizations, to take over from defaulting states'. Thus, beyond the states many actors are becoming powerful international players *per se*. Therein lies, declared Boutros Boutros Ghali, the then secretary-general of the United Nations, 'a legal and institutional framework which is not disturbing in the least and which does not seem to undermine the modern definition of sovereignty' (Boutros Ghali, 1993).

Constitutional Autonomy The 1970 Declaration on the Principles Governing Peaceful Relationships between States provided a general definition of the concept of constitutional autonomy: 'all states are free to choose and develop their political, economic, social and cultural systems'.

The International Court of Justice (ICJ) made some important advancements in the western Sahara issue. It clearly stated that 'there is no provision in international law that requires the state to have a given structure as this is evidenced by the diversity of state structures presently existing in the world'.[4] The same court commented in the case of military and paramilitary activities in Nicaragua that 'the adherence of a state to a specific doctrine is not in violation of international customary law'. A different conclusion would, according to the court, deprive of its meaning the fundamental principle of sovereignty of the states (a principle upon which all international law is based) and the freedom of the state to choose its own political, social, cultural and economic system.[5]

The findings of the ICJ translated the principle of peaceful coexistence that is enshrined in international law. However, since the downfall of the communist system and the establishment of a single political system at international level, the domestic organization of states is being approached in different terms, especially with regard to its implications on the keeping of peace and security at national, regional and, consequently, international levels. It is defined on the basis of a number of parameters that may secure the requirement of security. So much so that respect of democracy, rule of law and human rights directly derive from the respect of the United Nations Charter, as well as of other international commitments, thus reducing the choice in terms of domestic political organization. The evolution of international relations, even when it stresses respect for distinct cultural models of other societies, does not prevent 'other common values from becoming universal and established by general international law' (Bennouna, 1993: 46).

At the Vienna Conference on 14 June 1993 Boutros Boutros Ghali clearly reaffirmed the universal character of human rights, which was also the first item on the agenda at the conference. According to Boutros Ghali, this notion of universality is 'inherent' in the very concept of human rights. It cannot be decreed and 'is not an expression of some sort of ideological domination of a group of states over the rest of the world community' (Boutros Ghali, 1993).

Exclusive Areas of Competence   According to the Institute of International Law, exclusive areas of competence are those of state activities in which state competence is not bound to international law.[6] Nowadays, this is a well-established legal concept.

'Whether an issue lies within an exclusive area of competence of a state or not is a relative question: it depends on the development of international relations.'[7] The extent of this area varies according to the evolution of law. It means that 'international law evolves as a result of the behaviour of states through their normal conventional practices (conclusion of treaties in new areas) or their support for activities and initiatives of international organizations'.[8] Now, it is generally agreed that current state practices, at least by those able to assert themselves in the international arena, aim at protecting democracy and human rights directly by means of existing legal instruments. We also know that most states adhered to the various international instruments protecting human rights when these had a weak enforcement obligation.

Moreover, according to the definition of the International Law Institute, 'when an international commitment is taken in a matter falling under an exclusive area of competence, no party to said commitment may oppose the exceptional character of the exclusive area reserved for any issue relating to the interpretation or implementation of the said commitment'.[9]

Considering the importance of the instruments of human rights protection and the development, on that basis, of legal rules and practices, one can conclude that respect for the basic rights of individuals has clearly been excluded from areas of reserved state competence.

Speaking about Somalia in 1991, the UN secretary-general declared that 'one cannot lock oneself in the dilemma of the respect for sovereignty/protection of human rights. The United Nations should avoid any new ideological controversy. It is not the right of intervention that is at stake, it is the collective obligation of the states to provide help in situations of emergency where human rights are in danger.'[10]

Peoples' Rights   This principle is entrenched in Article 1 of the United Nations Charter and established by the Declaration on the Granting of Independence to Colonial Countries and Peoples. It is considered as the right of peoples to set up their own state.[11]

Whatever the opinion of those who thought that the right to self-determination was no longer relevant once decolonization was achieved, the concept of peoples' rights also incorporates an aspiration for democracy. By virtue of the Paris Charter for a New Europe and the World Declaration on Human Rights, the right to self-determination, which was recognized as a collective right, produces effects for individuals through the introduction of the right of peoples to choose freely their political institutions and leaders.

Moreover, it is also applied on a sub-national level through the right of national, ethnic, language and religious minorities (GA Res. 47/35, 18.12.1992) and the right of peoples to determine their own political status.

Recognition   This is merely the act whereby a state 'taking note of the existence of certain facts ... declares or implicitly accepts to consider them as the basis on which it will establish its legal relationships' (Sirey, 1960: 506). Such an act has become a unique opportunity for reminding newly formed states that the observance of certain criteria in their political organization shall condition the recognition of their statehood.

Hence, the member states of the European Community adopted on 16 December 1991 a declaration containing 'guidelines' for the recognition of new states in the former Soviet Union and Central and Eastern Europe. These guidelines subject the recognition of new states that emerged from the collapse of the Eastern Bloc to the respect for human rights, democracy and rule of law. Although this EU declaration has only a 'political bearing', it 'paves the way for recognition'. It intervenes within the framework of Article 20 of the Single European Act, which stipulates that 'the determination of common positions is a point of reference for all contracting parties', and assumes, on the basis of the expressed intent of the member states of the EU, the pressure they may exert on the new states (Charpentier, 1992: 343).

Indeed, pressure is at issue here. 'If the Twelve [now Fifteen] use recognition as a means of pressure in order to obtain some commitments, this must by no means be viewed as unorthodox, provided that the states concerned are free to express their refusal and if the commitment required is not contrary to the precepts of the international law' (ibid.: 353).

The conditions laid out in the European 'guidelines' are crystal clear; the aim is to lock the states formed after the collapse of communism into a network of formal commitments in order to ensure they respect the rules of democracy. In order to avoid the problem that conditions relating to the internal organization of states are contrary to the principle of constitutional autonomy and state sovereignty, the conditions were defined with reference to international commitments. Thus, respect for human rights, democracy and rule of law is presented as resulting from the observance of the UN Charter, the Universal Declaration on Human Rights and all other international human rights instruments as well as commitments in the framework of the OSCE.[12]

The Establishment of Human Rights in the European Legal Order

As from 1991 the EC introduced human rights and democracy in its relations with developing countries (resolution of 28 November 1991). The insertion of a human rights clause in all cooperation agreements with MPCs established respect of human rights and democracy as the 'foundations' of cooperation relations.

In 1992 an essential human rights clause was introduced in agreements between the EC and Brazil, the Andean Pact countries, the Baltic states and Albania. This provision gives a true normative effect to the principle of human rights and democracy in the agreements signed by the EU. In fact, by virtue of the provision mentioned above, the EU might consider any serious and sustained violation of human rights as a breach of an essential component of the agreement as provided in the Vienna Convention of 1969 on the Law of the Treaties. Thus, it may suspend or even terminate the agreement.

In its report on worldwide human rights (April 1995), the EP took a substantial and innovative initiative when it devoted the last part of the report to the promotion of democracy as the basis of the Common Foreign and Security Policy (CFSP). Furthermore, on the eve of the Inter-governmental Conference of 1996, it called for the merging of the foreign policies of all EU members (commercial, development and cooperation policies and CFSP) within the framework of one common policy based on the respect for human dignity. Since the Single European Act of 1987, the powers of the EP have increased significantly in the area of human rights, enabling it to oppose accession treaties and association agreements as well as financial protocols by refusing to give its assent. The EP asserted this right in the case of Morocco, Syria, Turkey and Israel.

Article F, paragraph 1 of the Maastricht Treaty states that 'the Union shall respect fundamental rights and the rights of peoples and minorities'. A clause was adopted by the EC on 21 March 1995 enabling the EU to suspend agreements concluded with MPCs as soon as it happens that they are violating those rights set out in the Universal Declaration on Human Rights.

Human Rights and Democracy within the
Euro-Mediterranean Partnership

If, for a long time, Europe was built without any reference to the Mediterranean, as soon as a new concept of security emerged, the EU announced at the European Council of Lisbon in 1992 that the 'Maghreb constitutes the Southern frontier of the Union' and adopted the concept of a 'Euro-Mediterranean Partnership' (EMP).

In its Communication to the Council and the EP on 1 July 1990, the European Commission reaffirmed its 'conviction that geographical proximity and the intensity of its relations of whatever nature, make the stability and prosperity of Mediterranean Non-Member Countries (MNCs) essential elements for the Community itself'. According to the conclusions of the Commission, 'the aggravation of the economic and social gap between the Community and MNCs on account of their respective levels of development would be intolerable to the Community itself' – in the sense that its security lies at stake.

In the beginning of the 1990s it became expedient for Europe to include neighbouring states within a framework guaranteeing peace and stability and to give them the legal and institutional instruments likely to sow the seeds of development. The Commission's opinions on the applications for membership of the Central and Eastern European countries to the EU require that candidate countries possess stable institutions that guarantee democracy, the supremacy of human rights, the existence of a market economy, the ability to withstand the pressures of competition due to the internal market, and to assume the obligations resulting from membership.

The EMP, which was launched in Barcelona in 1995 by the 15 EU member states and 12 Mediterranean partners, can be seen in similar terms. In fact, since the end of the Cold War liberal democracy has become the only legitimate political regime in the West. Therefore, Europe considers its safety guaranteed only if it is surrounded by other democracies.

In its Mediterranean policy, Europe declared the need to have at its frontiers countries and peoples who 'share the same democratic values, as well as a high level of prosperity'. Thus, in this perspective, it became 'indispensable to reinforce cooperation in the Mediterranean basin'.[13] Once the rules of the game were laid out, the EU proposed that its own founding values (democratic principles, respect for human rights, rule of law, political pluralism and economic liberalism) be inserted in the dialogue that it would open with its Mediterranean partners. These clauses are now incorporated in the association agreements between the EU and its partners. Any violation will warrant the application of the regulations of the Vienna Convention on the Law of the Treaties regarding the essential violation of an agreement.

In the same line of thinking, the EMP turned democracy into a cornerstone. It also entrenched the concept of conditionality. Partners must commit themselves to respect and develop the rule of law, human rights, fundamental freedoms, democracy, pluralism and diversity. In addition, it established a right of scrutiny leaving the way open for possible exchanges of information and for responding to requests for information made to different partners.

The Evolution of the Moroccan Legal Order

Morocco's association with the EU is based (according to the agreement) on historical links and values common to both partners. Its very foundations can be traced in the importance attached to respecting the principles of the United Nations Charter of Human Rights and Political and Economic Freedoms. It takes into consideration the progress accomplished by Morocco with regard to its aspiration to form an integral part of the global economy and of the community of democratic states.

'Nowadays, Morocco is witnessing a new step in its current history, a step marked by the establishment of a forward-looking democracy, carrying forth a spirit of progress likely to enhance the formation of a free, harmonious society mobilized to fully promote its human potential.'[14] The democratization process initiated in Morocco after many long, dark years helped to register 'important achievements in line with the principles aimed at establishing human rights, and in a lawful context, at restoring justice through the enforcement of its prerogative as supreme guarantor of such rights' (Youssoufi, 1998). The process was accomplished through significant institutional and legislative reforms. It resulted in the constitutional establishment of human rights as universally recognized through the signature or approval of various relevant international agreements, including the conventions on civil and political rights, on economic social and cultural rights, on the fight against torture, on the prohibition of discrimination against women, on the protection of children's rights and on the protection of migrant workers and members of their families. Political measures were also taken to grant the liberation of 'missing persons' and of practically all political prisoners, as well as the return of exiles and improved conditions of imprisonment.

Decentralization, the exercise of power at local level, participation in decision-making, consolidation of the rule of law, control of public spending, transparency, raising ethical standards of administration, equal opportunities, gender equality, civil society and initiatives by citizens – these and others are notions that in Morocco for a long time were considered taboo and are nowadays the subject of many debates.

Moreover, the creation in 1993 of a ministry in charge of human rights entrusted to a well-known activist for human rights confirmed, according to those in charge of this department, 'the institutional integration of respect, defence and promotion of human rights within government policy'.[15]

Morocco has been mobilized to 'on the one hand, implement all the texts directly or indirectly related to human rights and to work with a view to fill legislative gaps, and, on the other hand, to remove all that is misleading or likely to create ambiguities as regards executive and judicial powers' (ibid.). These declarations by governmental representatives are in reply to the increasing requests to claim the strengthening of the state of law. The government is now for the first time addressed by associations on issues such as corruption, women's rights, and the reform of legislation against human rights.[16]

Beyond these legal reforms, the combat undertaken has a much more general bearing, and participants (citizens, companies, political organizations or associations) converging towards the same objective have increased in number.

Conclusions

The Flexibility of the Concept of Democracy

The adherence of EU partners to the principles of human rights through different legal instruments is not always a choice. It is partly due to changes wrought on the international scene and can be explained by the economic precariousness that makes southern countries all the more dependent on foreign aid.

This situation is summed up in a declaration made by a European official who explained that 'ACP countries immediately understood that we were going to be more and more obdurate ... once the Soviet Union had been dismantled, they could no longer resort to the same means to exert pressure on us and at this stage we had too many friends and not enough money.'

As a result, the universalism of human rights remains an element of political discourse far removed from reality. Moreover, implementation of this theory is problematic for those advocating it, who find their principles contradicted. Their will to impose the same values on all states across the globe irrespective of their culture and social conditions calls to mind the methods deployed by a single party in the domestic political order.

Moreover, there is a patent contradiction between the assertion of the universalism of human rights as established in declarations and international covenants and the right of intervention claimed by the great powers. The universal promotion of human rights is a method that can be developed only in concrete, specific and varied situations. It may not be the fruit of any messianic or hegemonic persuasion (Chavrin and Sueur, 1997: 45).

Are we speaking of democracy *erga omnes*? Immediately after the Second World War, western European democracies asked themselves whether political parties propounding extremist ideologies should be tolerated or banned. They recalled that the Nazis rose to power through democratic means but then defeated the democratic mechanism of alternation.

In order to protect democracy, western lawyers had then drawn a distinction between the rules of procedure and the rules that form the unchangeable bulk of a constitution. The latter set out by constituent powers may not, by virtue of the principle of parallelism of form, be modified except by the people. Therefore, outlawing an extremist party that risks to distort this democratic rule is not an exception but rather the application of the democratic rule to which this extremist adheres.

Hence the banning of parties that constituted a threat to democracy was permitted. Such a ban was based on international instruments safeguarding human rights. In fact, Article 5, section 1 of the United Nations Covenant on Civil and Political Rights states that 'no provision of this Covenant may be construed as implying for a state, a group or an individual, the right to perform an activity or an act whose objective is to destroy the rights and freedoms recognized in this Covenant or to exert greater limitations on those provided under the said Covenant'. European instruments safeguarding human rights establish the same exception.

These conditional rights grant states a fair margin of latitude in the means they wish to deploy to exercise such rights. The European Court of Human Rights recognizes that 'the national legislator enjoys certain powers of appreciation. It [the court] certainly is not empowered to replace the judgement of national authorities by suggesting an alternative appreciation of what could be the best policy to follow in this area.'[17]

Elsewhere, in a case concerning the removal of foreigners, the court stresses 'its awareness of state interest ... It does not hesitate to legitimate the action taken by the states for the sake of "safeguarding" public order and to expressly justify the delivery of an order of removal, i.e. as a justified response to criminal activities of various sorts' (Labayle, 1997: 998).

In the Chahal versus the United Kingdom case of 15 November 1996, the European judge, when discussing the exercise of fundamental freedoms, underlined the 'enormous difficulties encountered by the states in our time to protect their populations from terroristic violence'.

On the one hand, the European notion of widening or narrowing the margin of appreciation depends on whether or not a common denominator may be observed among the different legal systems constituting the Council of Europe. As a result, it may not take into account the specificities of non-European states. On the other hand, different variations of case law on the extent of the margin of appreciation assign a purely relative value to the notion of a democratic society. In fact, limitations may be imposed if they are inspired by the need to safeguard national security, public safety, public order, health or morals, the rights and freedoms of others and so on. Thus, European countries are able to enjoy a substantial degree of latitude according to the situation. Double standards may even be used according to the interests at stake (e.g. the EC's very ambiguous attitude towards Algeria, Turkey and China).

Pluralism is 'an ideology that recognizes no unique ideal but claims the right for several ways of thinking to exist'.[18] At any rate, whatever the normative value of such a principle on an international level, its effectiveness remains a function of the diplomatic interests of the great powers. It is a well-known fact that diplomacy is always eager to restore 'the argument of opportunity, however hard it may be to reconcile it with the defence of human rights' (Badie, 1999: 264).

Democracy, Problems of Implementation

In order to conform to the new order, some Mediterranean partners have adopted political reforms that, however, require economic reforms with burdensome consequences. In this respect Morocco is an important case.

The structural adjustment programme adopted by some countries since the end of the 1980s, the development strategies implemented here and there during the last two decades, as well as the effort required to upgrade policies to meet the deadlines set for the EMP, have worn out the economies of the southern countries. The worsening of social disparities, regional gaps, unemployment, illiteracy and so on contribute to slowing down the fulfilment of the central objective of the EMP (security through the development and respect of human rights).

Nothing in the EU conception of partnership indicates any sort of relation between economic development and the protection of human rights. In other words, there is no order of priority for the fulfilment of the EMP's objectives. Such an observation is full of consequences as to the commitments taken by virtue of these agreements.

If one were to consider that the development of countries that are presently developed (including the new industrialized countries in south-east Asia) was accomplished at the expense of breaches of civil, political, economic and social rights, it could be very tempting to conclude that economic development comes prior to respect for human rights. This modernization theory, applied for several decades during the Cold War, allowed the western powers, for geo-political reasons, to close their eyes to the most staunch dictatorial regimes of the Third World, and financial institutions to implement their policies. Nevertheless, it did not lead to the expected levels of development.

At the same time, this theory raises the question of the intrinsic value of economic and social rights as an essential component of the protection system of human rights and, consequently, results in the fragmentation of human rights. Such a belief may allow for all sorts of abuses. Is it possible to imagine the EU suspending a partnership agreement for such a reason? In fact, in this case, the legal value of a universal principle cannot be applied unless it is compatible with the interests vested in each type of relationship.

At their present stage of economic and social development, the Mediterranean partners are not all in a position to implement either the economic and social rights, or the political and civil ones. As Mohamed Tozy rightly said when writing about political change in Morocco, this change is linked with 'a declaration of intent highlighting the discrepancies, the hurdles or the gaps. In fact, we are dealing with a complex process that is subject to change and which needs to be consolidated even in the soundest democracies. Temptations to resort to authoritarian methods are co-substantial with the democratic practices because the latter are artificial' (Tozy, 1999).

NOTES

1. Article 5.
2. In Namibia (Resolutions 632 and 640, 1989), in Nicaragua (Resolutions 637, 1989), in Haiti (Resolution 45/2, 1990).
3. Handyside Judgment 7 December1979. See also *Sunday Times* Judgment, 26 May 1979, § 66.
4. ICJ Opinion 1975, Rec. 1975/4, pp. 43–4.
5. ICJ Judgment, 27 June 1986, Military and para-military activities in Nicaragua, § 263, Rec. 1986, p. 133.
6. *Annuaire de l'Institut de Droit International*, 1954, vol. 45, II, p. 292.
7. Cour Permanente de Justice Internationale, *Décrets de nationalité*, B series, no. 4, p. 24.
8. Patrick Failler, Alain Pellet, DIP LGDJ-DELTA 1994, p. 426.
9. *Annuaire de l'Institut de Droit International*, 1954, vol. 45, II, p. 292.
10. Report on the 1991 organization's activities.
11. Resolution 1514, XV of 14 December 1960.
12. See article by Alain Pellet AFDI 1991, and H. R. Fabre AFDI 1992.
13. *Stratégie en Méditerranée*, Assemblée parlementaire (Strasbourg, Editions du Conseil de l'Europe Débats, 1995), pp. 69–70.
14. Son Altesse Royale, current King of Morocco, 'National Information Day', *Le Matin*, 20 November 1998.
15. First Report on the Implementation of the Convention on Children's Rights, Ministry of Human Rights, June 1995, p. 11.
16. Memorandum addressed to the prime minister by the Anti-Corruption Associations group dated 10 December1998.
17. Klass judgment 6 September 1978.
18. *Dictionnaire de la pensée politique*, Hommes et idées (Paris, Hatier, 1989).

8

Human Rights in the Framework of the Euro-Mediterranean Partnership: Overcoming the Culturalist–Universalist Divide

ABDELWAHAB BIAD

Introduction

The new interest expressed by Europe in its Mediterranean rim is linked to its perception of the risks to its security and stability. Once the Cold War was over and the corresponding threat, which was purely military in character, had been defused, the West spotted new risks of a 'multi-dimensional' and 'multi-directional' nature[1] stemming mainly from the South and taking different forms: the proliferation of weapons of mass destruction, terrorism or Islamism. Claims that a 'green peril' has supplanted the 'red peril' have been propounded not only in intellectual circles (Huntington, 1993b; 1996: 367) but also in western official fora and in particular NATO.[2] On the other side of the Mediterranean, the Gulf War has hardly contributed to improving the image of the western world as perceived in the South. Besides criticizing the West for its arrogance and its attempts to impose a new dominant international order, 'double standards' are traditionally denounced in the application of international law, cultural hegemony and political interference.

In the face of the risks implied by the widening gap between the two shores of the Mediterranean as far as development and mutual perceptions are concerned, it is imperative, now more than ever, to set up a global dialogue between North and South to discuss security and cooperation. Hence, the initiative the European Union (EU) took in 1995 to launch a partnership to enter into such a dialogue with its Mediterranean neighbours[3] was perceived rather well by the Arab world, weakened as it was at the time by the loss of its Soviet ally, partitioned on account of the Gulf War and shaken by a deep economic and political crisis.

The 27 countries participating at the Euro-Mediterranean Conference of Foreign Ministers convened in Barcelona in November 1995 adopted an important declaration defining the contents and objectives of the Euro-Mediterranean Partnership (EMP). Hence, the EMP appears to be an instrument of preventive diplomacy aimed at reinforcing security and stability in the Mediterranean on the basis of good neighbourly relations.[4] The EMP's main objectives are to create an area of peace and stability in the Mediterranean, to establish a free trade area by 2010 and to foster dialogue (including human rights and democracy issues) among peoples in the region.

Thus, in the preamble of the Barcelona Declaration, the participants declare that the EMP's general objective 'requires a strengthening of democracy and respect for human rights, sustainable and balanced economic and social development, measures to combat poverty and promotion of greater understanding between cultures'.

Human rights are mentioned more specifically in the first and third chapters of the Barcelona Declaration. In the first chapter, which is based on a Political and Security Partnership, participants make a number of commitments relating to security and human rights. In the third chapter, which is concerned with a Social, Cultural and Human Partnership, emphasis is laid on intercultural dialogue and human exchange with a view to improving mutual perceptions. As for the second chapter, comprising the Economic and Financial Partnership, also known as the 'engine' of the EMP, this involves a number of potential implications for those human rights resulting from reforms that are necessary for furthering economic transition and setting up a free trade area.

It is clear that the human rights issue is a major cause of concern within the EMP. Its inclusion among the principles and rules governing the EMP was the outcome of minimal political consensus. In fact, a background discussion in favour of a universalist alternative to cultural specificity ceaselessly divides European and Arab partners.

Human Rights: Minimal Consensus

Participants in the Barcelona Process undertake to carry out a 'strengthened political dialogue at regular intervals, based on the observance of essential principles of international law'.[5] It is obvious that some of the essential principles of international law concern the protection of human rights as defined principally in the Universal Declaration of 1948 and in the two covenants of 1966. To this end, the first paragraph of the chapter on the Political and Security Partnership stipulates that EMPs must undertake to 'act in accordance with the United Nations Charter and the Universal Declaration of Human Rights'. The declaration contains a list of the rights and freedoms of individuals that must be implemented by the states.

The Barcelona Declaration lists a number of rights and freedoms that were accepted by consensus, and insists on the role of civil society. It also suggests a number of concrete actions that fall short of the initial expectations.

Some Commonly Recognized Rights

The Barcelona Declaration contains explicit mention of a number of human rights,[6] including:

- freedom of expression;
- freedom of association;
- fundamental social rights;
- freedom of thought, conscience and religion; and
- non-discrimination.

The Universal Declaration of Human Rights provides for 'the right to freedom of opinion and expression'.[7] The Barcelona text contains no mention of freedom of opinion, a concept likely to be deemed unacceptable by the majority of southern regimes, who still consider it an undermining factor of state authority, indeed, a divisive element of the *Umma* (community of believers). By contrast, recognition of 'freedom of expression' does not seem problematic. In fact, it has been explicitly laid out in the text. Nevertheless, freedom of opinion and freedom of expression are so intimately linked that any attempt to separate them, as in the Declaration, is utterly absurd. Thus, in theory citizens may be free to express themselves but may not have an opinion! Recognition of freedom of expression is in itself positive, but in some southern countries there is no guarantee that it can be exercised.

Another human right that enjoys relative consensus is the right to 'freedom of association'. Hence, the free constitution of associations 'for peaceful purposes' is explicitly recognized in compliance with Article 20 of the Universal Declaration. However, this Article also provides for 'freedom of assembly',[8] which is not included in the Barcelona Declaration. Once again, the southern states are behind this omission. Not all of them have constitutionalized freedom of assembly,[9] perhaps out of fear that it may induce a higher degree of politicization. It is worth recalling that the recognition of 'freedom of association' is relative in so far as it is exercised at all times within the scope of existing legislation. Therefore, it is subject to prior authorization. Thus, it is up to the government concerned to evaluate on a case-by-case basis how freedom of association may be exercised. Bureaucratic hurdles to the establishment of independent associations may constitute a dissuading factor.

The Declaration mentions the protection of 'fundamental social rights'. How is 'fundamental' to be construed? In what way is this category different from other social rights? As these rights are not explicitly set out, each of the participating states is responsible for giving them an appropriate definition. Hence, the reference to economic and social rights unexpectedly places many southern and northern countries in a situation that is not in line with the relevant covenant of 1966. In fact, few countries may pride themselves on ensuring the enjoyment by their population of the right to work, accommodation, health and education.

The Barcelona Declaration also refers to 'freedom of thought, conscience and religion' as well as non-discrimination 'on grounds of race, nationality, language, religion or sex'. Nevertheless, although these principles seem to have been set out as a result of general consensus, the issue may present some very diverging positions between Europeans and Arabs in terms of cultural specificity. This problem will be dwelt upon in further detail later. The specificity issue also helps to explain the absence of so-called 'personal safety' rights, which concern the administration of justice, an area regulated in many Arab countries by Islamic law. All in all, the inclusion of these commonly recognized rights in a text regarding the EMP is a good initiative in itself. However, their implementation is subject to the existence of proactive civil societies.

The Driving Role Entrusted to Civil Society

EMPs undertake to encourage 'actions of support for democratic institutions and for the strengthening of the rule of law and civil society'.[10] Thus, they undertake not only to respect human rights but also to ensure they are actually exercised. The obligation here is not only to provide the means but also to ensure the outcome. In this respect, it is generally recognized that one of the guarantees for the implementation of human rights lies in a well-structured civil society.

The Barcelona Declaration underlines 'the essential contribution civil society can make in the process of development of the Euro-Mediterranean Partnership and as an essential factor of greater understanding and closeness between peoples'.[11] Decentralized cooperation, which is mentioned in the Barcelona Declaration, purports specifically to 'encourage the actions between those active in development', in particular, civil society operators such as academics, religious representatives, trade unionists and private individuals.[12] In this regard, emphasis is laid especially on youth exchanges as a 'means to prepare future generations for a closer cooperation between the Euro-Mediterranean partners'.[13]

With a view to furthering the dialogue, periodic meetings are proposed among non-governmental actors as well as common actions in the areas of cultural and creative heritage through theatre and film co-productions, translations and other means of cultural dissemination.[14] Clearly, a large and representative NGO presence within the EMP will be the key to its success.

The role of the media has been highlighted with regard to the responsibility of civil society actors in furthering dialogue between civilizations. Thus, Arab countries have often criticized the western media for their negative processing of information on the Arab Muslim world, the Gulf War being a prime example. They feel that the media contribute to disseminating stereotypes and negative images of Islam, which, as a result, add further fuel to mutual negative perceptions in the Mediterranean. The third chapter states in this regard that the media may play a pivotal role in the 'reciprocal recognition and understanding of cultures as a source of mutual enrichment'. The Barcelona Work Programme calls for close media interaction.

'Appropriate training' in human rights issues for civil society representatives is expressly stated among the commitments taken by the parties, but for opposite reasons. European countries intended to consolidate human rights as a whole, including the recognition of these rights by the citizens, while most Arab countries used this as an argument to emphasize that southern societies are lagging behind when it comes to implementing human rights. As a result, this very implementation may be delayed on the grounds that a whole generation needs to be educated beforehand in this area.

Within the framework of the EMP, in 1996 a programme of cooperation, MEDA Democracy, was launched on the initiative of the EP. Its specific objective is to promote human rights in the southern Mediterranean countries. The 62 projects developed by MEDA Democracy include human rights training and education activities.[15] Actions supported by this programme are modest in comparison with present needs, but this is an observation that can be made more generally about the implementation of the Barcelona Action Plan.

The Action Plan: Very Limited Results

The Action Plan annexed to the Barcelona Declaration includes five annexes. The first one is based on 'strengthening stability and democratic institutions'. In this respect, the document calls for the development of an understanding of issues pertaining to internal and external stability with the aim of aligning different points of view regarding the means to strengthen democracy, rule of law, human rights and fundamental freedoms. Thus, participants undertake to exchange information about human rights, fundamental freedoms, racism and xenophobia.[16] A questionnaire on this subject addressed to the High Officials Group was drawn up on the EU's initiative.[17] This information-sharing exercise is intended to serve as a confidence-building measure among partners.

At the second Euro-Mediterranean Conference of Foreign Ministers in Malta (April 1997), participants noted that some progress had been made by the High Officials Group in drawing up Annex 1 of the Action Plan, thereby implicitly acknowledging that the drafting of this annex still encountered difficulties. In fact, this document limits itself to mentioning as operational measures an information exchange on adherence to human rights instruments and a 'presentation by the Arab Group of the Islamic Declaration of Human Rights'. Clearly, the discussion on human rights is essentially confined to an exchange based on reciprocal perceptions of and approaches to the issue. It is therefore concerned with the sensitive problem of cultural specificity, for which the Action Plan advocates 'full respect'.

Human Rights: Discussion on Specificity

Even before the Barcelona Conference, the EP, in a resolution adopted on 31 July 1995, recommended that the EU presidency take a decisive stand in discussions on defining values of the European Union such as human rights, democracy, social justice and the rule of law, while at the same time being careful to take account of the ideas and values of our future partners so as to achieve a fruitful and useful debate. (European Parliament, 1995)

As for the Arab countries, although they declare their recognition of the interest of promoting human rights, they nevertheless deem that this issue must not serve as a cover-up for interference in their internal affairs, or as a breach of their system of values. Hence, national sovereignty and cultural specificity are two key arguments presented by the Arab countries that, incidentally, have given rise to an alternative rhetoric about human rights.

Respect for Sovereignty

Respect for sovereignty is a recurrent theme in the rhetoric used by developing countries when discussing human rights. Sovereignty acts as a shield, as it were protecting small countries from the pressure they feel they are subject to from great powers, especially in the area of human rights. In this respect, the Barcelona Declaration acknowledges that each state has the right 'to choose and freely develop its own political, socio-cultural, economic and judicial system'. This formulation is aimed at allaying the fears of the Arab nations as regards non-interference in areas of state sovereignty. The reference in the Barcelona Declaration to principles of international law relating to 'sovereign equality', to 'rights inherent to sovereignty' or to 'non-intervention in internal affairs'[18] is the result of the same effort to reassure those states that are mindful of their sovereignty.

Thus, it is clear that any form of pressure or political intervention criticizing, warning or carrying recommendations as to how human rights must be respected is considered unacceptable, irrespective of its origin. As a result, there are fundamental differences in approach of Arab and European partners. The latter consider that governments guilty of large-scale and systematic breaches of human rights may not invoke sovereignty to protect themselves and must account for their actions before the international community. Arab countries adopt a radically different perspective, which consists of proclaiming the supremacy of sovereignty over human rights. They reject, in practice, the notion of the 'right of intervention' (Bettati, 1996: 382). In this respect, the Barcelona Declaration contains a formulation that is relatively favourable to 'sovereignists' in so far as it invites states to 'refrain, in accordance with the rules of international law, from any direct or indirect intervention in the internal affairs of another partner'.[19]

Those who support the concept of the supremacy of sovereignty over human rights argue that in certain circumstances where the security and stability of the state are threatened, they have the right to override the human rights system. This position mainly concerns terrorism. Although the fight against terrorism enjoys the support of practically all EMP participants (states have undertaken to cooperate further in this area), this has sometimes served as an excuse to justify serious breaches of human rights.

Everybody is aware that the repression of terrorism is sometimes waged at a high cost for citizens' rights and freedoms. The case of Algeria provides a striking example. This country justified its suspension of the application of the 1966 Convention on Civil and Political Rights and of Protocol 1, to which it is party, on the grounds of national security. Algeria, supported by Egypt and indirectly by Israel, is responsible for the inclusion of a reference in the Barcelona Declaration to anti-terrorist cooperation that is to be considered 'a priority' in the Euro-Mediterranean Work Programme.[20] To this end a series of common measures were identified ranging from the sharing of intelligence to the assistance and training of anti-terrorist units.[21]

Besides the argument of respect for sovereignty, Arab countries invoke the prescriptions of Islam particularly in civil and criminal matters, which enables them to depart from the universal system of human rights.

Specificity

Bearing in mind that the Barcelona Process implies an ever-increasing interdependence between the EU and its Mediterranean partners, the Arab states succeeded in having an explicit reference to the respect for cultural identity to be inserted in EMP documents. Such a reference allows them to defend – at least rhetorically – their specificity *vis-à-vis* universalism. Nevertheless, this does not protect them from the effects of globalization on information, telecommunication and broadcasting networks, which stretch all over the globe and overwhelm them with programmes that are not commensurate with their cultural reference criteria. Clearly, in future, those advocating specificity will see their scope of action reduced under the effect of globalization.

It is worth stressing in this respect the delicate position of those countries that, while challenging the universalist doctrine, nevertheless adopt measures in the same vein by drawing up their own regional instruments.[22] This kind of behaviour tends to support the idea that as far as human rights are concerned, the southern countries are no doubt on the defensive. They react rather than take action. Such a position is even more uncomfortable inasmuch as these countries are confronted by the claims made internally within their own societies not to mention international pressure pushing for alignment with universal standards (Biad, 1997).

Arab countries stand to gain by the very fact that cultural specificity is expressly acknowledged in the Barcelona Declaration through a reference in the preamble to respect for 'the characteristics, values and distinguishing features peculiar to each of the participants' of the EMP. Specificity takes on a new and wider significance once 'freedom of thought, conscience and religion' and non-discrimination against women are at issue.

The Barcelona Declaration stipulates that the exercise of 'freedom of thought, conscience and religion' is carried out 'both individually and together with other members of the same group'. This is tantamount to recognizing the collective nature of these freedoms and thereby assigning a relative value to an individual exercise of the same. This is especially the case with religious freedom. In Muslim countries its application is subject to a prevailing restrictive notion that is contrary to the provisions of the Universal Declaration[23] and other international instruments relating to human rights. Thus, the conversion of a Muslim to another religion is an act of apostasy punishable by death and could hardly be considered the exercise of freedom of religion or conscience. In fact, this was the argument raised by Saudi Arabia against the Universal Declaration of Human Rights (Tavernier, 1992). Hence, what is the meaning of the reference in the Barcelona Declaration to 'freedom of conscience and religion' when it is well known that it may not be applied in Muslim countries on account of the decrees of the Koran and the *Shariah*?

Moreover, the principle of non-discrimination on the grounds of sex set forth in the Universal Declaration (together with nationality, language and religion) is also problematic. This does not mean in any way that the undertaking not to discriminate on the grounds of sex is respected in the Arab countries, most of which have adopted a Personal Status Code inspired, wholly or in part, by the *Shariah*, which instituted a legally unequal status for women. These codes are incompatible with the application of the universal principle of non-discrimination for whatever reason stated in relevant instruments of international law relating to human rights.

Nevertheless, the disunity of the Arab countries themselves in this regard is worthy of note. Three categories may be drawn up according to the positions adopted with regard to the issue of gender equality. The first category is reserved for the most progressive countries, including Tunisia, which have enshrined the principle of equality in the legislation. The more conservative ones are obviously the monarchies in the Persian Gulf, among which Saudi Arabia stands out as the most intransigent by its strict application of the principles of the *Shariah*. The other Arab countries lie somewhere in between. Algeria, Egypt and Morocco, in particular, have instituted a hybrid legal system with principles of modern law alongside those of Islamic law, most of all in civil matters (family, marriage, inheritance, etc.).

Nevertheless, the position of Arab states as regards human rights is not simply defensive. It has also materialized as an offensive rhetoric aimed at denouncing the Europeans.

Arab Counter-arguments for Human Rights

Arab countries consider that Europe, which has sermonized so much about human rights, does not have a spotless track record in this area either. They often mention racism and the treatment of migrant workers, as well as hurdles to the freedom of movement of persons in the Euro-Mediterranean area, as being equally an affront to human dignity.

In the Arab world – both at state and public opinion level – the growth of racism and xenophobia, mainly against Arab nationals and Muslims, is severely criticized. They believe that states in the West are not endeavouring in any decisive way to eradicate this phenomenon, which in itself endangers the pursuit of peace and dialogue in the Mediterranean. While European countries do not deny the criticism outright, they defend themselves by referring to their comprehensive legal resources, whose dissuasive force is strong enough to keep the phenomenon in check. Europeans may use the same argument to attack Islamist movements that they hold responsible for intolerance and hatred in the West.

The Barcelona Declaration expresses itself very clearly on this subject in its invitation to respective states to wage 'a determined campaign against racism, xenophobia and intolerance and [to] agree to co-operate to that end'.[24] Thus, by drawing a parallel between racism and intolerance, all EMPs are encouraged to assume their responsibilities in curbing social affliction in the Euro-Mediterranean area. In this regard, the Action Plan invites the partners to exchange information about their legislation and to compare their experiences in combating racism, xenophobia and discrimination and in promoting tolerance and coexistence.

The southern Mediterranean countries, from where most migrant workers originate, insisted that EMP participants undertake to guarantee protection for these workers against racist acts and, more generally, that their 'rights' are protected. However, European countries that are on the receiving end of these migration flows believe that no further action is necessary beyond respecting the 'rights recognized by existing legislation', thereby establishing the principle that foreign nationals admitted under a specific regime may not enjoy the same rights as their own nationals. They are also responsible for the inclusion in the Barcelona Declaration of the phrase 'legally established on their respective territories', which is explicitly targeted at denying illegal immigrants the rights set aside for foreigners in a legal situation. All the more significant is the inclusion in the declaration of a 'readmission' clause obliging the states concerned to take back those of their nationals who are in an illegal situation and of a reference to the need to 'reduce migratory pressures'.[25] Provisions are made to further dialogue on this subject, specifically through cooperation programmes.

Arab countries have also raised the issue of restrictive conditions applied for the acquisition of entry visas in Europe for their citizens, thereby implicitly criticizing the Schengen system. They believe these provisions could be contrary to the objective of the development of human exchange. As for the Europeans, they have stressed that the conditions for granting visas have only one objective, namely, to prevent certain categories of people from emigrating to Europe. It is worth mentioning at this stage that the stance adopted by European countries is contradictory in so far as they are defending in the same breath the freedom of movement of goods, services and ideas within the free trade area. How could one even think of selective freedom of movement in the Euro-Mediterranean area? Would it not be counter-productive to the inter-cultural dialogue and civil society exchanges which the EMP seeks to promote?

Arab countries too have adopted a paradoxical attitude. While defending tenaciously the principle of freedom of movement of people, they insist on keeping their own cultural identity immune from foreign influences. It would not have been unreasonable to expect them to adopt a position similar to that of the USSR, which consisted of discouraging human exchanges with the West to prevent the risk of 'ideological contamination'. By insisting on freedom of movement, Arab countries are perhaps responding to the need to use emigration as a safety valve to keep their own inward-looking political systems and ailing economies intact. Liberty of movement is a double-edged sword for these countries. This is because human exchanges not only support the dissemination of ideas but, in the long run, they also give rise to more forceful claims for democratization.

Another trace of the Arab counter-arguments in the discussion on human rights is the reference in the Barcelona Declaration to the 'right to development'. This is, by definition, a 'Third World' approach to collective rights and is defended by Arab countries, often at the expense of individual rights.[26] With regard to collective rights, the Barcelona Declaration mentions the right to self-determination, with a veiled reference to the Palestinian people.[27]

Conclusion

It is too early to draw up an assessment of the EMP. Even if developments have somewhat failed to match the ambitions laid out in Barcelona, the spirit of Barcelona still prevails. Issues related to the three chapters of the EMP have evolved at unequal speeds due to differences in the ways they were handled. Discussions on the implementation of the second chapter focused essentially on economic and financial aspects and progressed more rapidly than others. After all, southern countries require economic and financial cooperation. The same is not true of the first and second chapters where sensitive issues such as human rights, cultural values and the role of civil societies still give rise to serious diverging views among EU countries and the Arab Group.

One of the crucial problems for the EMP is its visibility *vis-à-vis* civil societies. Declarations of intent stressing this visibility are mere expressions of wishful thinking.[28] There is a disturbing contrast between the political mobilization both in the North and in the South in favour of the EMP and the indifference, or rather, the lack of interest of civil societies in a process that concerns them so intimately. The absence of, or insufficient networking among, non-governmental entities deprives the partnership of its leading actors. In spite of the existence of decentralized cooperation programmes, which work badly rather than properly, the EMP retains an intergovernmental character in so far as the importance of establishing good neighbourly relations and fostering exchange in the Mediterranean is secondary to state interests, often at the expense of human rights. Clearly, expressions in basic EMP texts, such as 'taking into account the evolution of the situation in the Mediterranean region' and 'when political circumstances allow', sound very much like reservations or conditions laid on the implementation of foreseen measures, especially human rights and democracy.[29] Such a context hardly helps to abate the pessimism hovering over the fulfilment of a constructive dialogue on human rights as foreseen by the EMP.

In spite of relatively greater openness towards human rights, Arab countries are still firmly locked in a conservative approach that clearly indicates their inability to relinquish the supremacy of the *Shariah* in criminal and civil matters (Personal Status Code) and to opt for legal and institutional systems worthy of modern states. Generally speaking, these countries continue to invoke the requirements of internal (the fight against Islamism) and external (the Arab–Israeli conflict) stability to refuse further commitment in a partnership they fear they have no hold on because of their unfavourable situation, at both a regional and an international level.

A recurring claim in Arab rhetoric on the EMP is the need for a fair and lasting peace in the Middle East on the basis of the 'land-for-peace' principle. Obviously, the breach of the rights of the Palestinian people and the sustained occupation of Arab territory by Israel in spite of the relevant provisions of international law are a major obstacle to the construction of an area of peace and stability in the Mediterranean. The unsuccessful Euro-Mediterranean Conferences further confirm this pessimistic, albeit realistic, observation.

NOTES

1. See the Alliance's Strategic Concept adopted at the North Atlantic Council's summit in Rome on 7 and 8 November 1991, §§ 8–15.
2. The former secretary-general of NATO, Willy Claes, stated in December 1994 that: 'Muslim fundamentalism is the most important challenge western Europe has to face since the end of the Cold War'.
3. This initiative may be considered a newer and more ambitious version of the 5+5 negotiating framework launched in the early 1990s between five southern European countries (Spain, France, Italy, Malta and Portugal) and the members of the Union of the Arab Maghreb (Algeria, Libya, Morocco, Mauritania and Tunisia), which was discontinued on account of the freezing of the UMA's activities and the embargo against Libya.
4. The idea is to create an area of peace and stability in the Mediterranean.
5. Barcelona Declaration, Chapter 1, preamble.
6. Barcelona Declaration, Political and Security Partnership, § 3.

7. Article 19: 'Everyone has the right to freedom of opinion and expression; this right includes freedom to hold opinions without interference and to seek, receive and impart information and ideas through any media and regardless of frontiers.'
8. Article 20: '(1) Everyone has the right to freedom of peaceful assembly and association; (2) Nobody can be obliged to be part of an association.'
9. Article 41 of the Algerian Constitution and Article 54 of the Egyptian Constitution expressly mention freedom of assembly. Nevertheless, the Egyptian Constitution further specifies that 'All citizens have the right to assemble in an orderly fashion without carrying arms and without prior authorization.' Only private meetings are at issue here. As far as public meetings are concerned, they are 'authorized within the limits of the law'.
10. Barcelona Declaration, Chapter 3, § 8.
11. Ibid., § 5.
12. Ibid., § 6.
13. Barcelona Declaration, Annex, Work Programme, Chapter 3.
14. Ibid.
15. For example, in 1997 the MEDA Democracy programme had a budget of €8 million. It provides grants, especially to associations, universities and research institutes, to implement projects aimed at promoting democracy, the rule of law and human rights in the 12 Mediterranean Partner Countries (MPCs) of the EU. A budgetary breakdown per category of rights is as follows: civic rights (32 per cent of the budget), women (15 per cent), youth and children (15 per cent) and trade unions (8 per cent) (European Commission, 1997).
16. 'Revised Draft of Action Plan for the Development of the Political and Security Chapter of the Barcelona Process', Annex 1 and Annex 3, A.
17. 'Political and Security Partnership: Inventory of Confidence and Security-Building Measures', EU document attached to the 'Revised Draft of Action Plan for the Development of the Political and Security Chapter of the Barcelona Process'.
18. Barcelona Declaration, Chapter 1, §§ 6 and 8.
19. Barcelona Declaration, Political and Security Partnership, § 8.
20. Barcelona Declaration, Chapter 1 (§ 11) and Chapter 3 (§ 12). The Work Programme provides for meetings to be held periodically among 'police, judicial and other authorities' (intelligence services) and to give consideration 'to stepping up exchanges of information and improving extradition procedures'. It is worth pointing out that Syria and Lebanon expressed their reservations on this score.
21. 'Revised Draft of Action Plan for the Development of the Political and Security Chapter of the Barcelona Process', Annex 5.
22. See the Cairo Declaration on Human Rights in Islam, adopted by the Organization of the Islamic Conference (1990) and the Arab Human Rights Charter adopted by the Arab League (1994).
23. Article 18 of the Universal Declaration provides for 'the freedom to change ... religion or belief'.
24. Barcelona Declaration, Chapter 3, § 14.
25. Ibid., §§ 10 and 11. The Work Programme calls for 'cooperation among police, judicial, customs, administrative and other authorities in order to combat illegal immigration'.
26. See the interesting confrontation between 'confirmed collective rights' and 'uncertain individual rights' regarding the Arab approach to human rights in Mahiou (1998).
27. Barcelona Declaration, Chapter 1, § 7.
28. In this regard the British Foreign Minister Robin Cook (1998) noted that: 'In our discussion of the Third Chapter, covering the partnership in social, cultural and human affairs, we recognized that this chapter provides the opportunity to make the Euro-Med process accessible to the peoples of our countries. We want improved visibility and awareness of the Partnership.' See also the Conclusions of the Second Euro-Mediterranean Conference (1997), General Aspects, § 2.
29. Ibid., Political and Security Partnership, §§ 3 and 4.

Part IV:

DIALOGUE BETWEEN CIVILIZATIONS

9

Speaking the Same Language:
The Benefits and Pitfalls of English

RAYMOND COHEN

Introduction

Most international systems since antiquity have depended for diplomatic communication on the use of international languages. An *international language* is a language, living or dead, used internationally beyond its home base and traditional linguistic boundaries. It may be spoken more or less widely, either by élites or the masses, and it may have narrower or wider functional uses, whether for communication between diplomats, scientific cooperation or chat networks between youngsters on the internet. In this chapter I propose to examine the role of English today within the context of some reflections on international languages, assessing both their advantages and disadvantages in a historical context.

My focus is on the world-view – philosophy and ethos – reflected in and transmitted by international languages. In brief, I argue that international languages are essential and their influence, on the whole, is benign. The fear that they may spread cultural homogeneity is exaggerated. While they permit interlocutors to communicate intelligibly by permitting the sharing of meaning across cultures and languages, the prior existence of alternative meanings and world-views should nevertheless not be forgotten. International languages also tend to be viewed fallaciously as in some way superior to other tongues, as though they were beyond idiosyncrasy, able to depict the world with privileged veracity. However, their limitations should be made clear and the equal merits of other languages vigorously defended, just as ecological diversity is promoted. Variety is inherently valuable and fruitful; uniformity imposes a dead hand on nations and cultures.

Two basic distinctions should be made at the outset. A lingua franca, strictly speaking, is not the same as an international language, although collo-quially the terms are confused. A lingua franca was originally a restricted, mixed language often used by traders and travellers speaking different native languages for conducting a limited range of transactions or activities. For instance, Baltic herring or timber traders in the Middle Ages used a mixture of

Scandinavian and German to do business. Frankish, a mixture of Italian and southern French (Occitan), was also spoken in the Middle Ages by travellers along routes to the Holy Land.

Another relevant term to be noted is *interlanguage*. This is a third language chosen by two non-native speakers as a common medium of communication. Immigrants from Russia and Ethiopia to Israel use Hebrew as an interlanguage, although it is not their native language or even in most cases their language of prayer. International examples would be the use of Russian by diplomats of the former Soviet republics of central Asia such as Turkmenistan and Uzbekistan, and German by Serbs and Turks. An interlanguage will often be an international language – although this is not necessarily the case – and this is helpful because special problems arise when the language being used is native to neither of the interlocutors.

The first international language known to us is Akkadian, which was written in cuneiform script on clay tablets and was used from about the middle of the third millennium BC to the mid-first millennium BC. By the end, Akkadian had been replaced for diplomatic purposes by Aramaic, though it continued as a literary language. Originally the language of Babylon, Akkadian spread throughout the entire ancient Near East as a language of learning, and was widely used for diplomatic and commercial purposes among peoples as varied as the Hittites, Hurrians, Assyrians, Babylonians, Egyptians, Canaanites, Mycenaean Greeks and Persians. Arguably, it was the use of Akkadian, and the specialized vocabulary of diplomacy and law developed in that language, that permitted diplomacy, and something resembling an international community, to emerge in the first place.

Other international languages throughout history include Greek, Persian, Sanskrit, Latin, Italian, French and English. Some international languages, such as French and now English, have reflected the politically hegemonic status of the nation speaking the language. But the use of Greek in the Mediterranean basin between about 200 BC and AD 400 did not reflect the status of Greece as a hegemonic power, rather the prestige and ascendance of its culture and ethos. Dead languages have also dominated international discourse. Akkadian and Latin remained international languages and reached a peak of use and influence despite the decline of their ancestral civilizations. Latin's history is a fascinating tale of expansion and very gradual contraction over many centuries. It retained its prestige and academic status long after it ceased to be the main medium of international communication. French was first used in the drafting of an international treaty in 1714, establishing itself as the international language *par excellence* thanks to the supremacy of France in Europe and the prestige of French letters. English was first given equal standing with French at the Congress of Versailles in 1919 because of the prominent roles of Woodrow Wilson and Lloyd George, and is now the pre-eminent international language for diplomacy, commerce, science and mass communication.[1] Unlike all international languages since Greek, its use has increasingly spread from the élites to the masses, making it a potent vehicle for the diffusion of ideas and popular culture.

It is language's function as disseminator of ideas that makes the choice of international language so consequential, and the topic of more than passing interest. Language is not just a neutral medium but a template and conveyor belt of culture, stamping its impression on those who use it. Greek philosophy and ethics, and later Christianity, were delivered by Greek into the collective consciousness of mankind. Indeed, the intellectual revolution perpetrated by Greek philosophers – the transformation of the way mankind perceived and thought about the world – was so far-reaching and innovative that it was best conveyed by the categories and concepts coined in the Greek language. The thought and language relationship was reciprocal. Second Temple Judaism, steeped in the ethical and ritual concepts of Hebrew and the legal themes of Aramaic, struggled against Hellenistic ideas and logic, which it saw as a threat to its religious world-view. In the end, it was as heavily influenced as were all the other cultures of the Mediterranean Basin by Greek thought and logic. The moment Greek, as the international language of the time, was spoken, the intellectual baggage of Greek culture was acquired along with it.

Later, Arabic was the vehicle for propagating the beliefs and values of Islam. Again, the world-view of the Holy Koran and *hawadith* were most conveniently transmitted by the language in which they had originally been expressed. In practical terms, Islamic categories of thought could not be accurately conveyed with full significance and nuance by another tongue. Equally, to acquire the language was, in effect, to ingest the philosophy of the parent civilization. Not by chance, states and religions with aspirations to hegemony vigorously promulgate their language as a means of shaping the concepts of speakers and thereby reinforcing political control. George Orwell may have exaggerated when he claimed in his great novel *Nineteen Eighty-Four* that by abolishing certain words Big Brother could make thoughts of freedom unthinkable. Nevertheless, the great powers of Europe are presumably convinced of the potency of their languages as a subtle mechanism for exercising influence and spreading ideas. Otherwise, they would hardly invest such funds and efforts in promoting them. Nor, conversely, would they restrict the use of rival languages, as China has done with English in Hong Kong schools.[2]

The Functions of International Languages

International languages are, first and foremost, undoubtedly a vital vehicle of communication and of functional cooperation. Interpreters have always been employed, but for easy communication and the development of personal relationships, hence of partnership in some shared endeavour, a common language is of great benefit. Once it is remembered that most work at international conferences takes place behind the scenes in discreet discussions, then it is clear that interpretation can never be more than an inferior substitute for direct contact and the unmediated exchange of views. This is as true of an academic conference, the joint work on an international project of engineers or scientists, the cooperation of aid agencies, the shared activities of Scouts at an international jamboree, as it is of the working of a military alliance or the negotiation of an international treaty. International languages, in short, are a great convenience for doing business, broadly defined, and may even be indispensable if spasmodic cooperation is to develop into something more sustained and comprehensive.

At the start of the third millennium we are witnessing an extraordinary proliferation of mass communication media, such as satellite television and the internet, and an enormous expansion of travel and international contact. Accordingly, international languages have acquired a new and decisive role, as intrusive as it is effective: purveying opinions, concepts, values, fads and fashions to hundreds of millions of people, especially young people, around the globe. The peer groups and opinion leaders of the young are no longer just friends at school or in the local community, but people on other continents, especially in media centres such as Los Angeles, London and New York. Suddenly, English, as the international language dominating the mass media and supplying fashionable ideas, becomes in itself irresistibly attractive and prestigious. The international language is reified into a desirable symbol of globalization.

Thus, beyond the convenience of communication, international language plays a part in creating a bond between individuals on a global scale. A sense of community, attachment to a group professing common purposes and values, necessarily entails 'possession of a common language', that is, a basic understanding of one's associates and an ability to converse with them. Actually, this common language may simply be the technical discourse of a science or a profession, the sacred language of a religion, the jargon of a peer group, or the kitchen talk of a family. It need not be a full-blown tongue. Physicians from different countries will usually be able to converse with sufficient shared technical vocabulary (and scientific knowledge) to allow them to work together. At the same time their common affiliation, their sense of partnership, is restricted to their profession. The more encompassing and pervasive the claims of membership of the community, of necessity the wider the scope of the common language. With some exceptions such as India, Indonesia and China, national identity – membership of a nation – is often marked by possession of a common or dominant mother tongue, the national language. Byzantine civilization was erected on the foundations of Greek language and culture, which then became a medium for propagating Christianity, the other indispensable glue of this originally multicultural empire. To be Maltese is to speak Maltese as one's mother tongue, with all the intimate knowledge of the secrets and nuances of the hearth and culture that this entails.

It is, therefore, surely no coincidence that most of the great international systems have possessed, together with a common body of international law and set of diplomatic customs and practices, an international language. The international language may have been known only by a cosmopolitan élite. Nevertheless, a working knowledge of it enabled those officials responsible for handling affairs across sovereignties to deal with each other with some sense of solidarity and even *esprit de corps*. The language provided the bond of a shared identity.

International languages create this link by establishing a common set of meanings, a notion of what the world is about, that speakers of different native languages can agree upon. After all, different languages do not simply sound different, saying exactly the same things using different words and grammatical conventions. Confusion arises in communication across languages because, while seemingly saying the same thing, in fact they may mean something quite different and untranslatable. The difficulty of translation of nontrivial texts has been convincingly demonstrated by George Steiner. The interpreter for Steiner is merely 'the intermediary who translates commercial documents, the traveller's questions, the exchanges of diplomats and hoteliers'. Complex abstract notions, 'the upper range of semantic events', the ideas of literature and philosophy, cannot 'be translated without fundamental loss' (Steiner, 1992: 265). The task of transferring the ideas of a Descartes or a Schopenhauer from French or German to English 'is to undertake an elaborate, finally "undecidable" task of semantic reconstruction' (ibid.: 255).

Without entering into an elaborate analysis of the difficulties of translation, it is clear that even at the level of the lexicon each language establishes its own unique cultural distinctions, ambiguities, conflations, niceties and valencies. The Italian *mediazione* and the English *mediation* appear to be the same word. But they denote, in a political context, very different kinds of activities, the one subtle and adroit, the other technical and disengaged. In French the distinction between the *fleuve* of the capital city and the *rivière* of a provincial town indicates a difference of political status, a focus on the centre of power. In English, which has no concern for this fine point, both terms are covered by *river*. *Temps* can mean either 'time' or 'tense'. This presents problems for the English translator when the French writer wishes to convey both meanings in the same sentence. Conversely, where the French speaker would use the undifferentiated term *bruit*, English prefers to distinguish between 'thumps', 'bumps', 'buzzes', 'screeches' and 'rustlings' (Kelly, 1994). These are shades of meaning between related languages within the same Standard Average European family. The difficulty is that much greater when translating across language families, from Semitic tongues such as Arabic and Hebrew, for instance, with their system of words based on common three-letter roots, into French and English.

The role of the international language is thus to bridge the semantic gap between disparate systems of meanings, creating conceptual common ground where there has previously been incompatibility and incomprehension. At the beginning of international relations in the mid-second millennium BC, when diplomacy extended the scope of its activity beyond the Mesopotamian heartland to the entire Near East, Akkadian did more than serve as an interlanguage. Importantly, it constituted, indeed set up, the elaborate set of concepts, roles, instruments and practices that permitted diplomacy in the first place. The idea of diplomacy is the precondition for the practice of diplomacy. Other civilizations, for instance in Africa, meso-America and pre-Columbian America, sent occasional messengers to other political entities and made transient alliances for war, but did not conduct diplomacy.

Diplomacy is not a one-off activity, but depends on continuity, professional training, institutional memory and hence a high level of literacy and written documentation in the form of letters, treaties, passports and records. It is not by chance that the word *diplomacy* derives from *diploun* (Greek) and *diploma* (Latin). Before there could be the institution of diplomacy the concepts of 'protocol', 'treaty', 'note', 'protest', 'ambassador', 'plenipotentiary', 'messenger', 'peace', 'passport', 'diplomatic gift', 'sovereignty', 'law', 'archive' and so on, had first to be invented, understood and generally accepted. Only when these complex ideas had been established could states engage in diplomacy, entering into diplomatic relations, communicating, negotiating, settling their disputes by judicial means and regulating their affairs by treaty. This major step forward in human affairs could occur only because the assumptions and ideas underpinning diplomacy were acquired at one and the same time together with the adoption of the international language. Although we take this for granted, international languages have performed much the same role throughout history, setting up a reality that they could then make propositions about.

By creating a world of understood conventions, international languages, used technically and precisely, can defuse and bypass the emotive charge of native speech. But the very strength of international languages may be their weakness: they sacrifice depth of meaning to precision; they are 'thin' rather than 'thick'. In the vernacular, words often have dense layers of significance, nuances and associations not possessed by equivalent terms in other languages. This is why poetry is so hard to translate. Mother tongue words are also frequently *polysemic*, that is, have multiple meanings, where only some of those meanings can be conveyed in translation.

The purpose of thin interlanguage is as much as possible to permit dispassionate discourse in a neutral third language by avoiding the misunderstanding that tends to arise in the transfer of meaning across thick native languages. The interlanguage, used as a diplomatic language possessing a dry, technical vocabulary of exact, defined terms, calms the negotiation down and enables negotiators to discuss the issues in a professional spirit while focusing on concepts with a clearly defined legal significance.

The Limitations of International Language

Interlanguages are without doubt beneficial in facilitating functional cooperation across languages and cultures. However, the very advantage of an interlanguage in enabling negotiators to work with a neutral, technical vocabulary
may also obscure the deeper sources of discord between the parties, particularly where the issues involve protracted, principled disagreement. Linguistic
precision and poverty are a convention and a convenience. But the reality of
vernacular richness and hence the potential for deep disagreement across
cultures over fundamental concepts should not be forgotten.

Efforts to resolve the Arab–Israeli conflict are a striking case in point. The
concepts and definitions of international law and diplomacy have been essential instruments in this peace process. At the same time, profound differences
on core questions of identity, justice and history cannot simply be swept under
the rug. For there to be reconciliation between the parties in the
Israeli–Palestinian dispute the emotive topics of historical responsibility,
refugees, the land and Jerusalem cannot be ignored. They may be postponed,
but must be tackled at some point.

Hebrew and Arabic are both languages that are inseparable from their
sacred texts, and their vocabularies are resonant with semantic, historical and
religious tones that are not evident in equivalent European words. Sometimes
these associations cannot be neutralized simply by switching into diplomatic
English or French. Some disagreements are not about legal definitions but
rather emerge from profoundly different ways of perceiving the world as
reflected in the vernacular. In these circumstances it may be best to bring
differences out into the open so that they can at least be understood, and if not
addressed, then bypassed. In the Arab–Israeli conflict peace and territory are
of the essence. But the connotations of these concepts to the disputants cannot
be adequately conveyed in English or French.

Take first the word *peace*. In Hebrew *shalom* covers a richer range of
meanings than the thin legal term 'peace'. In everyday use *shalom* means first
'greetings' followed by 'domestic well-being'. The international meanings of
'absence of war', 'harmony between nations', and importantly 'friendship',
appear only in third place. In addition, *shalom* significantly contains the idea
of 'safety' that is totally absent from European *peace, paix, pace, Friede*, etc.
Thus, when Israelis – even legal experts – talk about peace they are not just
thinking about an end to the state of war and the establishment of diplomatic
relations (as the West, relying on international law and diplomatic precedent,
implies), but instead mean something that is harder to fulfil: a harmonious state
of affairs in which states live in friendship, and their peoples enjoy safety and
well-being.

Another loaded term is *tatbi'*, the Arabic for *normalization*. Awkwardly for
peace negotiations between Israel and Syria, this important word can have the
meanings in Arabic of 'stamping, making an impression on metal', 'breaking

in a domestic animal (such as a horse)', and 'dirt'. Clearly, formidable substantive and not semantic problems divide Israel and Syria. Nevertheless, dissonant expectations of what normalization signifies and implies are not conducive to a meeting of minds on the final outcome of peace negotiations. Indeed, long, sterile debates over normalization marked the 1992–96 talks. By normalization (significantly rendered into Hebrew by the borrow-word *normalizatzia*), Israel's central aim in the negotiations, Israelis meant the construction of full, peaceful, cooperative relations, i.e., *shalom*. For Syria the goal of diplomacy was Israeli withdrawal from the Golan and a restoration of Syrian rights. Normalization was discussed unenthusiastically, because there was no choice. Sometimes the idea was interpreted as a mere ruse for Israel to extend its political and economic hegemony over the Middle East (Rabinovich, 1998: 202, 219; Savir, 1998: 272–7). There was no meeting of minds on the concept.

With the benefit of hindsight it is clear that both Israel and Syria were genuinely committed to achieving peace during the Rabin administration. The Israeli prime minister had communicated his willingness to withdraw from the Golan to the borders of 4 June 1967 before signing the Oslo Accords in 1994 with the PLO (Rabinovich, 1998: 4–13). Yet the opportunity this far-reaching concession presented was missed, despite intensive and protracted negotiations. Obviously, misjudgements were made on both sides about the time available and what the market would bear. But it was, not least, on the rock of contending understandings of normalization that the talks foundered.

The pitfalls of ignoring native language understanding of key diplomatic ideas by relying exclusively on English or French meanings are also demonstrated by an examination of the concept of land or territory, which is so central to the Arab–Israeli dispute. In Security Council Resolution 242, the starting point for all diplomacy since 1967, the key phrase 'withdrawal of Israeli armed forces from territories occupied in the recent conflict' is used. Discussion of the question of withdrawal has focused on the absence of the definite article in English and the ambiguity of the French text, as though the main problem was legal. Diplomats and other observers must not overlook the equally important point that the dispassionate word 'territories' conceals passionate feelings on both sides about the land. The dispute, in fact, is not about the merit of contending definitions, but a clash of national attachments.

Ard in Arabic, meaning 'land', 'region', 'plot of ground', 'soil', is the ancestral home, the source of one's identity and honour, the cherished possession of those close to the soil, symbolically, one's mother and father. *Eretz* in Hebrew, for its part (which is etymologically related to the Arabic), covers more or less the same semantic field as *ard* and also carries strong religious and ideological resonances. The belief that *Eretz* Israel was a gift of God to the Jewish people, and that its reclamation is a source of national redemption, has certainly not eased the task of a territorial settlement. But resolution of the bitter conflict could begin only when it was understood to derive from a principled, not cynical, mutual attachment to the land, *ard/eretz*. If questions of this kind – not only in the Arab–Israeli dispute – are only viewed from the technical, legal perspective of the international text then there is the danger that the source of disharmony will be missed.

Yet the point is not that an understanding of the contending conceptions of the protagonists can provide a panacea to solving their dispute. However, accurate diagnosis is certainly a precondition for developing a strategy for conflict resolution. And the best way to get at the perceptions and understandings of the contending parties is through a thick analysis of the language they use before domestic audiences when they describe the issues.

From the preceding discussion a clear conclusion follows. Exclusive reliance on texts translated into the international language, while ignoring native language understanding, risks perpetuating a one-sided, culture-bound view. Conflicts not only concern disagreement over aseptic concepts of international law best resolved in English or French, but also about festering ethnic disharmony expressed in the mother tongues of the rivals. For those for whom the international language is a supplementary language, a secondary interlanguage, the risk of misunderstanding and minimizing the visceral local issues at stake is perhaps less than it is for the great powers. Surveying the world from the lofty perspective of French or English, the latter may miss the passionate concerns of the involved parties that are expressed in the vernacular.

English is particularly prone to solecism. Because of the insular and continental location of the great Anglo-Saxon powers, English speakers have tended to ignore other living languages and cultures. Classical languages, once cherished in schools and universities, are now seldom taught. Combined with a certain educational provincialism on the part of the United States, a neglect of history, geography, regional studies and non-English literature, this results in a myopic world-view. But the world cannot be understood in all its complexity through the medium of any one international language, however competent its monitoring and translation services.

On repeated occasions American diplomacy has sought to tackle critical world issues without the necessary tools of local knowledge that are only accessible through a thorough grasp of native languages. Robert McNamara, secretary of defence during the Vietnam War, has belatedly acknowledged the cultural ignorance that marked the foreign policies of the Kennedy and Johnson administrations (McNamara, 1996: 43, 322). During the 1979 Iranian crisis and the fall of the Shah, the US embassy in Teheran employed few officials who understood Farsi and the local culture (Sick, 1985: 34, 66). A retired American diplomatist, Monteagle Stearns, bemoaned this impoverishment, arguing that it seriously affected the calibre of State Department recruitment and performance (Stearns, 1996).

Two factors aggravate the consequences of Anglo-Saxon ethnocentrism. One is that never in history has a nation had the global reach, monopoly of power, or ambition of the United States. Convinced of the God-given superiority of its political and economic systems, it remains committed to a mission to spread its singular version of democracy and economic organization to the ends of the earth. Were the United States not locked into a monolingual view of the world, it might be less dismissive about the merits of other cultures or deluded about their ripeness for conversion to the American way of life.

The other aggravating factor is the extraordinary scope for influence provided by the modern mass media of communication. Potentially, no corner of the globe accessible to a television or computer is out of range of the language and culture of the English-speaking world. Were the ideas displayed by these media of the loftiness and merit of those of Ancient Greece, Renaissance Italy or Enlightenment France, one would remain tranquil. But the culture peddled is crassly commercial, corrosive of traditional values (such as respect for family life), enamoured with guns, violence and crime, superficial, often obscene – and seductive. The conjunction of unquestioning self-confidence, absolute access and vulgarity is disturbing.

Conclusion

English achieved its unprecedented expansion because of four striking, inter-connected features of the modern world: globalization, interdependence, multilateralism and American hegemony. In an international system where people, money and information move around at extraordinary speed and on an unprecedented scale, where governments must cooperate with each other to ensure the safety and prosperity of their peoples, and where many problems can only be tackled at an international level and in multilateral forums, the emergence of a global language is inevitable.

Some writers have pointed to supposed inherent 'virtues' of English, such as its egalitarianism, the absence of a distinction between élite and popular forms of the language, and the everyday simplicity and directness of English style, to explain its general adoption. The absence of a language academy restricting the entry of borrow-words, hence the ability of the language to absorb enriching influences, has also been noted. Even if true, these feature seem to me to be irrelevant to the spread of a language that organically evolves to meet the needs of the community it serves.

In other circumstances French, Spanish, German, Italian or Russian might have become the global language. The diffusion of English is clearly associated with the inexorable rise of British and American power following the final defeat of Napoleon in 1815. Britain acquired an immense global maritime and imperial presence in the nineteenth century. In the twentieth century the decisive victory of the United States in 1945 resulted in an even vaster network of US-led alliances and American pre-eminence in international institutions. With the location of the United Nations in New York, and that of the World Bank and International Monetary Fund in Washington, English has become the dominant diplomatic language. The early lead of the United States in information technology and the invention of the internet were added assets.

However, English was not foisted or forced on an unwilling international system, it was seized upon by governments, firms and individuals looking for a universal means of communication. English first proved its utility as an inter-language in the Third World, on the Indian sub-continent. Significantly, ASEAN (the Association of South-East Asian Nations) adopted English as its interlanguage despite the Vietnam War. In Indochina, French was spoken by the élite, in Indonesia, the regional great power, Dutch. English was chosen as a regional interlanguage because it was most useful and convenient.

The benefits of international languages are undoubted. It is hard to imagine civilization without the sterling contributions of Akkadian, Greek and Latin. International communication and cooperation are greatly facilitated by a common language. The danger ostensibly arises when adoption of the international language comes at the expense of the mother tongue. However, the problem should not be overstated. It is worth pointing out that it is not English that endangers national tongues. The great national languages, such as French and Spanish, have the vitality, speech base and political support to look after themselves. Native languages have in almost all cases throughout history been threatened by political oppression, the calculated educational policies of central governments, the destruction of natural environments and the deliberate extermination of peoples and cultures.

The relative poverty of international languages as used by most – though certainly not all – non-native speakers should also put the 'English threat' into perspective. If the very advantage of an interlanguage is that it is thin, that is, precise, relatively simple and without confounding cultural depth, then it is hardly likely to oust the mother tongue, with its dense associations, intimacy and overlapping layers of semantic richness. English the threadbare interlanguage should not be confused with English the luxuriant native language of the Anglo-Saxons. An international language is useful; the mother tongue is indispensable.

The combination of a flexible international language and a vital vernacular may in fact prove a reciprocally beneficial combination. Maltese remains a vibrant, living language, the heart and soul of Maltese identity, despite Malta's proximity to and absorption of lexical elements of great European continental languages. The same is true of Hebrew, which was historically enriched by exposure to Aramaic, Persian, Greek, Latin, German, Russian, Arabic and now English.

Multilingualism opens up vistas not accessible to the single-language speaker. The distinctive features of a language and the world-view it reflects can only be revealed by comparison with the different outlook supplied by another language. The special contours of the western concept of peace (a product both of the Christian heritage and of long European experience of international law and diplomacy) are thrown into sharp relief when contrasted with *shalom/salaam*, resonating with the very different associations of the Bible/Koran, Judaism/Islam. Without the stereoscopic vision provided by another language and world-view one may never escape the fallacy that one's mother tongue is a kind of 'metalanguage', beyond culture, able to mirror the 'real world' with superior authenticity.

Rather than bemoaning the emergence of a global language, the advantages of a common interlanguage and the global sense of community it fosters should be recognized. At the same time, if two languages are good, three or four are even better. In the past an educated, well-rounded person was expected to know several living and classical languages. In the causes of cultural diversity and intellectual fecundity, this tradition should be revived. The Maltese – like the Dutch – have it about right when they preserve the vitality of their national language, speak English with ease, while at the same time mastering a second or even third foreign language to an enviable level of proficiency.

NOTES

1. For a historical survey of international languages see Goad (1956).
2. *International Herald Tribune*, 8 December 1997.

10

Towards a Viable Euro-Mediterranean Cultural Partnership

MOHAMMAD EL-SAYED SELIM

Recently there has been a revival of interest in the concept of culture in explaining international interactions at academic and policy levels. For the first time international relations theorists are using the concept of culture to account for various forms of conflict and cooperation among nations (Chay, 1994). This interest mushroomed as a result of the publication of Samuel Huntington's famous book, *The Clash of Civilizations* (1996), in which Huntington contended that civilizational struggle will be the major form of international relations in the future. It is now assumed that international relations are highly influenced by the cultural attributes of peoples and that the harmonization of such relations requires a manipulation of cultural variables as well. Such interest was also the outcome of the revival of ethnic and cultural identities in the post-Cold War world, and a result of the realization of the linkages between political, economic and cultural behaviours. Such behaviours are viewed as mutually supportive. Cultural cooperation reduces misperceptions and reinforces political and economic cooperation; joint achievements in the areas of politics and economics create an environment conducive to meaningful cultural contacts. Today, most projects for regional, transregional and global cooperation comprise a cultural dimension. For example, the Euro-Asian cooperation project, which was launched in 1996, included a major cultural dimension, and the Euro-Asian Foundation was established to promote such cooperation. UNESCO launched the concept of the 'culture of peace' as a major component of peace-building processes

Likewise, when proposals for Mediterranean and Euro-Mediterranean cooperation were submitted in the post-Cold War era, notions of cultural cooperation were included from the beginning. This was based on the assumption that if Euro-Mediterranean cooperation is to be sustainable, it has to address the gamut of human activities, including cultural ones. The first Interparlia-mentary Conference on Security and Cooperation in the Mediterranean held in Malaga in 1992 identified three areas of Mediterranean cooperation: political security; economic; and dialogue among civilizations, under which cultural cooperation was subsumed. Each delegation submitted a working paper outlining its views on civilization dialogue and cultural cooperation. The Final Document of the Conference referred to the development of cultural exchanges in all fields. Likewise, the Final Document of the Second Conference held in Valletta in November 1995 referred to cooperation in the fields of culture and sports. It referred to three main areas of cooperation: preservation of cultural heritage; cooperation in the fields of arts and publishing; and sports cooperation. When Egypt presented its proposal to establish Mediterranean Forum in 1991, it envisaged the forum as being a purely economic institution. However, as the Egyptian proposal was debated among the Mediterranean partners, it became clear that the issue of culture could not be ignored. At the first Mediterranean Forum ministerial meeting held in Alexandria in 1994 issues of cultural cooperation were included and even expanded in the following meetings. Finally, when the Euro-Mediterranean Partnership (EMP) proposal was laid down at the European Union (EU) Cannes Summit in June 1995, it was conceived from the beginning as a multi-dimensional project, including political, economic and socio-cultural dimensions. However, culture was considered one of the residual areas and was thus subsumed under the category of other areas of cooperation. Further, the EU adopted a narrow, élitist concept of cultural cooperation, which was mainly restricted to areas such as cultural heritage, cultural and artistic events, cultural co-productions, dissemination of the written word and translations. The Barcelona Declaration, which was the outcome of wider Euro-Mediterranean negotiations, allotted culture a more prominent position and adopted a broader concept of cultural cooperation. Culture was subsumed under the third chapter of cooperation (Partnership in Social, Cultural and Human Affairs). It also added the dimension of greater understanding between major religions, with the aim of breaking down prejudice and fostering cooperation at grass-roots level. The Conclusions of the Second Euro-Mediterranean Ministerial Conference held in Malta in April 1997 went a step further in operationalizing the concept of cultural cooperation. It focused on the dialogue between cultures and civilizations, dialogue between civil societies, cooperation in the fight against terrorism, etc. It also outlined certain projects for cultural cooperation. The third Euro-Mediterranean Conference of Foreign Ministers held in Stuttgart in April 1999 went a step further in the direction of elaborating the concept of cultural cooperation. The Stuttgart conference called for the involvement of a wide circle of actors outside central governments, and called for decentralized cultural cooperation. The Presidency Conclusions of the Fourth Euro-Mediterranean Conference of Foreign Ministers held in Marseilles in November 2000 referred to the initiation of new cultural cooperation projects such as the EuroMed Audiovisual II and EuroMed Human Sciences, and the need to develop the dialogue among cultures. It is obvious that as the EMP progressed, the concept of cultural cooperation was expanded and given more prominence on the Euro-Mediterranean agenda. It also moved from the level of strictly transregional cultural cooperation to the level of sub-state linkages, and from the level of general civilizational dialogue to the level of specific operational projects. The

EU has also initiated various cultural programmes for cultural cooperation within the EMP framework. These initiatives represent a major departure from the dominant paradigms of the 1970s, which focused almost exclusively on the political and economic dimensions of cooperation. For example, when the Euro-Arab Dialogue was launched in the mid-1970s, the Arabs expressed an interest in expanding the dialogue to include cultural issues, but Europe, according to a Jordanian participant in the dialogue, was not interested (Al-Assad, 1998). The initiatives also represent a shift of the paradigm of the 1980s towards a more grass-roots oriented paradigm. However, Euro-Mediterranean cultural cooperation still poses major problems along the road of the EMP. In my judgement, the viability and sustainability of the EMP will depend to a large extent on the paradigms that will be adopted in dealing with these problems. It is the argument of this chapter that Euro-Mediterranean cultural cooperation calls for a truly multidimensional and multicultural paradigm if such cooperation is to be sustained and to provide support to the political and economic dimensions of the EMP.

The objectives of this chapter are to identify the main problems that constrain cultural cooperation among Euro-Mediterranean actors, and to delineate the main elements of what are considered a viable Euro-Mediterranean cultural partnership in the light of the present programmes for cultural cooperation pursued within the EMP.

The Problems of Cultural Cooperation in the EMP

Cultural cooperation in the EMP encounters certain major problems. Comprehension of these problems is essential in order to embark on an effective cultural cooperation. This is because the policies and programmes of such cooperation will be designed to deal with these problems.

The main problems related to cultural cooperation in the EMP can be divided into three main categories: those related to the concepts of culture and cultural cooperation in general; those related to the cultural characteristics of the Euro-Mediterranean world; and finally those related to present conditions under which Euro-Mediterranean cultural cooperation has been initiated.

Although cultural variables are usually referred to as the third chapter in the EMP, which implies that they are the least important, and are usually referred to in the EMP literature as 'soft issues', these variables present the most difficult problems in initiating the EMP. This is because these variables are not only crucial, but also the least susceptible to change and manipulation. The cultural variables have been widely cited as major sources of the success and/or failure of development, and of conflict and/or cooperation among nations. The success of the countries of Pacific Asia in political/economic terms has been explained with reference to the particular cultural characteristics of the region (Preston, 1998). Also, 'there is some evidence that cultural differences between states are related to conflicts exchanged between them and those cultural similarities are associated with cooperative behaviour and high levels of transactions' (McGowan and Purkitt, 1979).[1] In discussing the notion of confidence-building measures (CBMs), various authors have suggested the introduction of cultural CBMs to buttress the military-political ones. This suggestion is based on the assumption that

> the cultural dimension of conflict resolution strategies helps to build confidence among people and find solution at the grass root level by promoting socio-cultural interaction among the people with divergent background ... The personal contact among people from various walks of life will remove some of the misunderstandings created by governments. (Qadeem, 1998)

However, despite their centrality in determining the prospects of development and cooperation, cultural variables can hardly be manipulated in ways to achieve the desired objectives. This is essentially because culture is a form of learned behaviour transmitted by primary socialization within the family, the kinship group, the media, and other forms of secondary socialization. It refers to people's preferred ways of life in the areas of language, religion, kinship organization, ideas and ideology, and values in general. Among all human variables, these forms and patterns are the least susceptible to change. This is not to argue that cultures do not change. In fact they do. But such change is an aberration, and it either occurs as a result of external traumatic events (a major military defeat) or through a long-term incremental process. Consequently, cultural cooperation will not bring immediate results; such results could only be expected in the long run.

Because cultures are the least susceptible to change, they call for a strategy that is different from the strategies pursued in political and economic cooperation. We can create free trade areas and nuclear-free zones but we cannot create culture-free areas in the Euro-Mediterranean world or anywhere else. Further, cultural cooperation cannot be achieved through central political decisions, or according to a master plan. It has to be achieved incrementally and involve the grass-roots population. Progress in the area of cultural cooperation cannot be directly assessed or measured, as it involves the perceptions, images and beliefs of the people. Further, peoples of the Euro-Mediterranean world belong to different cultures. In this world there are Arab Muslim, Jewish, Anglo-Saxon, Latin Roman Catholic and Orthodox Slavic cultures. The record of historical interaction between these cultures has not always been a positive one. For centuries, the Euro-Mediterranean world was plagued by various cultural conflicts. This was particularly true after the advent of Islam in the seventh century and the Arab Muslim conquest of the Orient, the Crusades in the eleventh century, the Ottoman expansion in Europe in the fourteenth century, and the European imperial onslaught on the Muslim world since the sixteenth century. These struggles have not only characterized North–South relations in the Euro-Mediterranean world, but also relations among the northern and southern actors. European powers have fought numerous religious and ethnic wars against each other, and similar wars were fought between the Ottomans and the Persians, between the Arabs and the Persians, and between the Ottomans and the Arabs. The cultural component was a major factor in these wars. The Catholic–Protestant and the Sunni–Shiite divides played a crucial role in these wars. The post-Second World War liberation wars in the southern Mediterranean against the European imperial powers reinforced these negative historical images. The influences of such a historical record are still haunting North–South Mediterranean relations. On the shores of the Mediterranean there are deeply distorted images of the other. Various Arab and European scholars have emphasized and documented the centrality of the distorted images of Arabs and Muslims in the western media, textbooks, and so forth. Mahmoud El-Sherif (1999) maintained that

> Arabs usually see the European individual as someone who is unsympathetic, if not hostile, towards the Arabs and their religion. This impression derives from the unfortunate succession of military confrontations between Europe and the Arab world ... The picture of invading Europe has left an indelible impression on the Arab subconscious; this impression has been reinforced in recent times by the role Europe played in the creation of Israel and the blind support it has given to the Jewish state while ignoring the plight of the Palestinian people.

Speaking from a European perspective, Kai Hafez (1999) also concluded that

> an important qualitative dimension of European and other Western media coverage is the considerable amount of stereotyping of Arabs, 'Orientals', and Islam ... In the 1960s and 1970s the Arabs and especially the Palestinians tended to be considered terrorists. Stereotyping still exists, but there has been a shift from the Arabs to Islam since the Iranian revolution of 1979.

Moreover, Marlene Nasr (1995) has also documented anti-Arab and Muslim bias in French textbooks. She found that these textbooks always portray Arabs and Muslims as aggressors in all encounters with the West and Israel. All of this has led some Arab scholars to suggest that these deep distortions are unlikely to change through dialogue and providing facts, and that all Euro-Mediterranean cultural conferences should be suspended until the question of these distorted images in the media and textbooks is resolved (El-Shalaby, 1998). Such controversy raises the question of the links between cultural cooperation and perception changes. Is it possible to bring about a change of perceptions through cultural cooperation? Or is it necessary to change perceptions in order to be able to embark on such cooperation? It is my argument that Euro-Mediterranean actors need to move on both tracks simultaneously.

Furthermore, a high level of socio-cultural and political duality characterizes the Euro-Mediterranean world. In the South there is a considerable socio-cultural polarization between the ruling élites and the masses, and the centrally controlled systems of governments. There are major political trends in the South whose political weight is not reflected in the governmental system and the political process. Southern governments tend to isolate their political critics (especially the Islamist trends) from the political process. The European world has managed to create over a long historical process of development a national consensus on the major issues and more representative and decentralized systems of government. Such differences have major implications for the cultural dimension of the EMP. Governments of the South have managed to exclude their political critics from Euro-Mediterranean cultural cooperation, and have attempted to use the EMP as a means to isolate them. Consequently, the Euro-Mediterranean cultural dialogue was turned into an élitist exchange between the élites who share more or less the same secular and western values and did not reach out to the wider social spectrum.

Finally, the initiatives of Euro-Mediterranean cultural cooperation are being launched under conditions of an emerging conflict in the Euro-Mediterranean world between the forces of cultural globalization and particularism. On the one hand, western victory in the Cold War created in the West a sense of confidence in the universality of its cultural values. This is evident in the approaches of western organizations in dealing with cooperation with other actors. Such actors are expected to accept western cultural values as the only way to enter into a real partnership with such organizations. For example, the Organization of Security and Cooperation in Europe (OSCE) and the EU have been persuading the MPCs to abolish the death penalty, although it is known that such a penalty is part of Islam. On the other hand, forces of nationalism and religious fundamentalism have been gaining momentum over the last few years. This process has been occurring across various societies and religions in the Euro-Mediterranean world. However, the articulation and impact of such forces is being mostly felt in the southern Mediterranean world. These forces tend to subscribe to notions of cultural particularism and exclusivity, and are mostly suspicious of the themes of intercultural communication. These fears have been reinforced as a result of the emergence of forces of cultural globalization. Various Arab analysts have detected and articulated these fears. For example, Amin Malouf, a Lebanese analyst, has warned that 'the same globalization that permits intercommunications has demonstrated the existence of a dominant global Anglo-Saxon culture which is perceived as an aggression towards the cultural identity of each people'.[2] Galal Amin (1999), a prominent Egyptian economist, also warned that globalization brings with it an onslaught on non-western cultures and religions and has warned against the endorsement of its arguments. Edward Said has contended that as a result of these factors the clash of civilizations has actually begun.[3] This has led some Arab and Islamist thinkers to conclude that under these conditions, a Euro-Mediterranean cultural communication is not possible. An Egyptian Islamist scholar has argued that because of the organic connection between European imperialist designs and the Zionist project in the Arab orient, it is hardly possible to envision a cultural relationship across the shores of the Mediterranean (Abdel-Kahalek, 1997). Another Islamist analyst contends that 'there is no room for a dialogue between the Islamic civilization and Latin and Anglo-Saxon civilizations because of their strong sense of supremacy and negation of the legitimacy of other civilizations' (Al-Bishry, 1998). Finally, Hassan Khalil (1998), a Syrian sociologist and Arab nationalist, concludes that under the present conditions of western hegemony, the Euro-Arab cultural dialogue will not be a dialogue among equals. Such dialogue, he asserts, would amount to 'a coercive imposition of the culture of the hegemon'. These mega-trends represent a major obstacle to the process of intercultural dialogue and cooperation in the Euro-Mediterranean world. Both the particularists and the globalists are not likely to look at the process of cultural dialogue with satisfaction. Whereas the particularists are likely to view it as a prelude to cultural assimilation, the globalists are also likely to perceive such cooperation as a slow-down of the globalization process.

The Prerequisites of a Viable Euro-Mediterranean Cultural Cooperation

The complexity and multi-dimensionality of the problems of cultural cooperation outlined above call for a new approach, one which would take them into account and enable the Euro-Mediterranean partners to establish a meaningful cultural partnership. Such an approach should address these problems and the vital prerequisites for a viable Euro-Mediterranean cultural cooperation. Once the prerequisites are defined and agreed upon, one could proceed to infer from them appropriate mechanisms. Outlining proposals for Euro-Mediterranean programmes of cooperation without setting their policy frameworks and outlining the assumptions of such frameworks is not likely to lead to viable policy options.

In my judgement, Euro-Mediterranean cultural cooperation is likely to develop and prosper only if it is based on three major policy stances. Such stances are prerequisites for the success of such cooperation.

Simultaneous Progress in the Political, Economic and Cultural Chapters of Euro-Mediterranean Cooperation

There are two main views on the relationship between the three chapters of cooperation in the EMP. These views reflect different perceptions of the linkages between cultural, political and economic cooperation, and advocates of both schools can be found on both shores of the Mediterranean. According to the first view, significant progress must be achieved in all chapters. However, progress in one chapter should not be necessarily linked to progress in the other chapters. Consequently, and because cultural dialogue is a less sensitive chapter, significant progress can be achieved in this area regardless of the possible stagnation of the other chapters. The Barcelona Declaration tacitly subscribes to this view. Although the declaration outlines three chapters of cooperation, there is no reference in it to the interrelationship between them.[4] Various European analysts have on different occasions advocated the argument that cultural cooperation should be depoliticized. Depoliticization refers to two main elements: the dialogue should not deal with political issues and lack of progress on political issues should not inhibit progress in the areas of cultural dialogue.

The second school of thought contends that human behaviour cannot be compartmentalized. Political, economic and cultural behaviours are all components of the totality of human behaviour, and as a result the dynamics of one component necessarily influence the dynamics of other ones. Consequently, no significant progress in the area of cultural dialogue can be achieved unless similar progress is achieved in the areas of economic and political cooperation. There are two variants to this view. The first variant emphasizes approaching cultural cooperation either after or in conjunction with the resolution of the main contentious political and economic issues that plague North–South and South–South relations. It is argued that unless such issues are resolved, cultural dialogue will be impaired, as such dialogue requires a certain political/ economic framework. This variant is dominant among southern Mediterranean scholars and professionals. A Tunisian scholar argued that as long as out-standing conflicts in the Mediterranean area remain unresolved, 'they will continue to divide nations, and no cooperation will be possible' (Chourou, 1998a). Although the second variant acknowledges the linkages between the three areas of cooperation, it prefers to focus on cultural cooperation, hoping that it would lead to better understanding and hence resolution of the main political and economic issues. This view was reflected in the French paper submitted to the Interparliamentary Conference on Security and Cooperation in the Mediterranean (Malaga, 1992). It was argued that 'cultural dialogue is essential for bridging the gulf in understanding between the peoples of the Arab world and those of Europe, for creating an atmosphere of confidence' (Group of France, 1992). Likewise, in 1998 a group of Mediterranean scholars issued the Mediterranean Charter, a document that emphasized the centrality of the indivisibility of security and the linkages between various forms of cooperation. It reiterated that intercultural dialogue and contacts among individuals and the peoples of the Mediterranean region contribute towards improved mutual understanding, peace and progress. Recently, Klaus Kinkel, the former German foreign minister, wrote an article on the relationship between Europe and the Muslim world in which he argued that 'what we need in all cases is to avoid the separation between the political dialogue and the civilizational dialogue. It is not possible to achieve progress in one of them isolated from the other' (Kinkel, 1999).

International relations theorists have long concluded that human transactions by themselves do not necessarily result in cooperation. In some cases it was found that human transactions had led to more conflicts. This was because these transactions have occurred under conditions of inequality. The partners drew unequal benefits from these transactions (Beer, 1981). Consequently, it is not enough to engage into human transactions. It is equally important that the economic and political framework of such transactions enhances the perception of mutual benefits. Accordingly, it is my argument that Euro-Mediterranean cultural cooperation will be tremendously enhanced if all the partners draw relatively equal benefits from it. The perception of the southern Mediterranean states that the EMP is an unequal economic partnership, or that Europe is providing certain actors a special treatment on economic and security issues, will not be conducive to a viable cultural dialogue, regardless of the number of conferences and programmes that are initiated in this field. The conclusion to be drawn from this analysis is that significant progress in the areas of equal economic partnership, South–South conflict resolution, and North–South security and political cooperation are essential for the advancement of Euro-Mediterranean cultural cooperation. Such cooperation will create new conditions for the stabilization and normalization of the newly created economic and political frameworks. The three chapters of cooperation must go hand in hand. Progress in one chapter will trigger forces of progress in the others. But the delinking of the chapters or the depoliticization of cultural cooperation will not result in significant achievements. After all, this linkage approach was the one adopted in the Helsinki Final Act, and the entire subsequent implementing processes.

A Paradigm of Euro-Mediterranean Multicultural Cooperation

The victory of the West in the Cold War seems to have unleashed forces of ideological and cultural uniformity. It is argued that western values are the ultimate model of human development, and as a result other cultures must strive to approach these values and the West must strive to persuade other countries to accept these values. Ideological manifestations of these arguments can be found in the *End of History* thesis (Fukuyama, 1992). At the policy level, terms of reference for the participation of southern Mediterranean actors in the security dialogue with some of the western institutions require the endorsement of some of the western cultural values. For example, in the OSCE, Mediterranean partners are expected 'to share OSCE principles and objectives as stipulated in its Code of Conduct'. Some of the principles of the code (such as the right of religious conversion, and unlimited personal freedoms) are incompatible with the cultures of those actors (Saif, 1998). As I have pointed out earlier, these trends have created fears of cultural domination and perceptions of cultural threat. Such perceptions call for a genuine multi-cultural paradigm of Euro-Mediterranean cooperation. Multiculturalism refers to the appreciation of the diversity of all cultures by all the actors. It includes various elements, such as (a) the prevalence of a non-hierarchical paradigm of cultures so that all cultures are considered equal in value and importance, (b) engagement in a genuine dialogue between the coexisting cultures based upon exchange of ideas and skills, (c) the pursuit of an anti-racist strategy, and (d) the participation of all the cultural groups in the institutions of cultural dialogue. Multiculturalism essentially means acknowledging and respecting cultural differences and acting to establish channels of communication between cultures.[5] This does not exclude the existence of common universal values, which cut across all cultures. However, the meaning and operational application of these values differ from one culture to the other.

Unfortunately, this is not the approach pursued by the EU. The EU's view of the cultural dimension of the projected partnership has been articulated in a document issued by the Council of the EU in its summit held in Portugal in June 2000 entitled *Common Strategy on the Mediterranean Region*. The Common Strategy contained some cultural elements, which run against the letter and spirit of multi-culturalism. Under Part 2, Article 7, entitled the objectives of the Common Strategy, the EU declares that it will strive to 'promote the core values embraced by the EU and its Member States – including human rights, democracy, good governance, transparency and the rule of law'. The document proceeds under Article 14 to assert that one of the Areas of Action and Specific Initiatives is to 'take measures to persuade all Mediterranean Partners to abolish the death penalty in accordance to the agreed EU guidelines'. The Common Strategy adds under Article 22 that one of these Areas is also 'to promote the identification of correspondences between legal systems of different inspirations in order to resolve civil law problems relating to individuals: laws of succession and family law, including divorce'. Taken together, these articles in the Common Strategy amount to a declaration by the EU that it will strive to promote its cultural values in the Mediterranean, and that it wants the Mediterranean countries to change their values to correspond with the European ones. Such declaration reflects the image of the existence of a hierarchy of cultures in the Mediterranean, and that the European cultures are the reference points in this hierarchy. If one recalls that some of these values are diametrically opposed to Islamic values (such as the reference to the death penalty, and family laws), and that changing these values actually means changing parts of Qur'an, the Holy Book for the Muslims, one can appreciate the extent to which the Common Strategy amounts to a declaration of European uniculturalism and eventually to a form of a cultural confrontation in the Mediterranean.

The Universal Application of Mutually Acceptable Cultural Norms

The value and credibility of the multicultural paradigm depends upon its universal and consistent application across the issues and the actors. An equal concern over human rights and cultural self-determination of all groups is likely to promote cultural exchange and promote confidence in Europe's firm commitment to such a paradigm. Unfortunately, the consistent pursuit of such paradigm is an exception in the Euro-Mediterranean world. Europe has advo-cated the cultural rights of the Iraqi Kurds, but not of the Turkish Kurds, or has punished ethnic cleansing in Yugoslavia, but not in Palestine. However, without the consistent pursuit of the multicultural paradigm, cultural dialogue is likely to be derailed. The selective application of cultural norms of conduct will erode their credibility.

The Structures and Processes of Euro-Mediterranean Cultural Cooperation

In thinking of operationalizing these prerequisites into viable mechanisms, one can conceive of Euro-Mediterranean cultural cooperation as having three main components: cultural dialogue, grass-roots cultural interaction, and joint ventures to reduce sources of image distortion. The first component refers to communication among Euro-Mediterranean élites and civil society groups concerning the pertinent issues. Such dialogue is crucial for the reduction of misperceptions and information distortions.

The question of cultural dialogue raises four main issues: the institutional framework of the dialogue; the role of civil society groups in the dialogue; the contribution of Euro-Mediterranean actors to the costs of the dialogue; and the substance of the dialogue. There is considerable disagreement within the Euro-Mediterranean world over the management of cultural cooperation. The EU advocates a decentralized form of cooperation based on direct contact between institutions of civil society without the direct involvement of the governments. European actors can choose directly their partners. The rationale for this approach is that it would enable European actors to reach out to the grass-roots institutions of southern Mediterranean civil society. This approach is clearly reflected in the Euro-Mediterranean documents. Advocates of the contending approach argue that the EMP is highly unbalanced, especially in the cultural field. The EU has a well-defined grand design of cultural cooperation. But, insti-tutions of civil society in the South are fragmented and have no clear vision of the objectives of the dialogue with the North. Further, European civil society institutions are more homogeneous and experienced than their southern counter-parts. Consequently, they call for the creation of a pan-Arab non-governmental institution, which will overlook the objectives and strategies of the Euro-Mediterranean cultural dialogue. Such an institution, it is argued, will ensure consistency, accumulation, and long-term engagement. It will also ensure a certain level of balance between the northern and southern partners, a balance which is viewed as essential for the success of cultural cooperation. Nasr El-Din Al-Assad (1998), a former Jordanian minister of higher education and an active participant in the old Euro-Arab Dialogue, advocated this approach. He justified it on the basis of the experience of the Euro-Arab Dialogue and his personal experience in various Euro-Mediterranean conferences. According to him, these conferences lacked a cumulative dimension, as there were no central institutions to prioritize the dialogues and draw the necessary lessons. Likewise, Mona Ebeid (1996), an active Egyptian contributor to Euro-Mediterranean cultural dialogues, has pleaded for 'an institutional mechanism within the EMP to activate the Euro-Arab civilizational dialogue'. In my judgement the two approaches are not mutually exclusive. Direct engagement of civil society institutions is essential. In fact, I argue for a wider participation of different social groups in Euro-Mediterranean cultural cooperation. This does not necessarily exclude the establishment of a pan-Euro-Mediterranean cultural forum. In the Asia–Europe cooperation a pan-Asia–Europe Foundation was established in Singapore with a view to orchestrating a programme of Euro-Asian cultural cooperation. In the Mediterranean, one can refer to the case of the Permanent Commission for Mediterranean Intercultural Exchange created by the Community Mediterranean Universities. The Arab side should also take the initiative to formulate a general non-governmental framework for cultural engagement with the EU.

Furthermore, the inclusion of civil society institutions in the cultural dialogue at the grass-roots level is likely to invigorate such a dialogue. The worst scenario for any dialogue is to insulate it from those who are likely to be influenced by its outcomes. If they are not involved in its structures and processes, they are likely to resist and even sabotage it. This dimension raises certain problems, because many southern governments are not likely to welcome such inclusion, especially if it is extended to include their political critics. If the Europeans insist on grass-roots inclusion, this will be perceived or portrayed as an intervention in domestic affairs. The solution lies in incrementalism and the gradual incorporation of wider segments of civil society through mutually beneficial programmes (Jünemann, 1998c).

So far, virtually all the programmes of Euro-Mediterranean cultural cooperation have been initiated and funded by the EU. Southern Mediterranean actors have played the roles of the respondent, beneficiary and receiver. Such a uni-dimensional contribution is not healthy for a sustainable cultural dialogue, as it reflects the lack of commitment on the part of the southern partners. In my judgement, the issue is not the availability of resources, but the lack of commitment. Lack of southern financial contributions also reduces the leverage of southern actors in setting the agenda of the dialogue, and generates forms of nepotism in managing the European resources allocated to the dialogue. If the Euro-Mediterranean cultural dialogue is to be sustainable, all actors must contribute to the costs of the dialogue according to their economic weight, as in the case of cultural cooperation with the Asia–Europe programmes.

Euro-Mediterranean cultural dialogue must address itself to the major issues of concern to all actors. The agenda of the dialogue must be acceptable to all actors and no single actor should have a veto power over the issues to be included. This is crucial in order to safeguard against the perception that the dialogue is a uni-dimensional framework through which the North is setting the agenda. Issues such as strategies of achieving regional peace, northern and southern concepts of democracy and human rights, the promises and limits of economic privatization in the South, ethnic conflicts in the Euro-Mediterranean world, southern immigration to the North, and inter-religious interactions could be included in the dialogue.

The second main component of Euro-Mediterranean cultural cooperation is grass-roots cultural interaction. It is crucial to pay special attention to younger generations, especially those who have a potential for future leadership. Those who are enrolled in secondary schools and institutions of higher education need programmes that portray the commonalities and differences between Euro-Mediterranean societies in a balanced way, with special emphasis on mutual interests. Personal communication programmes in the form of summer courses and joint seminars are also important. Groups such as scientists, social scientists, and private sector specialists can contribute to a pooling of knowledge, the early identification of problems, and the enrichment of the policy-making process. Finally, increased interaction in the fields of art, music, theatre and architecture could be greatly advantageous. The objective is not only to expand interaction among artists but also to acquaint Euro-Mediterranean peoples with trends in diverse artistic fields, and to couple that with a deeper understanding of the cultural roots of Euro-Mediterranean societies.

I have referred earlier to the impact of distorted images on both shores of the Mediterranean on the prospects of cultural cooperation. Cognizant of such a negative impact, the European Parliament issued a declaration in 1991 calling for a correction of stereotypes and distorted public images of the Arab and Islamic world.

There are two main channels for the creation and reinforcement of distorted images in the Euro-Mediterranean world: mass media and textbooks. Hafez (1999) suggested four strategies to deal with the role of mass media in reducing negative images: (a) the creation of media watchdog groups and intellectual élites, who evaluate media content; (b) an agreement on a Euro-Mediterranean code of ethics for journalism; (c) the establishment of a journalistic early warning and crisis management system by the media – such a system would address conflicts early on and recommend peaceful resolutions to crises; and (d) the establishment of multinational professional dialogues among journalists in the Euro-Mediterranean world.

Whereas most of the work on the mass media will be done by their own people, Euro-Mediterranean governments themselves are called upon to change the negative narratives and images of others mentioned in textbooks. This does not mean changing the facts, but filling the history gaps and correcting false images. For example, it was found that in most European textbooks on history and philosophy, the Arab Islamic heritage and its role in the preservation of Greco-Roman civilization is almost lacking. Furthermore, secondary schools and institutions of higher education should develop courses and reading lists that portray both the commonalities and differences among Euro-Mediterranean societies.

177

Conclusion

In this chapter I have argued that the viability of the EMP calls for an emphasis on its cultural component. Unless Euro-Mediterranean cultural cooperation is upgraded to the level of the other chapters and linked with progress in them, the projected partnership is not likely to endure. Further, the sustainability of the EMP will largely depend on the pursuit of a truly multi-cultural and multi-dimensional cultural paradigm. For centuries, civilizations and cultures have prospered and co-existed on both shores of the Mediterranean. Today, they could provide support to the projected politico-economic partnerships if the diversity of their cultures is acknowledged, the linkages between the various baskets of cooperation are established, and the common cultural values are consistently applied. The EU's approach of linking Euro-Mediterranean coop-eration to the endorsement of its values by the Mediterranean actors is likely to result in cultural warfare rather than cooperation. Arab countries in the Mediterranean must also contribute actively to the programme of cultural cooperation at the level of agenda setting and programme setting. Further, the cultural dialogue must reach out to incorporate various segments of the civil society. An elitist cultural dialogue will have limited impacts on the overall cultural processes in the Euro-Mediterranean world. Some work is needed to promote inter-cultural dialogue at the élite and civil society levels and to change the present negative images reinforced by the mass media and the text-books. This is the most practical way to provide southern Mediterranean peoples with a sense of cultural security and give them a vested interest in the promotion of the projected partnership.

NOTES

1. McGowan and Purkitt found that the cultural attribute variables of black African states are asso-ciated with certain patterns of foreign policy behaviour. For example, they found that black African states that engage in conflictual foreign policy behaviour are culturally plural and polit-ically divided by ethnicity (McGowan and Purkitt, 1979: 58). Further, Jandord (1999) also argues that there is a relationship between culture and war-making and war-fighting patterns.
2. Amin Malouf, interview with *InfoMed* (Barcelona), February 1999.
3. In 'Barbarians at the Gates', *The Star* (Jordan), 13 March 1999, Said argued that this continuing series of US aggressions, 'in my opinion, is the clash of civilizations, or rather the clash of untrammelled barbarism with civilization, with a vengeance'.
4. A Tunisian scholar argued that 'such separation cannot be attributed to chance alone, or to styl-istics, or to the need of facilitating the presentation of the various points' (Chourou, 1998a). He added that the issue is not one of oversight but one of conceptualization, and cited the EU–Tunisia Association Agreement as a case in point.
5. See the example mentioned above concerning the death penalty, which is one of the fundamen-tals of Islamic *Shariah*. For Muslims, the abolition of the death penalty means questioning the validity of their religion. Such European endeavour runs against the spirit of multiculturalism.

Conclusion

Towards a Mediterranean Cultural Identity

STEFANIA PANEBIANCO

Mediterranean Identity through Constructivist Lenses

The analysis of the Euro-Mediterranean Partnership (EMP) institutional framework and of some of the main issues dealt with in the third *volet* of the Barcelona Declaration (i.e. democracy, civil society, human rights and cultural dialogue) contained in this volume highlights both the powerful and weak points of this regional integration process, which aims at eventually developing a multicultural Mediterranean society. The fundamental question throughout has been whether the Mediterranean can currently be regarded as a bridge or a barrier between the two shores of the Mediterranean; the former allowing for lasting cooperative relationships, the latter leading the way to conflictual ones. Or maybe an alternative option to a dichotomic vision can be envisaged, due to the current unstable elements of a compromise between conflict and cooperation.

Historically, patterns of conflict and cooperation have characterized the Mediterranean, but the EMP has set the basis for North–South relations across the Mediterranean on cooperation and partnership rather than on confrontation and conflict. The end of USA–USSR rivalry has opened up new opportunities for the European Union (EU) to act as an influential political power in the Mediterranean and promote regional integration. Both economic and political reasons are currently pleading for regional integration and cooperation between the EU and southern Mediterranean countries, rather than closure and conflict (see the Introduction). But, paradoxically, the end of the Cold War was followed by the rise of different forms of extremism, including the rise of ethnic nationalism and religious fundamentalism. Thus Euro-Mediterranean countries are faced with the dilemma of conflictual competition vs. a cooperative zone of peace, prosperity and tolerance.

Moving from inter-state relations to society interaction, Arab and European societies can no longer be regarded as separated worlds. Through migration European society has got in touch with Muslim cultural traditions and vice versa. As a consequence of migration flows, the western world and Islam have become closely intertwined and characterized by continuous exchanges.[1] Geographical barriers cannot prevent flows of people who bring with them their culture, their religion, their habits, their tradition, and who adapt themselves to a different social setting. It is essential, then, to redefine community identity, considering that the changing of society produces identity adaptation.

The reformulation of EU Mediterranean policy, which in 1995 led to the EMP, entailed a move from a purely economic and commercial level of cooperation to security and human rights issues. The comprehensive concept of security that forms the basis of the EMP allowed for new fields of cooperation to be dealt with, such as migration, international crime, xenophobia and racism. Moving away from the purely military concept of security to embrace a human dimension of security, the cultural and human aspects have become an important field of cooperation. The EMP aims at integrating the southern Mediterranean countries through a comprehensive project to improve the local economic conditions and favour political stability, by supporting at the same time the development of democratic institutions and civil societies. The EMP has committed 27 Euro-Mediterranean countries to support democratic processes, to strengthen the role of civil society and to protect human rights. In fact, the EMP has envisaged a prominent ground for cooperation: statements about basic principles (e.g. democratic principles and human rights), provisions for political dialogue, agreement on the free circulation of goods and institutional arrangements. The common interest of the 27 partners is to adopt a common strategy to face the challenges that menace Mediterranean security.

The projects adopted within the EMP framework aim at avoiding the clash of civilizations as foreseen by some authors (e.g. Huntington, 1998), through the practice of mutual respect and the coexistence of cultural traits. Notwithstanding the existence of both differences and commonalities between the EMP partners, the Barcelona Process aims at dispelling any leaning to cultural exclusion and leads instead towards a multicultural society that shares a minimum of common values and interests. The early 1990s were marked by lively debate about an eventual *clash of civilizations*, particularly the West and Islam. There have been frightening assumptions that coexistence of western and Islamic society is not possible due to the 'continuing and deeply conflictual relation between Islam and Christianity' (Huntington, 1998: 209). Islam and the western world have been depicted as two antithetic value systems and styles of life. Conversely, the constructive approach of the EMP assumes that in order to achieve the goal of peace and stability in the Mediterranean, it is necessary to profit from the gains of disclosing a Mediterranean identity that shares common values and principles without renouncing cultural specificity.

The contributions to this volume all in all avoid any dark forecasts. Despite the reference to some existing controversies among Mediterranean societies (Chapter 10), the main focus has been to highlight elements of coexistence and common traits that might eventually lead to a common cultural identity.

Without denying the existence of elements leading to ethnic conflicts, factors allowing coexistence and mutual respect have been investigated. The basic assumption remains that civilizations are not monolithic entities. A static concept of civilization does not provide for the changes and evolutionary processes within them. Similarly, cultural identities are a mixture of elements that are not homogeneous. They are not fossil or static structures, but a process evolving through history (Kodmani-Darwish, 1998: 43).

The Mediterranean as a Community-Region?

The Barcelona Declaration is the result of a European approach aimed at constructing – in the long run – a community region or eventually a security community in the Mediterranean.[2] In a community region 'people imagine that, with respect to their own security and economic well-being, borders run, more or less, where shared understandings and common identities end' (Adler, 1997: 250). The role of individuals, such as political leaders and statesmen, and international and transnational institutions, is essential to construct such communities. EMP institutions and actors seem to play such a role. The long-term aim of the Barcelona Process is in fact the creation of an area of peace and stability in the Mediterranean based upon dialogue, exchange and cooperation. The Barcelona Declaration, together with its Work Programme, the Conclusions adopted at Foreign Affairs Ministerial level and the Charter on Peace and Stability (which is still in the pipeline but for the time being has been frozen), represent the new normative framework for Euro-Mediterranean relations. Agreement on some basic values has allowed the partners' commitment in official documents where clear reference is made, for instance, to democracy, the rule of law and human rights. Yet we are still experiencing the declaratory stage, which might precede the creation of a security community based upon early warning, conflict prevention, crisis management, peace-building, arms limitation, and so on.[3]

Confidence-building measures (CBMs) are an essential community-building mechanism based upon the social construction of mutual trust (Adler, 1997: 273). Accordingly, within the EMP framework specific partnership-building measures (PBMs) have been adopted to achieve the aims of peace, stability, prosperity and mutual understanding, which in the long run will lead to the construction of a foundation for community practices and behaviour. The EMP can be regarded as a social construction. EMP institutions provide a forum in which state and non-state representatives debate and bargain about their understandings and interests. The institutionalized civil fora, which are creating epistemic communities dealing with environmental issues, human rights and industrial affairs, are proof of the emerging of a regional civil society.

The EMP is a constructivist project based upon liberal values; it is through the spreading of liberal values, norms and practices that it aims to shape a new trans-national identity. However, this is a long and tortuous process, since the Mediterranean partners are often critical of the affirmation of liberal values, in so far as they are interpreted as being synonymous with 'western/ imperialist' values.

Basic agreement on the definition of concepts and the perception of values is essential in view of the challenges to the cultural dialogue among Mediterranean partners coming from the stereotypes and misperceptions which offer a wrong image of the other (Panebianco, 2001a).[3] In particular, it is widely acknowledged that a wrong perception of the other, namely of the different societal groups comprising the Euro-Mediterranean area, can slow down the process of community/region- building. There still are some social tensions that have to be appeased. On the one hand, European societies are coexisting with 10 million immigrants who bring with them different cultural traditions; on the other, southern societies are inevitably experiencing a modernization and westernization process. In both cases there is a 'contami-nation' of local identities and threats to the cohesion of society. The resulting cleavage is the preservation of cultural purity vs. multiculturalism. The strategy that is suggested by the EMP is clearly based upon the latter. Differences leading to a cultural conflict must be appeased through tolerance, the recognition and coexistence of cultural pluralist tendencies in society. Cultural pluralism permeates the EMP, claiming that a multicultural Euro-Mediterranean area can exist only through the enhancement of common values, the expansion of common institutions and practices helping peaceful coexistence.

The EMP tends to 'invent' a cultural identity (Willa, 1999) through the enhancement of existing commonalities. The EMP project can be regarded as the framework for the creation of a new community and the definition of a 'we' concept that can overcome the cleavages around which state action takes place. But the Euro-Mediterranean project cannot be constructed upon one single identity or an exclusive belonging. It is not a question of encouraging southern countries to become the same as European countries; it is how cultural differentiation can reconcile identity affirmation with a new univer-sality (Kodmani-Darwish, 1998: 45 ff).

In constructivist terms, the community-belonging, or 'we-feeling', can be developed through socialization actors who can help with belief in a common destiny and a common identity. Community regions are socially constructed by actors and institutions, and transcend national borders. Therefore, international and trans-national institutions play a critical role in the social construction of these communities (Adler, 1997: 250). In order to explain the relationship between the national and the trans-national community, Emanuel Adler refers to concentric circles of allegiance:

> national 'imagined communities' are not about to disappear ... [but] people have begun to imagine new communities ... Growing numbers

of people have begun imagining that they share their destiny with people of other nations who share their values and expectations of proper behaviour in domestic and international political affairs. (ibid.: 250)

Although 'the social construction of a cognitive region out of intersubjective understandings, values, and norms enables people to achieve a community life that transcends the nation-state and indeed any territorial base' (ibid.: 254), it is not possible to affirm that Mediterranean people (in Adler's terms) 'are tenuously starting to perceive as "home" ... a transnational region where they imagine sharing a common destiny and *identity*' (ibid.: 252). This is primarily because the evolution towards socially constructed and spatially differentiated trans-national *community regions* is a long process. As long as the EMP partners remain suspicious and see each other as the origin of potential security threats, the construction of a cognitive region is delayed.

The EMP normative framework, which has been adopted by the 27 partners, is based upon the promotion of reciprocally non-threatening practices (i.e. the institutionalization of political dialogue, seminar diplomacy, non-governmental actor interaction, etc.). Since the long-term objective of the EMP is to create in the Mediterranean an area where disputes are settled peacefully, shared understanding and mutual trust are fostered through PBMs, disaster management mechanisms are foreseen, the EMP is set to act as a 'security community-building institution', which diffuses and institutionalizes values, norms and shared understanding, the multi-level EMP institutional framework, by means of multilateral dialogue and community-building practices, should end up with the creation of a Mediterranean trans-national cognitive/ community region whose people possess collective identities and share other normative and regulatory structures, but this is not a linear nor an irreversible process.

So far, the Barcelona Process represents one of the regional arrangements of security partnership that have been set up to deal with regional stability and security. A 'security partnership arrangement' is based upon 'a group of inter-related international and internal measures ... created to improve the security conditions and defend the geopolitical stability of the region' (Attinà, 2001: 8). Within the EMP, the set of accords including one or few 'fundamental agreements' and a number of related 'operative agreements' that the security partnership is based upon (ibid.) already exist.

The distinctive trait of the EMP is that throughout the Mediterranean a feeling of belonging to the same community is still missing. However, identity studies have explained the socialization process that leads people to internationalize an identity. In order to answer the question 'Who am I?' one has to depict one's specificity in relation to the 'other', how one perceives and defines oneself. Alexander Wendt (1996) insists upon the cognitive process through which common identities are created. Identity cannot be understood in exclusive terms; instead a concentric circle of identities exists: 'under normal circumstances most human beings can live happily with multiple identifications and enjoy moving between them as the situation requires' (Smith, 1992: 59). People are able to hold several identities in parallel, just as they play different roles in society. In western Europe, a European identity is developing that does not replace national identities. Although the latter remain strong, the 'feeling European' is added to national, regional and local allegiance as proof of a multiple identity (Panebianco, 2001b).

By focusing on the cultural dimension and common traditions, the conclusion this book arrives at is that differences and commonalities coexist even within the same civilization (e.g. Jewish or Christian fundamentalism). In every civilization one can find debates and discussions, diversity in culture, language, religion, etc. The European integration process has been characterized by the (re)birth of nationalist movements whose primary aim is to protect cultural specificity. Not even EU countries are totally homogeneous societies: domestic tensions are created by nationalist movements such as, for instance, ETA in Spain.

Openness and dialogue must guide the coexistence of different peoples. Cultural diversity has to be regarded as a source of richness, rather than the source of conflict. Indeed, the risks of transposing some cultural values are high, as counterproductive effects can be produced whenever one cultural model is assumed as the 'real one'. The sterile imposition of western views of democracy and civil society without popular support or inner requests might lead to dissatisfaction (Joffé, 1998). It is risky, for instance, to include in the EMP the apology of liberal democracy is the 'optimum' to which partners must aspire, assuming that liberal democracy has emerged as the 'peak' of political experience (Fukuyama, 1992) and that it should be exported as such. A European attitude that does not acknowledge western democracy's contradictions might provoke fierce opposition of the partners. Undeniably, the EMP institutional setting needs to be revised so as to allow the partners to be more actively involved in the planning stage, in order to contribute with their specific needs and ideas to create projects and initiatives that are not just imposed on the partners by the EU via the European Commission.

The basic assumption of the EMP is that the existence of democratic states with civil pluralist societies favours regional integration. Some chapters tackle these subjects, *de facto* contesting that the Islamic tradition is not compatible with the values and institutions of democracy or human rights (e.g. Chapters 2 and 7). Some common cultural traits exist already and have to be enhanced. Moreover, beyond intergovernmental relations, in the Mediterranean a network of non-state actors exists that is closely interrelated (Chapter 5) and this is the level that is required in order to accomplish the clearly stated aim of the third *volet* of the EMP, namely to bring people closer. Moving to the cultural level, the historical perspective offers examples of cultural unity in the Mediterranean that date back to Hellenistic and Roman times, when a common imprint characterized the area. Today, in contrast, the Mediterranean is an artificial construction. Beyond a historical concept it does not yet correspond to an objective reality that is spontaneously conceived. The definition of Mediterranean as a fluid continent (*continent liquide*) (Kodmani-Darwish, 1998: 45) is a formula that reflects the construction of a region which combines at the same time the dense exchange between the two shores with economic disparities. Thus the Mediterranean can be conceived as a region under construction, or a would-be community region.

A Glance through the Book

This volume's contributors have focused their attention upon some key issues of the human dimension of security dealt with by the third *volet* of the Barcelona Declaration. By reviewing issues tackled directly or indirectly by the EMP, this volume puts together visions of democracy, human rights, civil society and cultural dialogue that are still the object of lively debate along the North–South, West/Middle East, secular/fundamentalist cleavage. Democracy, civil society, human rights and dialogue among civilizations are not always granted common definitions in all the EMP partner countries. Nevertheless, this volume aims to highlight the potential of North–South cooperation in creating a Mediterranean community region. This book discusses differences and highlights common traits that bring the EMP partners closer, by following the assumption 'to know to have a better understanding, to understand for a better action' (Khader, 1996: 8).

The democratization process affecting Mediterranean countries has been the subject of Part I. Assuming that security and democracy are interdependent, support for democratic transition is one of the overtly stated aims of the EMP. By including the strengthening of democratic processes in the Barcelona Declaration, democracy has become an element of EU foreign policy. But the implementation of democratic processes encounters contradictions both in aspiring democracies in the South and in EU countries overtly in favour of democratic changes (with the aim of preserving stability, the EU has on occasion supported undemocratic countries). In Chapter 1 Béchir Chourou was rather sceptical about the 'wave of democratization' that is taking place in some areas of the world, but rarely in the southern Mediterranean. He stresses that the move towards democratization must come from the Arabs themselves, and western support of democracy is often just a façade. He sarcastically uses a metaphor to describe the democratic process in MPCs, saying that 'one can hardly deny that democracy in MPCs is about as present as water is in the deserts that dominate their landscapes'.

The debate over the (in)compatibility of the Arab world and democracy is reflected in several contributions. In Chapter 2, by exploring terms such as *shura* (consultation) or *umma* (community), Rodolfo Ragionieri pleads for the compatibility of democracy and Islamic political culture.

Chapter 3 highlights the contradictions of the EU support of democracy and human rights, arguing that beyond the declaratory stage, EU promotion of democracy and human rights has not yet taken off. In this perspective, by means of the 'civilian power' concept applied to the EU, Stelios Stavridis and Justin Hutchence go beyond rhetoric to analyse the EU political discourse of the 1990s, which claimed that the aim of Europe was the promotion of democracy and human rights. In particular they focus on concrete cases where *realpolitik* prevailed, showing that the principle of conditionality that supposedly regulates EU development aid can be easily overcome by the need of stability and security.

Part II is devoted to one of the aspects of novelty of the Barcelona Process: the non-governmental cooperation level. The Barcelona Declaration refers to the strengthening of the role played by civil society as a clear example of an open and democratic society. Civil society has become a relatively recurrent notion, an encompassing label including at the same time NGOs, consumers' associations, environmentalists, chambers of commerce, industrialists or small and medium enterprises. In Chapter 4 Fifi Benaboud refers to a broad concept of civil society, that is to say to all that is outside politics and the state. The activity of civil society is often associated with democratic transitions, but in the southern Mediterranean region, civil society encounters several difficulties, as a number of limitations are placed, for example, on free assembly; associations also face legislative problems and restrictive pressures. A difficult social and institutional environment is often justified by states because it is necessary to preserve stability. Benaboud shapes the difficulties encountered by civil society in southern Mediterranean societies and stresses the necessity for a new 'social contract', arguing that the contradictions of southern Mediterranean societies, facing economic restrictions and dissatisfaction, allow for 'Islamic organizations to successfully compensate for deficiencies of the welfare state'.

In Chapter 5, by devoting specific attention to the civil fora that have accompanied the interministerial meetings from Barcelona to Marseilles, Annette Jünemann's overview of the role of civil society within the EMP points out the existence of a plurality of actors. However, she admits that in some cases a sort of state control has been exerted through the presence at such occasions of members of southern Mediterranean governments. This reveals a form of state influence and control on civil society within MPCs, which limits the independent promotion of societal interests *vis-à-vis* the state.

In dealing with civil society in the Middle East, in Chapter 6 Youssef Mouawad insists upon the necessity of separating politics from religion in Arab society. He denounces the lack of individualism in favour of Arab collectivism (based upon a 'clan society' made up of close family ties), where religion still regulates most aspects of life. His sceptical view on civil society has in a way counterbalanced Benaboud's optimistic belief in the potential role of civil society and the necessity of strengthening its role in the Mediterranean arena.

In Part III the discussion focuses upon human rights meeting universal standards. Jamila Houfaidi Settar describes the establishment of human rights in the European legal order. In particular, she analyses the Mediterranean area and the Moroccan legal order in order to explore the efforts the Moroccan state is making to enter the community of democratic states. However, this process is not taking place without contradictions.

In Chapter 8 Abdelwahab Biad reviews the freedoms enshrined in the Barcelona Declaration by comparing them with the Universal Declaration of Human Rights. He highlights some contradictions and some resistance of Arab countries in granting human rights on a full scale as long as some freedoms (e.g. freedom of assembly or of expression) are still regarded as a source of domestic instability. The wave of democracy the Arab world experienced in the last decade of the twentieth century has helped the process of opening up Arab polities, granting civil society – including human rights advocates – a greater role in society. But unfortunately governmental approval of such groups is still required in most Arab countries.

The cultural divide between the West and the Islamic world was tackled in Part IV. In Chapter 9 Raymond Cohen identifies English as an international language, that is to say a vehicle of communication that brings people closer and creates a 'bond between individuals on a global scale'. However, an international language has some limitations, because it risks becoming a language that is relatively simple, thereby losing the nuances of meaning. Unique cultural distinctions can only be expressed by a mother-tongue language, and so the combination of a flexible international language and a 'vital vernacular' remains a beneficial combination.

Chapter 10 analyses the Euro-Mediterranean cultural partnership. Mohammad Selim stresses the lack of a truly multicultural and multi-dimensional cultural paradigm in the EMP. In fact, Arab visions should be taken into much more account. He argues that a bigger role should be played by southern Mediterranean countries in the EMP; they should be granted an increased participation in all stages of the Barcelona Process, from agenda-setting to the implementation stage.

The contributions to this volume explore the possibility of spreading global issues with respect to western–Islamic cultural differences. Too often Europe and the Arab world are posed as rivals, historical examples recall opposing actors such as colonizers vs. colonized, developed vs. underdeveloped people, exploiters vs. exploited. More optimistically, we deem that the EMP approach can eventually lead to a fruitful cooperation within the Mediterranean. However, we do not deny differences in values or approaches. Clearly a too extreme culturalist approach could create distinct worlds of closed clusters. On the contrary, the approach adopted in this volume is that of pluralism and tolerance leading to enrichment and mutual respect. This book does not claim to be exhaustive; on the contrary, it aims at raising some critical aspects of Euro-Mediterranean cooperation. The path marked by the EMP seems to be the best option currently available to grant peaceful coexistence between Mediterranean countries. However, the goals stated in the Barcelona Declaration are far from being accomplished. If only criticism is accepted, then improvements to the EMP general framework can be brought about. By a better knowledge of the partners involved, the obstacles deriving from misunderstanding and cultural difference can be faded away. The same can be said for the tortuous path towards a Mediterranean pluralist identity of shared values. The basis of the dialogue among civilizations has to be revised, avoiding any competition attitude wherein each part believes that its own values are superior. The EMP fundamentals are fostering understanding and mutual trust, that is, exchange among representatives of civil society as it is broadly conceived. Some basic common elements lie already at the basis of a Mediterranean cultural identity to be 'constructed', which is still in the making.

NOTES

1. According to Stefano Allievi (2000) it is impossible to keep two 'uncontaminated' societies separated because of the emergence of a 'European Islam' with peculiar traits. For instance, in European Islam individuals acquire a more prominent role, as here Islam has become an individual choice (ibid.: 20). The community of 'converted' (i.e. Europeans converted to Islam) also plays an important role as mediator between Islam and Europe.
2. For a thorough analysis of the concepts of 'community-region' and 'security-community' see Adler (1997).
3. For a thorough review of the potential of the EMP joint actions for peace-building see Tanner (1999).

Bibliography

Abdel-Khalek, N. (1997), 'The Mediterranean Project: The Cultural Dimensions', in N. Mustafa (ed.), *Egypt and the New Regional Projects in the Area*, Cairo, Cairo University, Centre for Political Research and Studies.

Acharya, A. (1998), 'Collective Identity and Conflict Management in Southeast Asia', in E. Adler and M. Barnett (eds), *Security Communities*, Cambridge, Cambridge University Press, pp. 198–227.

Adler, E. (1997), 'Imagined (Security) Communities: Cognitive Regions in International Relations', *Journal of International Studies*, 26, 2: 249–77.

Adler, E. (1998), 'Seeds of Peaceful Change: The OSCE's Security Community-Building Model', in E. Adler and M. Barnett (eds), *Security Communities*, Cambridge, Cambridge University Press, pp. 119–60.

Agénce Europe, 17 April 1997.

Ahlswede, S. (1999), 'Israel's Policy Towards the EU and Germany after the Cold War', paper presented at the 1998/99 departmental seminar series, Politics Department, University of Reading, 23 February.

Al-Assad, N. (1998), 'Means of Understanding and Rectification of Errors and Mutual Respect Between the Europeans and the Muslims', in M. El-Arnaout et al. (eds), *Europe and Islam*, proceedings of the Second International Conference, Jordan 1996, Al-Mafrik, Al Al-Bayt University Press.

Al-Azmeh, A. (1994), *Populisme contre démocratie. Discours démoctratisants dans le monde arabe*, in G. Salamé (ed.), *Démocraties sans démocrates: politiques d'ouverture dans le monde arabe et islamique*, Paris, Fayard, pp. 233–52.

Al-Bishry, I. (1998), 'Dialogue with Europe is Difficult Unless Certain Conditions are Met', *Al-Hayat*, 8 June.

Al-Khatib, H. A. G. (1994), *The General Factors for the Collapse of Democracy in Lebanon*, London.

Allen, D. and M. Smith (1998), 'The European Union's Security Presence: Barrier, Facilitator, or Manager?', in C. Rhodes (ed.), *The European Union in the World Community*, Boulder, CO/London, Lynne Rienner, pp. 45–63.

Allievi, S. (2000), *Nouveaux protagonistes de l'Islam européen. Naissance d'une culture euro-islamique? Le rôle des convertis*, EUI Working Papers, European University Institute, RSC no. 18, Florence, Mediterranean Programme Series.

Al-Najjar, M. (1981), *Hikayat al-shuttar wa al-'ayyarin fi al-turath al-'arabi*, Kuwait, Collection 'Alam al-ma'rifa, pp. 161–2.

Amin, G. (1999), *Globalization*, Cairo, Dar Al-Ma'aref.

Amin, S. (1993), 'The Issue of Democracy in the Contemporary Third World', in B. Gills et al. (eds), *Low Intensity Democracy*, London, Pluto Press.

Amnesty International (1996), *Turkey: No Security without Human Rights*, London, Amnesty International.

Anderson, L. (1995), 'Democracy in the Arab World: A Critique of the Political Culture Approach', in Brynen et al. (1995a), pp. 77–92.

Attinà, F. (1996), *Regional Co-operation in Global Perspective. The Case of the 'Mediterranean' Regions*, University of Catania, Jean Monnet Working Papers in Comparative and International Politics, JMWP 04.96, http://www.fscpo.unict.it/EuroMed/jmwp04.htm

Attinà, F. (1998), 'La Partnership EuroMediterranea. Politica e sicurezza', in F. Attinà et al. (eds), *L'Italia tra Europa e Mediterraneo: il bivio che non c'è più*, Bologna, Il Mulino, pp. 91–116.

Attinà, F. (2001), 'The European Security Partnership, NATO and the European Union', *The European Union Review*, 6, 1: 135–51.

Ayubi, N. (1997), 'Islam and Democracy', in D. Potter et al. (eds), *Democratization*, Cambridge, Polity Press, pp. 345–66.

Ayubi, N. (1999), *Overstating the Arab State, Politics and Society in the Middle East*, London, I.B. Tauris.

Badie, B. (1986), *Les Deux états*, Paris, Fayard.

Badie, B. (1992), *L'État importé*, Paris, Fayard.

Badie, B. (1995), *La fin des territoires*, Paris, Fayard.

Badie, B. (1997a), *Les Deux états: pouvoir et société en Occident et en terre d'Islam*, Paris, Fayard.

Badie, B. (1999), *Un Monde sans souveraineté*, Paris, Fayard.

Barakat, H. (1985), *Al-mujtama' al-'arabi al-mu'aser, Bahth istitla'i ijtima'i*, Beirut, Markaz dirasat al-wahda al-'arabiyya, 2nd edn.

Barbé, E. (1995), 'Reinventar el Mare Nostrum: el Mediterráneo como espacio de cooperación y seguridad', *Papers*, 46: 9–23.

Barbé, E. (1998), Interview, Faculty of Political Science, Autonomous University of Barcelona, 9 November 1998.

Barber, B. (1992), 'Jihad vs. McWorld', *Atlantic Monthly*, 269, 3.

Barcelona Declaration (1995), adopted at the Euro-Mediterranean Conference, 27–28 November 1995, Brussels, European Commission.

Barnett, M. (1995), 'Sovereignty, Nationalism and Regional Order in the Arab States' System', *International Organization*, 49, 3: 479–510.

Beer, F. (1981), *Peace Against War*, San Francisco, W. H. Freeman.

Bennouna, M. (1993), *L'Obligation juridique dans le monde d'après guerre froide*, Paris, Annuaire Français de Droit International.

Bettati, M. (1996), *Le Droit d'ingérence: mutation de l'ordre international*, Paris, Odile Jacob.

Biad, A. (1997), 'Les Droits de l'homme: un nouvel enjeu pour le monde arabe', *Mediterranean Journal of Human Rights*, 1, 1: 9–17.

Bin, A. (1997), *Mediterranean Diplomacy. Evolution and Prospects*, University of Catania, Jean Monnet Working Papers in Comparative and International Politics, JMWP 05.97, http://www.fscpo.unict.it/EuroMed/ jmwp05.htm

Bishara, A. (1998), *Al-mujtama' al-madani, dirasa naqdiyya*, Beirut, Markaz dirasat al-wahda al-'arabiyya.

Blunden, M. (1994), 'Insecurity on Europe's Southern Flank', *Survival*, 36: 134–48.

Boeck, A. (1992), 'Entwicklungstheorien – Eine Rückschau', in D. Nohlen and F. Nuscheler (eds), *Handbuch der Dritten Welt*, vol.1, *Grundprobleme, Theorien, Strategien*, 3rd edn, Bonn, Verlag J. H. W. Dietz Nachf. GmbH, pp. 110–30.

Boutaleb, A. (1995), *Le Monde islamique et le project du nouvel ordre mondial*, Paris, Presses Universitaires de France.

Boutros Ghali, B. (1993), *Déclaration liminaire du secrétaire général de l'ONU à la conférence mondiale des droits de l'homme*, brochure of the United Nations Department of Information, DPI/1394-93630, pp. 11–15.

Bromley, S. (1997), 'Middle East Exceptionalism: Myth or Reality?', in D. Potter et al. (eds), *Democratization*, Cambridge, Polity Press, pp. 1–40, 321–44.

Brynen, R., Korany, B. and Noble, P. (eds) (1995a), *Political Liberalization and Democratization in the Arab World*, vol. 1, *Theoretical Perspectives*, Boulder, CO/London, Lynne Rienner.

Brynen, R., Korany, B. and Noble, P. (1995b), 'Introduction: Theoretical Perspectives on Arab Liberalization and Democratization', in Brynen et al. (1995a), pp. 3–28.

Buchan, D. (1993), *Europe – the Strange Superpower*, Aldershot, Dartmouth.

Buirette-Maurau, P. (1985), 'Les Difficultés de l'internationalisation des droits de l'homme à propos de de la Convention de Lomé', *Revue Trimestriel de Droit Européen*.

Bull, H. (1983), 'Civilian Power Europe: a Contradiction in Terms', in L. Tsoukalis (ed.), *The European Community, Past, Present and Future*, Oxford, Basil Blackwell, pp. 149–64.

Burckhardt, J. (1958), *Civilisation de la Renaissance en Italie*, vol. 1, Livre de Poche, Biblio Essais, Paris, Fayard.

Cacciari, M. (1994), *Geofilosofia dell'Europa*, Milan, Adelphi.

Cacciari, M. (1997), *L'Arcipelago*, Milan, Adelphi.

Cacciari, M. (1999), 'L'Arcipelago Europa', *Micromega*, 2: 21–34.

Cahen, C. (1958), 'Mouvements populaires et autonomisme urbain dans l'Asie Musulmane du Moyen-Age', I, *Arabica*: 245–6.

Cahen, C. (1959a), 'Mouvements populaires et autonomisme urbain dans l'Asie Musulmane du Moyen-Age', III, *Arabica*, vol. 6: 250.

Cahen, C. (1959b), 'Mouvements populaires et autonomisme urbain dans l'Asie Musulmane du Moyen-Age', II, *Arabica*, vol. 6: 26–7.

Cahen, C., *Ahdath*, Encyclopedia of Islam (EI).

Cahen, C., *Futuwwa*, Encyclopedia of Islam (EI).

Calleya, S. (1997), *Navigating Regional Dynamics in the Post-Cold War World*, Aldershot, Dartmouth.

Camau, M. (1991), *Changements politiques au Maghreb*, Paris, Éditions CNRS.

Charillon, F. (1998), 'La Stratégie européenne dans le processus de paix au Moyen-Orient: politique étrangère de proximité et diplomatie du créneau', in M.-F. Durand and A. Vasconcelos (eds), *La PESC-Ouvrir l'Europe au monde*, Paris, Presses de Sciences-Po, pp. 195–225.

Charpentier, J. (1992), 'Les Déclarations des douze sur la reconnaissance des nouveaux états', *Revue Générale de Droit International Public*.

Chaunu, P. (1970), *La Civilisation de l'Europe classique*, Paris, Arthaud, Collection Les Grandes Civilisations.

Chavrin, R. and Sueur, J. J. (1997), *Droits de l'homme et libertés de la personne*, Paris, Litec.

Chay, J. (ed.) (1994), *Culture and International Relations*, New York, Praeger.

Chomsky, N. (1993), 'The Struggle for Democracy in the New World Order', in B. Gills et al. (eds), *Low Intensity Democracy*, London, Pluto Press.

Chourou, B. (1997), 'The Euro-Mediterranean Partnership Agreements: a Shortcut to El Dorado via Utopia?', Amsterdam Middle East Paper no. 11, Amsterdam, Amsterdam International Studies.

Chourou, B. (1998a), 'Re-defining Mediterranean Security: a View from the South', in A. Marquina (ed.), *Mutual Perceptions in the Mediterranean*, Madrid, UNISCI.

Chourou, B. (1998b), 'Measures Towards Achieving Mediterranean Security: a Proposal from the South', in A. Marquina (ed.), *Mutual Perceptions in the Mediterranean*, Madrid, UNISCI.

Chourou, B. (1998c), 'The Free-trade Agreement between Tunisia and the European Union', *Journal of North African Studies*, 3, 1 (spring).

Chourou, B. (2000), 'Security Partnership and Democratisation: Perception of the Activities of Northern Security Institutions in the South', in H. G. Brauch, A. Marquina and A. Biad (eds), *Euro-Mediterranean Partnership for the 21st Century*, London, Macmillan.

Chourou, B. (2001), 'The (Ir)relevance of Security Issues on Euro-Mediterranean Relations', paper presented at the workshop 'The EU and the Mediterranean', Geneva Centre for Security Policy, 5–6 March 2001, Geneva (unpublished).

Chryssochoou, D., Stavridis, S. and Moschonas, A. (2000), 'Greek Political Parties and European Integration after Amsterdam', in A. Mitsos and E. Mossialos (eds), *Contemporary Greece and Europe*, Aldershot, Ashgate, pp. 183–204.

Chryssochoou, D., Tsinisizelis, M., Stavridis, S. and Infantis, K. (1999), *Theory and Reform in the European Union*, Manchester, Manchester University Press.

Cohen, J. L. and Arato, A. (1995), *Civil Society and Political Theory*, Cambridge, MA, MIT Press.

Cohen, R. (1994), 'Pacific Unions: a Reappraisal of the Theory that "Democracies Do Not Go to War with Each Other"', *Review of International Studies*, 20: 207–333.

Cohn-Bendit, D. and Rieu, M. (1998), *Rapport de mission*, mission à Alger, 8–12 February.

Cook, R. (1998), 'Concluding Statement', EUROMED *ad hoc* ministerial meeting, Palermo, 3–4 June.

Corten, O. (1996), *Droit, force et légitimité dans une société internationel en mutation*, RIEJ, 37.

COWI Consulting Engineers and Planners (1998), 'Evaluation of Aspects of EU Development Aid to the Mediterranean Region – Final Synthesis Report', November.

Dahrendorf, R. (1997), *After 1989: Morals, Revolution and Civil Society*, New York, St Martin's Press.

De Schoutheete, P. (1986), *La Cooperation politique européenne*, Brussels, Labor, 2nd edn.

Diamond, L. (ed.) (1993), *Political Culture and Democracy in Developing Countries*, Boulder, CO/London, Lynne Rienner.

Ebeid, M. (1996), 'The Cultural and Social Challenges on Both Shores of the Mediterranean: the Post-Barcelona Era', *Al-Hayat*, 22 October.

Economist, 10 January 1998, http://www.economist.com/archive/view.cgi (printed 8 March 1999).

Edwards, G. and Philippart, E. (1997), 'The Euro-Mediterranean Partnership: Fragmentation and Reconstruction', *European Foreign Affairs Review*, 2, 4: 465–89.

Edwards, G. and Regelsberger, E. (eds) (1990), *Europe's Global Links – the European Community and Inter-regional Co-operation*, London, Pinter.

Elias, N. (1991), *La Société des individus*, Paris, Collection Fayard, Agora.

El-Shalaby, G. (1998), 'The Image of Arabs and Islam in Western Media: the French Case', in M. El-Arnaout et al. (eds), *Europe and Islam*, proceedings of the Second International Conference, Jordan, 1996, Al-Mafrik, Al Al-Bayt University Press.

El-Sherif, M. (1999), 'The Arab Perceptions of European Culture', in *The Role of NGOs in the Development of Civil Society in Europe and the Arab Countries*, proceedings of a seminar held in Jordan, 6–7 December 1997, Amman, Arab Thought Forum.

EMHRN (ed.) (1998), *Report: Second General Assembly of the Euro-Mediterranean Human Rights Network*, Copenhagen, 12–13 December 1997.

Entelis, J. P. (1995), 'Civil Society and the Authoritarian Temptation in Algerian Politics. Islamic Democracy Versus the Centralized State', in A. R. Norton (ed.), *Civil Society in the Middle East*, vol. 1, Leiden, E. J. Brill, pp. 45–86.

Esposito, J. and Voll, J. (1996), *Islam and Democracy*, Oxford, Oxford University Press.

European Commission (1994), *Strengthening the Mediterranean Policy of the European Union: Establishing a Euro-Mediterranean Partnership*, COM(94)427 final, 19/10/1994, Annex II.

European Commission (1996), *Manuel des programmes MED. Votre guide pour le Partenariat Euro-Méditerranéen*, DG IB.

European Commission (1997), *MEDA-Democracy. Euro-Mediterranean Partnership*, Information note no. 2, 1 September 1997, Unit 1 B/A.

European Commission (1999a), *Programmation budgétaire 1996–1998– Méditerranée: Algerie*, http://www/europa.eu.int/en.comm.dg1b (printed 22 March 1999).

European Commission (1999b), *Information Note*, 1 April 1999, Unit 1 B/A.

European Commission (2000), *Progress Report on Turkey*, 8 November 2000.

European Parliament (1995), *Resolution on the Mediterranean Policy of the European Union with a View to the Barcelona Conference*, Foreign Affairs, Security and Defence Policy Committee, COM (95) 0072 final and COM (94) 0427 final, 31 July 1995.

European Parliament (1998), *Report of the ad hoc Delegation on the Visit to Algeria (8–12 February 1998)*. Committee on Foreign Affairs, Security and Defence Policy Ad Hoc Delegation for Algeria, Luxembourg, European Parliament.

Fawcett, L. and Hurrell, A. (eds) (1995), *Regionalism in World Politics*, Oxford, Oxford University Press.

Feliu, L. (1997), 'The European Union as a Mediterranean Actor', in R. Ragionieri (ed.), *Politica ed economia nell'area mediterranea*, Quaderni Forum, XI, 2: 21–39.

Ferhad, I. (1995), 'Die arabische Debatte über Zivilgesellschaft', in I. Ferhad and H. Wedel (eds), *Probleme der Zivilgesellschaft im Vorderen Orient*, Opladen, Leske and Budrich, pp. 23–48.

Ferhad, I. and Wedel, H. (eds) (1995), *Probleme der Zivilgesellschaft im Vorderen Orient*, Opladen, Leske and Budrich.

Fierlebeck, K. (1998), *Globalizing Democracy. Power, Legitimacy and the Interpretation of Democratic Ideas*, Manchester, Manchester University Press.

Filali-Ansari, A. (1999), 'Muslims and Democracy', *Journal of Democracy*, 10, 3: 18–32.

Fondazione Laboratorio Mediterraneo (1998), *II Forum Civile Euromed. Obiettivi e mezzi per il partenariato euromediterraneo*, Naples, Edizioni Magma.

Foreseen (Observatoire International des Tendances Sociologiques) (1997), *Le Retour des clans. Après l'ère de l'individualisme, entrons-nous dans l'ère des clans?*, Paris, Editions Denoël.

Fotopoulos, T. (1997), *Towards an Inclusive Democracy*, London, Cassell.

Foundation for International Studies (ed.) (1997), *Intercultural Dialogue in the Mediterranean*, EuroMed Civil Forum Malta, selected papers, University of Malta.

Fukuyama, F. (1992), *The End of History and the Last Man*, New York, Free Press.

Fülberth, G. (1991), 'Zivilgesellschaft als Nationalreligion', *Konkret*, 5: 46–51.

Galtung, J. (1973), *The European Community: A Superpower in the Making*, London, Allen and Unwin.

Gardet, L. (1961), *La Cité Musulmane, vie sociale et politique*, Collection Études Musulmanes, Librairie Philosophique, Paris, J. Vrin.

Georgiades, H. (2000), 'Greece and the EU–Turkish Relationship', in A. Mitsos and E. Mossialos (eds), *Contemporary Greece and Europe*, Aldershot, Ashgate.

Germ (1996), *Annuaire de la Méditerranée*, Publisud Éditions.

German Foreign Ministry (1999), 'Förmliche Schlußfolgerungen des Präsidenten', press communication, Third Euro-Mediterranean Conference of Ministers of Foreign Affairs, Stuttgart, 15–16 April 1999.

Ghalioun, B. (1992), 'Bina al-mujtama' al-madani al-'arabi: Dawr al-'awamel al-dakhiliyya wa al-kharijiyya', in *Al-mujtama' al-madani fi al-watan al-'arabi wa dawruh fi tahqiq al-dimuqratiyya*, Beirut, Markaz dirasat al-wahda al-'arabiyya.

Ghalioun, B. (1995), *Hiwarat min 'asr al-harb al-ahliyya*, Beyrut, Al-mu'assasa al-'arabiyya lid-dirasat wa'l-nashr.

Ghalioun, B. (1997), *Islam et politique. La modernité trahie*, Paris, Éditions La Découverte.

Gillespie, R. (ed.) (1997a), 'The Euro-Mediterranean Partnership', *Mediterranean Politics*, special issue, 2, 1.

Gillespie, R. (1997b), 'Northern European Perceptions of the Barcelona Process', *Revista CIDOB d'Afers Internacionals*, 37: 65–75.

Ginsberg, R. (1989), *Foreign Policy Actions of the European Community – the Politics of Scale*, Boulder, CO/London, Lynne Rienner.

Gleditsch, K. and Ward, M. (1998), 'Democratizing for Peace', *American Political Science Review*, 92, 1: 51–61.

Gleditsch, N. P. and Risse-Kappen, T. (eds) (1995), 'Democracy and Peace', *European Journal of International Relations*, special issue, 1, 4.

Goad, H. (1956), *Languages in History*, Harmondsworth, Penguin.

Gordon, P. (1998), 'Storms in the Med Blow Towards Europe', *World Today*, 54, 2: 42–4.

Gowa, J. (1995), 'Democratic States and International Disputes', *International Organization*, 49, 3: 511–22.

Group of France (1992), *Strengthening Security and Developing Cooperation in the Mediterranean: Dialogue among Civilizations and Human Rights;*

Mutual Respect; Cultural Cooperation and the Human Dimension, Inter-Parliamentary Conference on Security and Cooperation in the Mediterranean, Malaga, 15–20 June.

Guillaume, A. (1990), *Islam*, Harmondsworth, Penguin.

Guney, A. (2001), 'Turkey: Beyond the Customs Union?', in F. Attinà and S. Stavridis (eds), *The Barcelona Process and Euro-Mediterranean Issues from Stuttgart to Marseille*, Milan, Giuffrè, pp. 201–25.

Hafez, K. (1999), 'Perceptions of Arab Politics and Culture in European Mass Media: Towards a Reform of Foreign Reporting', in *The Role of NGOs in the Development of Civil Society in Europe and the Arab Countries*, proceedings of a seminar, Jordan, 6–7 December 1997, Amman, Arab Thought Forum.

Hanafi, H. (1990), *Hiwar al-Mashreq wa al-Maghreb*, Casblanca, Dar Toubaqal.

Harthy, F. (1999), 'Institutionalisation and Political Development in Saudi Arabia', paper presented at the Italian–Saudi conference, Rome, 3–5 March.

Heinrich Böll Foundation (1999), 'EuroMed Ministerial Conference in Stuttgart – German Delegation Receives Representatives of Environmental Civil Forum', press communication, Stuttgart, 15 April.

Heinz, W. (ed.) (1995), *La Société civile aux pays du Maghreb. Réalités et perspectives*, Brussels, Conférence à Bruxelles.

Heinz, W. (ed.) (n.d.), *La Société civile dans les pays du Maghreb. Discours et réalités*, Brussels.

Helmich, H. and Lemmers, J. (1999), 'Analysis of the History and Status of the Concept of Civil Society', in Arab Thought Forum/ Bruno Kreisky Forum (ed.), *The Role of NGOs in the Development of Civil Society: Europe and the Arab Countries*, Amman/Vienna, pp. 12–25.

Hill, C. (1990), 'European Foreign Policy: Power Bloc, Civilian Power – or Flop?', in R. Rummel (ed.), *The Evolution of an International Actor – Western Europe's New Assertiveness*, Boulder, CO, Westview Press, pp. 31–55.

Hill, C. (1991), 'The European Community: Towards a Common Foreign and Security Policy?', *World Today*, 305–28.

Hill, C. (1993), 'The Capability–Expectations Gap, or Conceptualizing Europe's International Role', *Journal of Common Market Studies*, 31, 3: 305–28.

Hill, C. (1998), 'Closing the Capabilities–Expectations Gap?', in J. Peterson and H. Sjursen (eds), *A Common Foreign Policy for Europe? – Competing Visions of the CFSP*, London, Routledge, pp. 18–38.

Hollis, R. (1997), 'Europe's Incremental Influence', *International Affairs*, 73, 1: 15–29.

House of Lords, Select Committee on the European Communities, Session 1994/95, (1995), *Relations between the EU and the Maghreb Countries*,

London, HMSO Books. http://www.europaeu.int/comm.enlargement/turkey/index.htm#Overview

Hudson, M. (1995), 'The Political Culture Approach to Arab Democratization: The Case for Bringing it Back Carefully', in Brynen et al. (1995c), pp. 102–25.

Huntington, S. (1993a), *The Third Way: Democratization in the Late Twentieth Century*, Norman, OK, University of Oklahoma Press.

Huntington, S. (1993b), 'The Clash of Civilizations', *Foreign Affairs,* 72, 3: 22–49.

Huntington, S. (1998), *The Clash of Civilizations and the Remaking of World Order*, London, Touchstone Books; 1st edn 1996: New York, Simon and Schuster.

Hutchence, J. (2001), 'The Middle East Peace Process and the Barcelona Process', in F. Attinà and S. Stavridis (eds), *The Barcelona Process and Euro-Mediterranean Issues from Stuttgart to Marseille*, Milan, Giuffrè, pp. 171–98.

Ibrahim, S. E. (1993), 'Crises, Elites and Democratization in the Arab World', *The Middle East Journal*, 47, 2: 292–305.

Ibrahim, S. E. (1995), 'Democratization in the Arab World', in J. Schwedler (ed.), *Towards Civil Society in the Middle East?*, Boulder, CO/London, Lynne Rienner, pp. 37–8.

Ibrahim, S. E. (1996), *Al-mujtama' wa al-dawla fi al-watan al-'arabi*, Beirut, Markaz dirasat al-wahda al-'arabiyya.

Ifestos, P. (1987), *European Political Cooperation – Towards a Framework of Supranational Diplomacy?*, Aldershot, Gower.

Institut Català Mediterrània (ed.) (1996), *Towards a New Scenario of Partnership in the Euro-Mediterranean Area*, Barcelona, EuroMed Civil Forum.

International Institute for Strategic Studies (1998), *The Military Balance 1998/99*, Oxford: Oxford University Press.

Ismail, S. (1995), 'Democracy in Contemporary Arab Intellectual Discourse', in Brynen et al. (1995a), pp. 93–112.

Jandord, J. (1999), 'War and Culture: a Neglected Relation', *Armed Forces and Society*, 25, 4.

Jannuzzi, G. (1988), 'European Political Cooperation and the Single European Act', in P. Tsakaloyannis (ed.), *Western European Security in a Changing World: from the Reactivation of the WEU to the Single European Act*, Maastricht, EIPA, p. xxxx.

Joffé G. (1998), *Relations Between the Middle East and the West: the View from the South*, in B. Roberson (ed.), *The Middle East and Europe: The Power Deficit*, London, Routledge, pp. 45–73.

Joffé, G. (1999), 'The Euro-Mediterranean Partnership Initiative: Problems and Prospects', in G. Joffé (ed.), *Perspectives on Development: the Euro-Mediterranean Partnership*, London, Frank Cass, pp. 247–66.

Johnson, M. (1986), *Class and Client in Beirut. The Sunni Muslim Community and the Lebanese State 1840–1985*, London, Ithaca Press.

Jünemann, A. (1997), 'Die Euro-Mediterrane Partnerschaft vor der Zerreißprobe? Eine Bilanz der zweiten Mittelmeerkonferenz von Malta', *Orient*, 38, 3: 465–75.

Jünemann, A. (1998a), 'Europe's Interrelations with North Africa in the New Framework of Euro-Mediterranean Partnership – a Provisional Assessment of the "Barcelona-concept"', in European Commission (ed.), *Third ECSA-World Conference – The European Union in a Changing World*, Brussels, a Selection of Conference Papers, 19–20 September 1996, pp. 365–84.

Jünemann, A. (1998b), 'Democratization – Reflections on the Political Dimension of the Euro-Mediterranean Partnership', in P. Xuereb (ed.), *The Mediterranean's European Challenge*, Malta, European Documentation and Research Centre, University of Malta, pp. 89–118.

Jünemann, A. (1998c), 'Cultural Aspects of Euro-Mediterranean Cooperation and the German Point of View', in S. Hegazy (ed.), *Egyptian and German Perspectives on Security in the Mediterranean*, Cairo, Friedrich-Ebert-Stiftung, pp. 143–57.

Jünemann, A. (1999), 'Europas Migrationspolitik im Mittelmeerraum – Strategien im Spannungsfeld zwischen Festungsmentalität und neuem Partnerschaftsgeist', in A. Schulte and D. Tränhardt (eds.), *International Migration and Liberal Democracies: Internationale Migration und freiheitliche Demokratien*, Münster, Jahrbuch Migration 1999/2000, Lit-Verlag.

Kamrava, M. (1998), 'Non-Democratic States and Political Liberalization in the Middle East – a Structural Analysis', *Third World Quarterly*, 19, 1.

Kandil, A. (1995), *Civil Society in the Arab World*, Washington, DC, Civicus.

Kaplan, R. D. (1997), 'Was Democracy Just a Moment?', *Atlantic Monthly*, 280, 6.

Katz, J. (1984), *Hors du ghetto, émancipation des juifs en Europe, 1770–1870*, Paris, Hachette Littérature.

Katzenstein, P. (1996), 'Regionalism in Comparative Perspective', *Co-operation and Conflict*, 31, 2: 123–59.

Kawtharani, W. (1988), *Al-sulta wa al-mujtama' wa al-'amal al-siyasi min tarikh al-wilaya al-'uthmaniyya fi bilad al-sham*, Beirut, Markaz dirasat al-wahda al-'arabiyya, PhD thesis collection.

Kawtharani, W. (1992), *Al-mujtama' al-madani wa al-dawla fi al-tarikh al-'arabi in Al-mujtama' al-madani fi al-watan al-'arabi wa dawruh fi tahqiq al-dimuqratiyya*, Beirut, Markaz dirasat al-wahda al-'arabiyya.

Kelly, L. G. (1994), 'Translatability: Limits', in R. E. Asher (ed.), *The Encyclopedia of Language and Linguistics*, Oxford, Pergamon Press.

Keohane, R. (1993), 'Institutional Theory and the Realist Challenge after the Cold War', in D. Baldwin (ed.), *Neorealism and Neoliberalism: the Contemporary Debate*, New York, Columbia University Press, pp. 269–300.

Khader, B. (1996), *L'Europa e il mondo arabo. Le ragioni del dialogo*, Torino, L'Harmattan Italia.

Khalil, H. (1998), 'Arab Culture and the Dialogue Among Civilizations', *Al-Risalat* (Damascus), 2, 10, November.

Kienle, E. (1998), 'Destabilization through Partnerships? Euro-Mediterranean Relations after the Barcelona Declaration', *Mediterranean Politics*, 3, 2: 1–20.

Kinkel, K. (1999), 'Islam is Our Neighbor', *Frankfurter Allgemeine*, 8 February (Arabic translation in the *Journal of World Journals* [Cairo], Egypt's State Information Service, 23 February).

Kirchner, E. (1989), 'Has the Single European Act Opened the Door for a European Security Policy?', *Journal of European Integration*, 13, 1: 1–14.

Kodmani-Darwish B. (1998), 'Pulsions et impulsions: l'euro-méditerranée comme enjeu de société', *Politique Étrangère*, 1: 35–51.

Kodmani-Darwish, B. and Chartouni-Dubarry, M. (1994), *Perceptions de sécurité et stratégies nationales au Moyen Orient*, Editions Masson.

Kramer, H. (1997), 'The Cyprus Problem and European Security', *Survival*, 39, 3: 16–32.

Kukathas, C. (1998), 'Islam, Democracy and Civil Society', *Liberal Düsünce Quarterly* (Turkey), summer: 37–9.

Labayle, H. (1997), RFDA, September–October.

Lapidus, I. (1988), *History of Islamic Societies*, Cambridge, Cambridge University Press.

Laroui, A. (1990), *Islam et modernité*, Paris, Éditions La Découverte.

Laroui, F. (1999), *Méfiez-vous des Parachutistes*, Paris, Julliard.

Lewis, B. (1998), *The Multiple Identities of the Middle East*, London, Weidenfeld and Nicolson.

Leca, J. (1994), 'La democratisation dans le monde arabe: incertitude, vulnerabilité et légitimé, in G. Salarné (1994), pp. 35–94.

Mabro, R. (1999), 'Civil Society in the History of Ideas and in European History', in Arab Thought Forum/Bruno Kreisky Forum (ed.), *The Role of NGOs in the Development of Civil Society: Europe and the Arab Countries*, Amman/Vienna, pp. 29–48.

Maffesoli, M. (1988), *Le Temps des tribus. Le déclin de l'individualisme dans les Sociétés de Masse*, Paris, Livre de Poche.

Mahiou, A. (1998), 'La Charte arabe des droits de l'homme', in Mélanges Hubert Thierry, *L'évolution du droit international*, Paris, pp. 305–20.

Maougal, M. L. (1997), 'Recognition – the Cardinal Stake of Violence: an Essay in the Neurotic Structure of the Algerian Cultural Élite', *Journal of Algerian Studies*, 2: 1–26.

Marks, J. (1999), 'The European Challenge to North African Economies: the Downside to the Euro-Med Policy', in G. Joffé (ed.), *Perspectives on Development: the Euro-Mediterranean Partnership*, London, Frank Cass, pp. 47–58.

Maspéro, F. (1997), *Balkans-Transit*, Paris, Collection Fiction and Cie, Éditions du Seuil.

Massignon, L. (1963), *Les Corps de métier et la cité Musulmane, Opera Minora.*, Beirut, Collection Recherches et Documents, Dar Al-Maaref, vol. 1.

Mayer, A. (1995), *Islam and Human Rights*, Boulder, CO, Westview Press.

McGowan, P. and Purkitt, H. (1979), *National Character in Black Africa: Comparative Study of Culture and Foreign Policy Behavior*, Denver, CO, University of Denver Press.

McGrew, A. (ed.) (1997), *The Transformation of Democracy?*, Cambridge, Polity Press.

McNamara, R. S (1996), *In Retrospect: the Tragedy and Lessons of Vietnam*, New York, Vintage Books.

Merkel, W. and Lauth, H.-J. (1998), 'Systemwechsel und Zivilgesellschaft – Welche Zivilgesellschaft braucht die Demokratie?', *Aus Politik und Zeitgeschichte*, 30 January, pp. 3–12

Messarra, A. (1995), *Al-mujtama' al-madani wa al-tahawwul al-dimuqrati fi Lubnan*, Cairo, Ibn Khaldun Centre.

Monar, J. (1998), 'Institutional Constraints of the European Union's Mediterranean Policy', *Mediterranean Politics*, 3, 2: 39–60.

Monteil, V. M. (1987), *La Pensée arabe*, Paris, Collection Clefs, Seghers.

Moore, B. (1966), *Social Origins of Dictatorship and Democracy: Lords and Peasants in the Making of the Modern World*, Boston, Beacon Press.

Morlino, L. (1986), 'Democrazie', in G. Pasquino (ed.), *Manuale di scienza politica*, Bologna, Il Mulino, pp. 83–135.

Morlino, L. (1998), *Democracy between Consolidation and Crisis*, Oxford, Oxford University Press.

Moten, A. (1996), *Political Science. An Islamic Perspective*, London, Macmillan.

Moussali, A. (1995), 'Modern Islamic Fundamentalist Discourses on Civil Society, Pluralism and Democracy', in A. Norton (ed.), *Civil Society in the Middle East*, Leiden, E. J. Brill, vol. 1, pp. 79–119.

Mozaffari, M. (1998), 'Can a Declined Civilization be Reconstructed?', *International Relations*, 14, 3: 31–48.

Nabhani, T. (1990), *Nizam al-hukm fi'l-Islam*, from the Manshurat Hizb at-Tahrir.

Nasr, M. (1995), *The Image of Arabs and Islam in French Text Books*, Beirut, Centre for Arab Unity Studies.

Nienhaus, V. (1999), 'Euro-Mediterrane Freihandelszone: Intensivierung der Wirtschaftsbeziehungen und Förderung nachhaltiger Entwicklung?', in W. Zippel (ed.), *Die Mittelmeerpolitik der EU*, Baden-Baden, Nomos Verlag, pp. 91–114.

Norton, A. (1993), 'The Future of Civil Society in the Middle East', *Middle East Journal*, 47, 2: 211.

Norton, A. (ed.) (1995), *Civil Society in the Middle East*, vol. 1, Leiden, E. J. Brill.

Nugent, N. (1997), 'Cyprus and the European Union: a Particularly Difficult Membership Application', *Mediterranean Politics*, 2, 2: 53–75.

Nuttall, S. (1988), 'Where the European Commission Comes in', in A. Pijpers et al. (eds), *European Political Cooperation in the 1980s – a Common Foreign Policy for Western Europe?*, Dordrecht, Martinus Nijhoff, pp. 104–17.

Olsen, G. (1998), 'The European Union and the Export of Democracy: Ad Hoc Policy with Low Priority', Copenhagen, Centre for Development Research (mimeo).

Ó Tuathail, G. (1996), *Critical Geopolitics. The Politics of Writing Global Space*, London, Routledge.

Ouannes, M. (1997), *Le Phénomène associatif au Maghreb*, El Taller.

Panebianco, S. (2001a), 'The EMP's Innovative Dimension of a Cultural Dialogue: Prospects and Challenges', in F. Attinà and S. Stavridis (eds), *The Barcelona Process and Euro-Mediterranean Issues from Stuttgart to Marseille*, Milan, Giuffré, pp. 99–120.

Panebianco, S. (2001b), 'European Citizenship and European Identity: from Treaty Provisions to Public Opinion Attitudes', in E. Moxon-Browne (ed.), *Who are the Europeans Now?*, Aldershot, Ashgate, pp. 19–38.

Patai, R. (1983), *The Arab Mind*, New York, Charles Scribner's Sons.

Peters, J. (1997), *Europe and the Middle East Peace Process: Emerging from the Sidelines*, http://www.rdg.ac.uk/EIS/GSEIS/emc/pubs.html

Piening, C. (1997), *Global Europe – the European Union in World Affairs*, Boulder, CO/London, Lynne Rienner.

Pijpers, A. (1988), 'The Twelve Out-of-Area: a Civilian Power in an Uncivil World?', in A. Pijpers et al. (eds), *European Political Cooperation in the 1980s – a Common Foreign Policy for Europe?*, Dordrecht, Martinus Nijhoff, pp. 143–64.

Pinn, I. and Wehner, M. (1995), *Euro Phantasien. Die islamische Frau aus westlicher Sicht*, Duisburg, DISS.

Politis, N. (1927), *Les Nouvelles Tendances du droit international*, Paris, Presses Universitaires de France.

Potter, D. (1997), 'Explaining Democratization', in D. Potter et al. (eds), *Democratization*, Cambridge, Polity Press, pp. 1–40.

Preston, P. W. (1998), *Pacific-Asia in the Global System*, Padstow, Blackwell Publishers.

Pridham, G. (ed.) (1991), *Encouraging Democracy: the International Context of Regime Transition in Southern Europe*, Leicester, Leicester University Press.

Prodromou, E. (1998), 'Reintegrating Cyprus: the Need for a New Approach', *Survival*, 40, 3: 5–24.

Project Outline of the Conférence Méditerranéenne Alternative, http//www.pangea.org/events/cma95/eng/about/html

Qadeem, M. (1998), 'CBMs and Conflict Resolution as Approaches to the South Asian Security: How Relevant and Pragmatic?', in M. Ahmar (ed.), *Internal and External Dynamics of South Asian Security*, Karachi, Fezleesons (PVT).

Rabinovich, I. (1998), *The Brink of Peace*, Princeton, Princeton University Press.

Raymond, A. (1973–74), *Artisans et commerçants au Caire au XVIIIème siècle*, Damascus, Institut Français de Damas.

Rhode-Liebenau, S. (1996), *Menschenrechte und internationaler Wandel*, Baden-Baden, Nomos Verlag.

Rich, P. and Joseph, S. (1997), *Algeria: Democratic Transition or Political Stalemate?*, London, Saferworld.

Richter, E. (1997), 'Die europäische Zivilgesellschaft', in K. Wolf (ed.), *Projekt Europa im Übergang?*, Baden-Baden, Nomos Verlag.

Risse-Kappen, T. (1995), 'Democratic Peace – Warlike Democracies?', *European Journal of International Relations*, 1, 4: 491–517.

Rodinson, M. (1992), *Islam. Politique et croyance*, Paris, Fayard.

Romeo, I. (1998), 'The European Union and North Africa: Keeping the Mediterranean "Safe" for Europe', *Mediterranean Politics*, 3, 2: 21–38.

Rosenau, J. (1997), 'The Complexities and Contradictions of Globalisation', *Current History*, 96, 613: 360–4.

Rummel, R. (1988), 'Speaking with One Voice and Beyond', in A. Pijpers et al. (eds), *European Political Cooperation in the 1980s – a Common Foreign Policy for Europe?*, Dordrecht, Martinus Nijhoff, pp. 118–42.

Russett, B. (1993), *Grasping the Democratic Peace*, Princeton, NJ, Princeton University Press.

Saadah, A. (1978), *Al-Athar al-Kamila, Al-Rasail*, Beirut, Manshurat Al-Hizb al-Suri al-Qawmi al-Ijtima'i, vol. 1, 1st edn.

Sabá, K. (1996), 'Spain: Evolving Foreign Policy Structures – from EPC Challenge to CFSP Management', in F. Algieri (ed.), *Synergy at Work. Analysen zur Europapolitik des Instituts für Europäische Politik*, Bonn, Europa Union Verlag GmbH, pp. 81–205.

Saif, M. (1998), 'The Mediterranean Policy of Western Security Institutions: an Egyptian Perspective', in S. Hegazy (ed.), *Egyptian and German Perspectives in the Mediterranean*, Cairo, Friedrich Ebert Stiftung.

Salamé, G. (ed.) (1994), *Démocraties sans démocrates: politiques d'ouverture dans le monde arabe et islamique*, Paris, Fayard (*Democracy without Democrats? The Renewal of Politics in the Muslim World*, London, I. B. Tauris, 1995).

Santoro, C. M. (1998), *Occidente. Identità dell'Europa*, Milan, Angeli.

Sartori, G. (1993), *Democrazia. Che cos'è?*, Milan, Rizzoli.

Savir, U. (1998), *The Process*, New York, Random House.

Sayyid, M. (1994), 'The Third Wave of Democratization in the Arab World', in D. Tschirgi (ed.), *The Arab World Today*, Boulder, CO/London, Lynne Rienner.

Schwedler, J. (ed.) (1995a), *Towards Civil Society in the Middle East?*, Boulder, CO/London, Lynne Rienner.

Schwedler, J. (1995b), *Introduction – Civil Society and the Study of Middle East Politics*, in J. Schwedler (ed.), *Towards Civil Society in the Middle East?*, London, Lynne Rienner, pp. 1–32.

Sharabi, H. (1988), *Neo-Patriarchy: A Theory of Distorted Change in the Arab World*, Oxford, Oxford University Press.

Shils, E. (1966), *The Prospect for Lebanese Civility*, in L. Binder (ed.), *Politics in Lebanon*, New York, John Wiley and Sons (quoted in A. Hourani, *Political Society in Lebanon, an Historical Introduction*, Papers on Lebanon Collection, Centre for Lebanese Studies, Lebanon, n.d.).

Sick, G. (1985), *All Fall Down: America's Fateful Encounter with Iran*, London, I. B. Tauris.

Sirey (1960), *Dictionnaire de la terminologie du droit international*.

Sjostedt, G. (1977), *The External Role of the European Community*, Farnborough, Saxon House.

Smith, A. (1992), 'National Identity and the Idea of European Unity', *International Affairs*, 68, 1: 55–76.

Smith, K. (2000), 'The End of a Civilian Power Europe: a Welcome Demise or Cause for Concern?', *The International Spectator*, 35, 2: 11–28.

Spencer, C. (1996), 'Islamism and European Reactions: the Case of Algeria', in R. Gillespie (ed.), *Mediterranean Politics*, London, Pinter, vol. 2, pp. 121–37.

Spencer, C. (1998a), 'Rethinking or Reorienting Europe's Mediterranean Security Focus?', in W. Park and G. Wyn Rees (eds), *Rethinking Security in Post-Cold War Europe*, London, Longman, pp. 135–54.

Spencer, C. (1998b), 'Who Killed the Monks?', *World Today*, 54, 8/9: 203–4.

Stavridis, S. (1991), 'Foreign Policy and Democratic Principles: the Case of European Political Co-operation', unpublished Ph.D. thesis, London, LSE.

Stavridis, S. (1997a), 'The Democratic Control of the CFSP', in M. Holland (ed.), *Common Foreign and Security Policy: the Record and Reform*, London, Pinter/Cassells, pp. 136–47.

Stavridis, S. (1997b), 'The CFSP of the EU: Why Institutional Arrangements are not Enough', in S. Stavridis, E. Mossialos, R. Morgan and H. Machin (eds), *New Challenges to the European Union: Policies and Policy-Making*, Aldershot, Dartmouth, pp. 85–121.

Stavridis, S. (1999), 'Double Standards, Ethics and Democratic Principles in Foreign Policy: the European Union and the Cyprus Problem', *Mediterranean Politics*, 4, 1: 95–112.

Stavridis, S. (2001a), 'Failing to Act Like a Civilian Power: the European Union's Policy Towards Cyprus and Turkey (1974–2000)', *Studia Diplomatica*, 54, 3: 75–102.

Stavridis, S. (2001b), *Why the 'Militarising' of the EU is Strengthening the*

Concept of a 'Civilian Power Europe', EUI Working Papers Series, RSC No. 2001/17, RSCAS, Florence, June.

Stavridis, S., Couloumbis, T., Veremis, T. and Waites, N. (eds) (1999), *The Foreign Policies of the European Union's Mediterranean States and Applicant Countries in the 1990s*, London, Macmillan.

Stearns, M. (1996), *Talking to Strangers*, Princeton, NJ, Princeton University Press.

Steiner, G. (1992), *After Babel*, Oxford, Oxford University Press, 2nd edn.

Strange, S. (1997), 'The Erosion of the State', *Current History*, 96, 613: 365–9.

Sudre, F. (1997), *Droit international et européen des droits de l'homme*, Paris, Presses Universitaires de France.

Sulayman, S. (1993), *Athar al-bannain al-ahrar fi al-adab al-lubnani (1860–1950)*, Beirut, Nawfal Publications.

Tanner, F. (1996), 'An Emerging Security Agenda for the Mediterranean', *Mediteranean Politics,* 1, 3: 279–94.

Tanner, F. (1999), 'Joint Actions for Peace-building in the Mediterranean', *International Spectator*, 34, 4: 75–90.

Tavernier, P. (1992), 'Des États arabes, l'ONU et les droits de l'homme', *Cahiers de l'Orient*, 19, 3: 183–97.

Taylor, C. (1989), 'Die Beschwörung der Civil Society', in M. Von Krzysztof (ed.), *Europa und die Civil Society*, Stuttgart, Castelgandolfo-Gespräche.

Tocqueville, A. de (1981), *De la démocratie en amérique*, Paris, Flammarion.

Touraine, A. (1994), *Qu'est-ce que la démocratie?*, Livre de Poche Biblio Essais, Paris, Fayard.

Tovias, A. (1999), 'Regionalisation and the Mediterranean', in G. Joffé (ed.), *Perspectives on Development: the Euro-Mediterranean Partnership*, London, Frank Cass, pp. 75–88.

Tozy, M. (1999), *Confluences Méditerranée sur la transition démocratique au Maroc*, Paris, L'Harmattan.

Tsakaloyannis, P. (1997), 'The EU and the Common Interests of the South?', in G. Edwards and A. Pijpers (eds), *The Politics of the European Treaty Reform – the 1996 Intergovernmental Conference and Beyond*, London, Pinter, pp. 142–58.

Turan, I. (1997), 'The Military in Turkish Politics', *Mediterranean Politics*, 2, 2: 123–35.

Valinakis, Y. and Pitsarou, E. (1996), 'Greece's Position on the Revision of the CFSP', in P. Kazakos et al. (eds), *What is the Future of the EU? The Maastricht Treaty Review* (bilingual), Athens, Sideris for ELIAMEP, pp. 155–76.

Vatikiotis, P. (1991), *Islam and the State*, London, Routledge.

Virally, M. (1983), *Cours général de droit international public*, Recueil des Cours de l'Académie de droit internationale, 193.

Waites, N. and Stavridis, S. (1999), 'The European Union and the

Mediterranean', in S. Stavridis et al. (eds), *The Foreign Policies of the European Union's Mediterranean States and Applicant Countries in the 1990s*, London, Macmillan, pp. 22–39.

Walker, M. (1998), 'Algeria Highlights EU's Impotence', *Guardian*, 20 January.

Weber, M. (1967), *L'Éthique protestante et l'esprit du capitalisme*, Paris, Librairie Plon.

Wendt, A. (1996), 'Identity and Structural Change in International Politics', in Y. Lapid and F. Kratochwil (eds), *The Return of Culture and Identity in IR Theory*, Boulder, CO/London, Lynne Rienner, pp. 47–64.

Wessel, R. (1997), 'The International Legal Status of the European Union', *European Foreign Affairs Review*, 2: 109–29.

White, G. (1996), 'Civil Society, Democratization and Development', in R. Luckham and G. White (eds), *Democratization in the South – the Jagged Wave*, Manchester, Manchester University Press, pp. 178–219.

Whitehead, L. (1996), 'Concerning International Support for Democracy in the South' in R. Luckham and G. White (eds), *Democratization in the South – the Jagged Wave*. Manchester, Manchester University Press.

Whitman, R. (1998), *From Civilian Power to Superpower? – the International Identity of the European Union*, London, Macmillan.

Willa, P. (1999), *La Méditerranée comme espace inventé*, University of Catania, Jean Monnet Working Papers in Comparative and International Politics, JMWP 25.99, http://www.fscpo.unict.it/EuroMed/jmpwp25.htm

Xenakis, D. (1998), *The Barcelona Process: Some Lessons from Helsinki*, University of Catania, Jean Monnet Working Papers in Comparative and International Politics, JMWP 17/98, http://www.fscpo.unict.it/EuroMed/jmpwp17.htm

Xenakis, D. (1999), *Mediterranean Complexities, Cyprus and the EU's Enlargement*, University of Reading, Euro-Med Research Paper no. 99/2, http://www.rdg.ac.uk/EIS/GSEIS/emc.pubs.html

Ya'qub, M. M. (1997), 'Fi al-dimuqratiyya wa al-mujtama' al-madani', *Abwab Quarterly* (Lebanon): 40–68.

Youssoufi (Moroccan prime minister) (1998), 'Speech at the National Information Day', *Le Matin*, 20 November.

Zeine, Z. N. (1973), *The Emergence of Arab Nationalism*, New York, Caravan Books.

Zielonka, J. (1998), *Explaining Euro-Paralysis – Why Europe is Unable to Act in International Politics*, London, Macmillan.

Index